DIAMONDS

3RD EDITION

The Antoinette Matlins Buying Guide

How to Select, Buy, Care for & Enjoy Diamonds with Confidence and Knowledge

Antoinette Matlins, P.G.

RUPA

2011 Third Edition, Quality Paperback, First Printing

First published by GemStone Press

Published 2012 by
Rupa Publications India Pvt. Ltd.
7/16, Ansari Road, Daryaganj,
New Delhi 110 002

Sales Centres:

Allahabad Bengaluru Chennai
Hyderabad Jaipur Kathmandu
Kolkata Mumbai

Cover Design: Stacey Hood
Interior Design: Chelsea Cloeter
Photo Credits: See pages 215-16

By arrangement with
GemStone Press, USA

This edition is for sale in the Indian subcontinent only.

Printed in India by
Nutech Photolithographers
B-240, Okhla Industrial Area, Phase-I,
New Delhi 110 020, India

DIAMONDS

3rd Edition

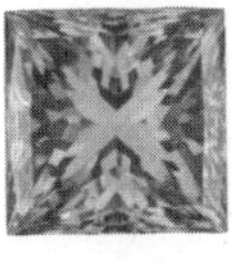

By the same author

Colored Gemstones: The Antoinette Matlins Buying Guide

Contents

PART THREE

Design & Style

Getting the Look You Want ... and Keeping It That Way

PART FOUR

Important Advice Before & After You Buy

Appendix

Index 217

Price Guides

Special Charts and Tables

Color Photograph Section

Acknowledgments

There are many people who have helped me learn and understand the complexities of this exciting field—too many to try to mention all of them here. Nonetheless, there are a few people who have been especially influential and supportive of the work I have done, and I would like to take a moment to acknowledge them. In addition to my father, I would like to thank my brother, Kenneth Bonanno, F.G.A., P.G., and my sisters, Karen Bonanno DeHaas, F.G.A., P.G., and Kathryn Bonanno Patrizzi, F.G.A., P.G., from whom I continue to learn, and with whom I enjoy sharing and debating gemological issues. I would also like to thank, in particular, C.R. "Cap" Beesley, founder and former director of American Gemological Laboratories, New York; he has been a great teacher, and his research and leadership have benefited the entire gem and jewelry community.

I would also like to thank the late Robert Crowningshield, former vice president of Identification Services, Gemological Institute of America (GIA) Gem Trade Laboratory. A wonderful friend to my father, he was always generous in the time he gave me to address questions or issues I might have had. Mr. Crowningshield's work for the past half-century in the field of diamonds and gemstones, and his contributions to the gemological literature, have helped shape the world of gemology as we know it.

At GemStone Press I would like to thank Sandra Korinchak, Polly Mahoney, and Bridgett Taylor, with whom it has been a pleasure to work, and who have made the project fun.

And last, but not least, I want to thank my husband, Stuart Matlins, for his unfailing support and encouragement, and for his willingness to spend many lonely nights while I'm traveling around the world to pursue my work.

Dedication

This book is specially dedicated to my father, Antonio C. Bonanno, who died in 1996. He inspired me as a child and filled my world with awe and wonder. He was my teacher, my mentor, and my coauthor on three books. Although his name is not on this cover, his knowledge and wisdom—his words, his ideas, his values—fill its pages. My gratitude is eternal.

Preface to the Third Edition

From the time I was a small child, I had the pleasure of being surrounded by beautiful gems and had a unique opportunity to learn the gem business. Having a father who was a well-known gemologist, appraiser, and collector—described as the "father of modern, practical gemology" prior to his death—I was able to spend hours marveling at stones, those in his own private collection as well as those brought to him to be professionally identified and evaluated.

Dinner conversation always centered on the day's events at my father's office. Sometimes he would thrill us with an account of a particularly fine or rare gem he had had the pleasure of identifying or verifying. But too often the subject would turn to some poor, unknowing consumer who had been victimized. It might have been a soldier who thought he had purchased genuine diamonds while visiting Africa, and learned sadly that they were inexpensive quartz pebbles; or a housewife who bought a "diamond" ring at an estate sale, only to learn the stone was a colorless zircon or a white sapphire. It might have been a doctor who thought he had purchased a rare "canary" color diamond as a gift for his wife, who learned to his dismay that the beautiful bright yellow color was not natural at all but the result of special treatment, so the stone was not worth anywhere near what he had paid for it.

I grew up with a deep appreciation and passion for diamonds, but also with a keen awareness of the pitfalls of the gem trade. This led to my first book, *Jewelry & Gems: The Buying Guide*—the first book ever written to help consumers and laypeople understand what they were really buying. After seven editions and over 500,000 copies in seven languages—Arabic, English, Greek, Hungarian, Japanese, Spanish, and Russian—there have been so many changes in the diamond field that a book focused exclusively on diamonds was needed.

For those who love diamonds *and* color, one of the most exciting developments since the previous edition of this book is the rapidly growing popularity of "fancy-color" diamonds in every hue and shade! For those who desire an unusual and distinctive gem, nothing rivals the combination of color and the brilliance and fire of diamond. Whatever color you prefer, diamond's fiery character sets it in a class apart from all other gems.

The latest rage is "brown" diamonds, from pale beige to rich cognac. The most affordable of the fancy colors—and more affordable than colorless and near-colorless diamonds—they have moved into the spotlight with fashion and jewelry designers alike; today no fashion-conscious woman wants to be without one! Ranging from just a few hundred dollars per carat to under $10,000 per carat in larger sizes and deeper shades, these make a statement at a fraction of the price of colorless diamonds.

The heightened popularity of fancy-color diamonds has created increased demand, and even in the less rare colors, prices have strengthened. On the other end of the spectrum, diamonds in the rarest colors—red, pink, blue, and green—are setting one world record after another, impervious to the global financial rollercoaster. As costs continue to rise, however, so too does the incidence of fraud and misrepresentation by unscrupulous sellers. Diamond buyers must be especially cautious when buying any fancy-color diamond. (See chapter 12 for more information on the risk of fraud with fancy-color diamonds.)

Additionally, new treatments have been developed to make natural diamonds appear whiter and also to transform undesirable tints into rare "fancy" colors. As long as you know that the color of such diamonds is not natural, and pay an appropriate price, these treated diamonds provide beautiful, affordable alternatives to their rarer natural counterparts. Let's take the rarest and costliest of all gems—red diamonds—for example. Natural diamonds can be treated to create a "red" color, which may make it possible to afford and enjoy wearing a real diamond in red. Altering color is costly, and the stones are not inexpensive, but they are sold at a fraction of the price of natural-color red diamonds!

Not all treatments, however, are desirable or permanent. One new treatment posing serious problems for consumers is the application of *temporary surface coatings* that are not permanent—the color of such stones may change back at some future time to their original, much less desirable color. *This is especially true for small fancy-color diamonds in rare pink and blue colors; there has been a dramatic increase in surface-treated pink and blue diamonds being used in pavé jewelry pieces.*

In the field of synthetic diamonds, we are seeing advances. *Colorless synthetic diamonds* are now available in larger sizes, and polished stones in the one-carat range can now be found. Synthetic diamonds are also available in a wider range of colors, including not only various shades of yellow, but also in the "rarest" diamond colors, including red, blue, and pink. Here again, caution is advised. In the rarest colors, stones even as small as one-tenth carat may have a lab report, but typically diamonds under one-fifth carat will not have laboratory documentation. It is essential to verify that these stones are natural diamonds with natural color if they have been represented and priced as such.

Another serious concern now coming to light is the possible over-grading of a diamond's color as a result of changes made in the type of lighting used for color grading. Until this issue has been rectified by the jewelry trade, you'll need to know how to make sure you are paying the right price and getting the color you really want. (See chapter 6 for more on fluorescence and color grading.)

As with my other books, the purpose of this book is to provide a basic but complete consumer's guide to buying a diamond, whether for your own personal pleasure, as a gift, or as an investment in something beautiful to pass on as a treasured heirloom. It is designed and written for a wide market—for husbands, wives, or parents buying a sparkling gift for a loved one to mark a special moment; for young couples looking for the perfect stone for an engagement ring; for tourists, business travelers, and servicemen or servicewomen hoping to pick up a diamond at a "bargain" price while near the mines or cutting centers; and for collectors and connoisseurs who simply love diamonds and want to know more about them. It is written to give you information you need, in relevant terms you can understand.

In the following pages you will find what you need to know to make wise choices and avoid costly mistakes. I wish to stress, however, that my purpose is not to give you false confidence, nor is it to frighten you or discourage you from buying diamonds and jewelry. My primary purposes are to make you less vulnerable to the allure of *bargains* and more aware of the importance of buying from knowledgeable, reputable jewelers; to make you a more knowledgeable shopper and to help transform a confusing—often frightening—experience into one that is truly interesting, exciting, and safe.

I hope you enjoy *Diamonds: The Antoinette Matlins Buying Guide* and find it to be indispensable. Most of all, I hope it will remove your fear and enable you to experience the wonder, surprise, and romance that should be part of discovering the "perfect" diamond, a special stone that, when you look upon it, will bring the "sparkle" of delight to your eyes!

Antoinette Matlins

Introduction

Throughout history, diamonds have been prized above all other gems. Their beauty, rarity, and inherent "magical powers" have made them the symbol of kings, of power, of wealth, and of love. Every civilization, every society, grandly exhibits its fascination with and desire to possess these sparkling creations. And so it continues to this very day. We are no different from the generations that have come before, and global diamond sales continue to reach new heights.

With each passing year there are new developments in the world of diamonds—stunning new designs, new shapes, and "fancy" colors. Major new diamond deposits have also been discovered in new places, including Colorado and Canada; Canada is rapidly emerging as a major source of fine-quality diamonds. And believe it or not, we even have diamonds that *sing* (see chapter 1)!

But along with all the wonderful new developments come more things to *look out* for, and more reasons *not* to base your choice on price alone:

- **Diamonds are being treated in new ways to alter color**—including more sophisticated high pressure/high temperature methods to transform common tinted diamonds into more highly desirable colorless gems and exotic "fancy" colors, and simple methods like *surface coating* (see chapter 10).
- **New lasering techniques and glasslike fillers** are being used to improve clarity (see chapter 7).
- **Synthetic diamonds** are available in larger sizes and more colors, sometimes erroneously identified and sold as natural gems (see chapter 10).
- **New diamond *imitations* can fool some electronic diamond testers** (see chapter 10).

Adding to the complexity of buying a diamond today is the marketplace itself, and determining *where* to buy. The retail marketplace is more competitive than ever, with no fewer than ten jewelry stores in every major mall. Showrooms claiming to sell to the public at "wholesale" prices are popping up in almost every state. And Internet commerce, including online auction sites, has entered the diamond arena!

Diamond Branding Makes Its Debut

In an effort to attract customers and reassure them on matters of reliability, integrity, and the quality of products being offered, many companies are now *branding* what they sell. We find names we recognize and trust—such as De Beers—now selling "De Beers diamonds" directly to consumers. There is certainly name recognition in the De Beers brand, and it also carries with it a reputation for unparalleled expertise in the diamond field; the company hopes the brand identification will instill confidence in consumers to buy their product over another.

Retailers and designers are also getting into the branding act. You will find specially commissioned diamond cuts such as Tiffany's unique *Lucida*™ diamond cut available only at Tiffany, the *Escada*® designed exclusively for the famous fashion house, the well-known Movado company's own *Movado Diamond*, and the unique *Noble Cut*™ commissioned on an exclusive basis by designer Doron Isaak for his Couture Gems collection. Even diamond *cutters* are branding their product in an effort to reassure consumers that the diamond they are considering exhibits maximum beauty resulting from precision cutting. Currently, some of the best-known cutting brands—brands that help assure consumers of precision cutting—include the *Lazare Kaplan Ideal*®, *EightStar*®, *Hearts on Fire*®, *Gabrielle*®, *Context*®, *Tiana*™, and the *Spirit Sun*®. You will find more on cutting considerations and innovations in chapter 5. Branded diamonds are specially marked so that they can be identified and verified. This is currently done using laser technology to inscribe pertinent information along the diamond's edge—usually the brand name and logo, and a registration number that corresponds to the certificate issued with the diamond.

More and more brands are entering the market, but today most diamonds sold have no brand identification. There are many beautiful diamonds that have no "signature" but are equally dazzling; some may also offer better value. Furthermore, trademarked cuts are already being duplicated with minor alterations, sometimes so closely resembling the original that differences can only be seen with magnification. Keep in mind also that a brand name isn't always a guarantee of quality, especially in the secondary market—estate sales, auctions, pawnshops, and so on. There have already been reports of *faked* brand identification where a respected brand name—complete with logo and number—was laser inscribed on a diamond in order to represent it as a diamond of much better quality. It is relatively easy and inexpensive to laser inscribe diamonds, so we cannot ignore the possibility that the incidence of this type of fraud might increase. New technology may provide a solution; *ion beam technology,* for example, offers some promise in this area (see chapter 9).

The future of diamond branding is still unknown. Whether or not consumers will find it helpful or more confusing, only time will tell. But whatever the case, branding is no substitute for knowledge.

Now more than ever, understanding as much as possible about what you are buying is the key to getting what you really want, paying the right price, and enjoying your diamond purchases for years to come. In *Diamonds: The Antoinette Matlins Buying Guide,* you will find the information you need, including:

- The factors affecting quality differences in diamonds.
- Diamond grading reports and how to interpret what the information really means.
- How to compare prices.
- How to spot differences in stones that may *appear* to be the same quality.
- Fraudulent practices to guard against.
- How to protect yourself from misrepresentation.
- How to select the right style and design.
- Questions to ask when buying any diamond.
- What to get *in writing*.
- How to select a reliable jeweler, appraiser, and insurer.
- How to get what you want within your budget.
- … and more.

The experience of buying a diamond doesn't have to be confusing, overwhelming, intimidating, or terrifying. Within the following pages you will find the key to experiencing its magic, excitement, and pleasure.

Antoinette Matlins

PART ONE

Appreciating Diamonds

CHAPTER ONE

The Magic of Diamonds

The substance that possesses the greatest value, not only among the precious stones, but of all human possessions, is the diamond ... which for a long time was known to kings only, and to very few of them.

From the *37th Booke of the Historie of the World*, by Roman historian C. Plinius Secundus, published in the year 77 CE

The diamond has been one of the most coveted gems in history. Uncut diamonds adorned the suits of armor of the great knights; cut diamonds have adorned the crowns of kings and queens throughout the ages, and today the diamond is internationally recognized as a symbol of love and betrothal. Diamond, nature's hardest substance—uniquely able to resist both fire and steel, and therefore all of humankind's early efforts to alter it—epitomized unyielding power and invincible strength. It seemed truly indestructible. The word *diamond* comes from the Greek word *adamas* and its Roman equivalent *diamas,* which meant "the unconquerable."

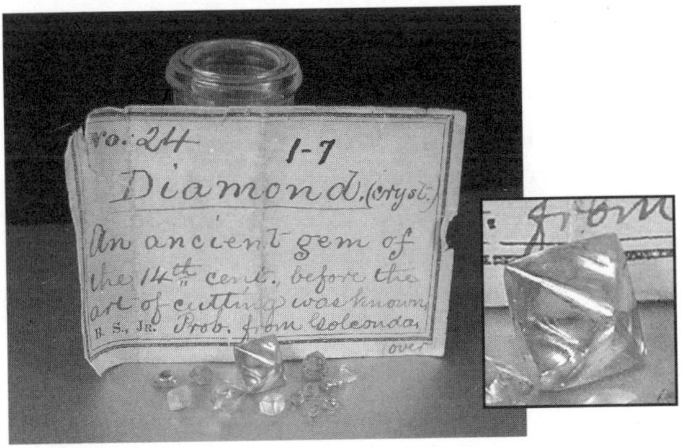

Natural diamond crystals from .05 to 3.18 carats
from the Benjamin Silliman Jr. Collection, Cornell University.
Photo: E. A. Skalwold

Legends of the diamond's mythical properties have been passed along for centuries. In India, where diamonds were first discovered several thousand years ago, the diamond was valued more for its strength and magic than for its beauty. The diamond was thought to protect its wearer from snakes, fire, poison, illness, thieves, and all the combined forces of evil.

As the gemstone of the zodiac house of Aries, symbolized by the ram, the diamond was believed by ancient astrologers to be powerful for people born under the planet Mars. They thought diamonds could provide fortitude, strength of mind, and continuous love in marriage, as well as ward off witchcraft, poisons, and nightmares.

Each culture has prized the diamond for its unique properties. The Romans believed that a diamond worn against the skin of the left arm would help them remain brave and daring in battle and give them victory over their enemies. An ancient passage reads: "He who carries a diamond on the left side shall be hardy and manly; it will guard him from accidents to the limbs; but nevertheless a good diamond will lose its power and virtue if worn by one who is incontinent or drunken." Another Roman practice was to set diamonds in steel to serve as a charm against insanity.

The diamond has been credited with many magical powers. At one time it was considered the emblem of fearlessness and invincibility; the mere possession of a diamond would endow the wearer with superior strength, bravery, and courage. It was also believed that a diamond could drive away the devil and all spirits of the night.

During the 1500s, diamonds were looked upon as talismans that could enhance the love of a husband for his wife. In the Talmud, a gem that from its description was probably a diamond was worn by the high priest and served to prove innocence or guilt. If an accused person was guilty, the stone grew dim; if the person was innocent, it shone more brilliantly than ever!

Aside from colorless varieties, diamonds occur in every color of the rainbow. The Hindus classed diamonds according to the four castes. The Brahmin diamond (colorless) gave power, friends, riches, and good luck; the Kshatriya (brown/champagne) prevented old age; Vaisya (the color of a kodali flower) brought success; and the Sudra (a diamond with the sheen of a polished blade—probably gray or black) brought all types of good fortune. Red and yellow diamonds were exclusively royal gems, for kings alone.

Diamonds have been associated with almost everything from inducing sleepwalking to producing invincibility and spiritual ecstasy. Even sexual prowess has been strongly attributed to the diamond. There is a catch, however, to all the mythical powers associated with this remarkable gem. One must find the diamond "naturally" in order to experience its magic, for it loses its powers if acquired by purchase. However, when a diamond is offered as a pledge of love or friendship, its potency may return—another good reason for its presence in the engagement ring!

Diamonds to Delight the *Ear* as Well as the Eye

Diamonds are creating a new sensation, quite literally, as they move from the visual realm to the realm of *sound*. Now, in addition to liking the way a diamond looks, you may soon be able to decide if you like the way it sounds!

Advanced technology now makes it possible to translate lightwave patterns into soundwaves—sound that can be consistently reproduced and recorded. Each diamond has a unique pattern that creates a unique sound. This new, patent-pending innovation called *Diamond Melody* was pioneered by Gabi Tolkowsky, world-renowned diamond cutter and cousin of Marcel Tolkowsky (father of the modern American ideal-cut diamond), and Gemprint, the Canadian company specializing in diamond laser identification (see chapter 17).

At a conference I attended several years ago, Gabi Tolkowsky played a CD that filled the room with a dreamy, abstract sound. There was an almost otherworldly dimension to what we were hearing, random yet beautiful. We then heard another work, this one clearly a different composition, but with the same absorbing, new-age sound. And then we were told who the composers were: two diamonds! I recently purchased two diamonds, had CDs made, and played them at a gala event at which I was the featured speaker here in Woodstock, Vermont. They were a hit … and it was magical!

One day in the near future, it may well be possible to go to a jewelry store and select a diamond not only because of its visual characteristics, but because of its unique sound. The diamond of the twenty-first century may do more than dazzle the eye—it may also enchant the ear!

CHAPTER TWO

Becoming Familiar with Diamonds

Diamonds should never be bought casually—there are too many risks and the uneducated consumer will always lose. This is a basic rule of thumb. The best way to take the risk out of buying a particular diamond is to familiarize yourself with the stone. While the average consumer can't hope to make the same precise judgments as a qualified gemologist, whose scientific training and wealth of practical experience provide a far greater database with which to operate, the consumer can learn to judge a stone as a "total personality" and learn what the critical factors are—color, clarity (also referred to in the trade as "perfection"), cut, brilliance, and weight—and how to balance them in judging the diamond's value. Learning about these factors and spending time in the marketplace looking, listening, and asking questions before making the purchase will prepare you to be a wise buyer more likely to get what you really want, at a fair price.

Try to learn as much as you can about the diamond you want to buy. Examine stones owned by your family and friends, and compare stones at several different jewelry stores, noting differences in shades of colors, brilliance, and cut. Go to a good, established jewelry store and ask to see fine stones. If the prices vary, ask why. Let the jeweler point out differences in color, cut, or brilliance, and if he can't, go to another jeweler with greater expertise. Begin to develop an eye for what constitutes a fine stone by looking, listening, and asking good questions.

Before you consider buying any stone, ask yourself:

- Is the color what *you* desire?
- Is the shape what *you* want?

- Is it lively? Does it have the character or personality that *you* like?
- Do *you* feel excited by it?
- Can you afford it?

If you answer yes to all of these questions, you are ready to examine the specific stone more carefully.

The Six Key Steps in Examining a Stone

1. *Whenever possible, examine stones unmounted.* They can be examined more thoroughly out of their settings, and defects cannot be hidden by the mounting or side stones.
2. *Make sure the diamond is clean.* If you are buying a stone from a retail jeweler, ask that it be cleaned for you. If you are not in a place where it can be cleaned professionally, breathe on the stone in a huffing manner in order to steam it with your breath, and then wipe it with a clean handkerchief. This will at least remove the superficial film of grease.
3. *Hold the unmounted stone so that your fingers touch only the girdle* (the edge where top and bottom meet). Putting your fingers on the table (top) and/or pavilion (bottom) will leave traces of oil, which will affect color and brilliance.

   The *careful* use of tweezers instead of fingers is recommended only if you feel comfortable using them. Make sure you know how to use them, and get the permission of the owner before picking up the diamond. It is easy for the stone to pop out of the tweezers and to become damaged or lost, and you could be held responsible.
4. *View the diamond under proper lighting.* Many jewelers use numerous incandescent spotlights, usually recessed in dropped ceilings. Some use special spotlights that can make any stone—even glass imitations—look fantastic.

   Fluorescent lights are what professionals use for diamond grading, but they *adversely* affect the appearance of the stone. Diamonds will not show as much brilliance and fire, as much sparkle, when viewed under fluorescent lighting. I recommend looking at diamonds in several types of light, including daylight when it is available (sometimes the jeweler will let you walk to a window or go outside to better see the stone's personality).

The light source should come from above or behind you, shining down and through the stone, so that the light traveling through the stone is reflected back up to your eye.

5. *Rotate the stone in order to view it from different angles.*
6. *If you are using a loupe, focus it both on the surface and into the interior.* To focus into the interior, shift the stone slowly, raising or lowering it, until you focus clearly on all depths within it. This is important because if you focus on the top only, you won't see what is in the interior of the stone.

How to Use a Loupe

A loupe (pronounced *loop*) is a special type of magnifying glass. The loupe can be very helpful in many situations, even for the beginner. With a loupe you can check a stone for chips or scratches or examine certain types of noticeable inclusions more closely. Remember, however, that even with a loupe, you will not have the knowledge or skill to see or understand the many telltale indicators that an experienced jeweler or gemologist could spot. No book can provide you with that knowledge or skill. Do not allow yourself to be deluded or let a little knowledge give you false confidence. Nothing will more quickly alienate a reputable jeweler or mark you faster as easy prey for the disreputable dealer.

The loupe is a very practical tool to use once you master it, and with practice it will become more and more valuable. The correct type is a 10x, or ten-power, "triplet," which can be obtained from any optical supply house. The triplet type is recommended because it corrects two problems other types of magnifiers have: traces of color normally found at the outer edge of the lens, and visual distortion, also usually at the outer edge of the lens. In addition, the loupe must have a black housing around the lens, not chrome or gold, either of which might affect the color you see in the stone.

The loupe *must* be 10x because the United States Federal Trade Commission requires grading to be done under ten-power magnification. Any flaw that does not show up under 10x magnification is considered nonexistent for grading purposes.

With a few minutes' practice you can easily learn to use the loupe. Here's how:

1. Hold the loupe between the thumb and forefinger of either hand.
2. Hold the stone or jewelry similarly in the other hand.
3. Bring both hands together so that the fleshy parts just below the thumbs are pushed together and braced by the lower portion of each hand just above the wrists (the wrist acts as a pivot point).
4. Now move both hands up to your nose or cheek, with the loupe as close to your eye as possible. If you wear eyeglasses, you do not have to remove them.
5. Get a steady hand. With diamonds it's very important to have steady hands for careful examination. With your hands still together and braced against your face, put your elbows on a table. (If a table isn't available, brace your arms against your chest or rib cage.) If you do this properly you will have a steady hand.

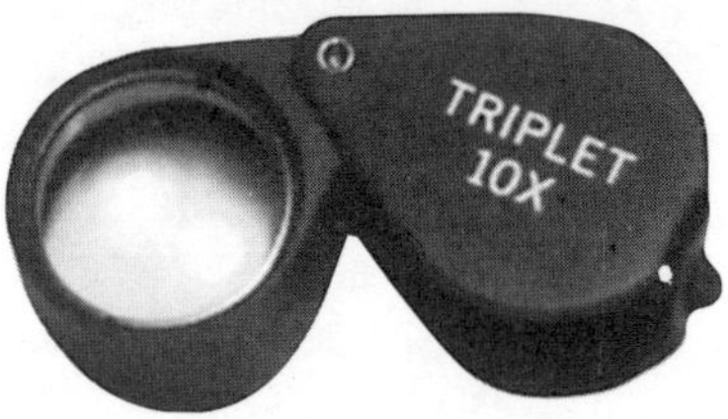

A 10x Triplet Loupe

How to hold a loupe when examining a stone

Practice with the loupe, keeping it approximately one inch (more or less) from your eye, and about an inch from the object being examined. Learn to see through it clearly. A 10x loupe is difficult to focus initially, but with a little practice it will become easy. You can practice on any object that is difficult to see—the pores in your skin, a strand of hair, a pinhead, or your own jewelry.

Play with the item being examined. Rotate it slowly, tilt it back and forth while rotating it, and look at it from different angles and different directions. It won't take long until you can focus easily on anything you wish to examine. If you aren't sure about your technique, a knowledgeable jeweler will be happy to help you learn to use a loupe correctly.

What the Loupe Can Tell You

With practice and experience (and further education if you're really serious), a loupe can tell even the amateur a great deal. For a gemologist it can help determine whether the stone is natural, synthetic, or glass, and reveal characteristic flaws, blemishes, or cracks. In other words, the loupe can provide the necessary information to help you know whether the stone is in fact what it is supposed to be.

For the beginner, the loupe is useful in seeing these features:

- *The workmanship that went into the cutting.* For example, is the symmetry of the stone balanced? Does it have the proper number of facets for its cut? Is the proportion good? Few cutters put the same time and care into cutting glass as they do into a diamond.
- *Chips, cracks, or scratches on the facet edges, planes, or table.* White zircon, for example, looks very much like diamond because of its pronounced brilliance and relative hardness, but it chips easily. Therefore, careful examination of a zircon will often show chipping, especially on the top and around the edges. Glass, which is very soft, will often show scratches. Normal wear can cause it to chip or become scratched. Also, if you check around the prongs, the setter may even have scratched it while bending the prongs to hold the stone.
- *The sharpness of the facet edges.* Harder stones will have a sharp edge, or sharper boundaries between adjoining planes or facets, whereas many imitations are softer, so that under the loupe the edges between the facets are less sharp and have a more rounded appearance.
- *Bubbles, inclusions, and flaws.* Many flaws and inclusions that cannot be seen with the naked eye can be seen with the loupe. But remember, many are not easily seen unless you are very experienced. With minimal experience, however, even the amateur can learn to spot the characteristic bubbles and swirl lines associated with glass.

When you use a loupe, remember that you won't see what the experienced professional will see—clues about the diamond's quality, authenticity, and durability—but with a little practice, it can still be a valuable tool and might save you from a costly mistake.

CHAPTER THREE

Looking for a Diamond That's a "Cut Above"

One of the most important things to learn is how to look at a diamond, even if you won't see all that a gemologist will. Let's begin by making sure you understand the terms you will be hearing and using to describe what you want—especially terms pertaining to the stone's "cut" and the names for the parts of a cut stone.

It's important to be familiar with a few general terms that are commonly used in reference to faceted stones. The parts of a stone can vary in proportion and thus affect its brilliance, beauty, and desirability. This will be discussed later in greater detail.

- *Girdle.* The girdle is the edge or border of the stone that forms its perimeter; it is the edge formed where the top portion of the stone meets the bottom portion—its "dividing line." This is the part usually grasped by the prongs of a setting.
- *Crown.* The crown is also called the *top* of the stone. This is simply the upper portion of the stone: the part above the girdle.
- *Pavilion.* The pavilion is the bottom portion of the stone, the part from the girdle to the "point" at the bottom.
- *Culet.* The culet is the lowest part or point of the stone. It may be missing in some stones, which can indicate damage.
- *Table.* The table is the flat top of the stone and is the

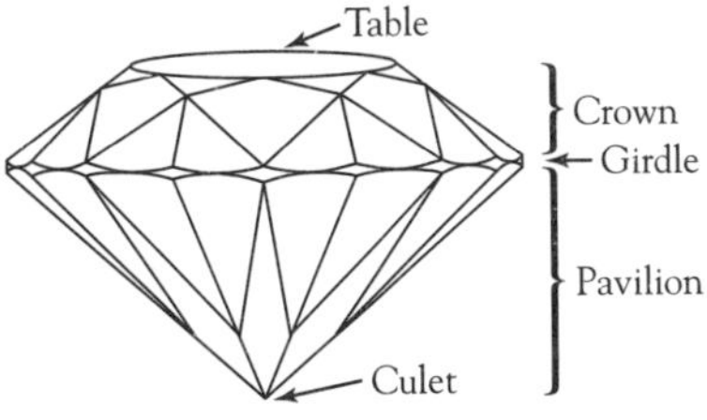

Parts of a faceted stone

stone's largest facet, often called the *face*. The term *table spread* is used to describe the width of the table facet, often expressed as a percentage of the total width of the stone.

The Cut of the Stone

The most important—and least understood—factor that must be evaluated when one considers any gem is the *cutting*. When we talk about cut, we are not referring to the *shape* but to the care and precision used in creating a finished gem from the rough. There are many popular shapes for diamonds. Each shape affects the overall look of the stone, but if the stone is cut well its brilliance and value endure no matter what shape it is. For the average consumer, choosing a shape is simply a matter of personal taste. Some of the most popular shapes are pictured. New shapes are discussed in chapter 5.

Classic Shapes

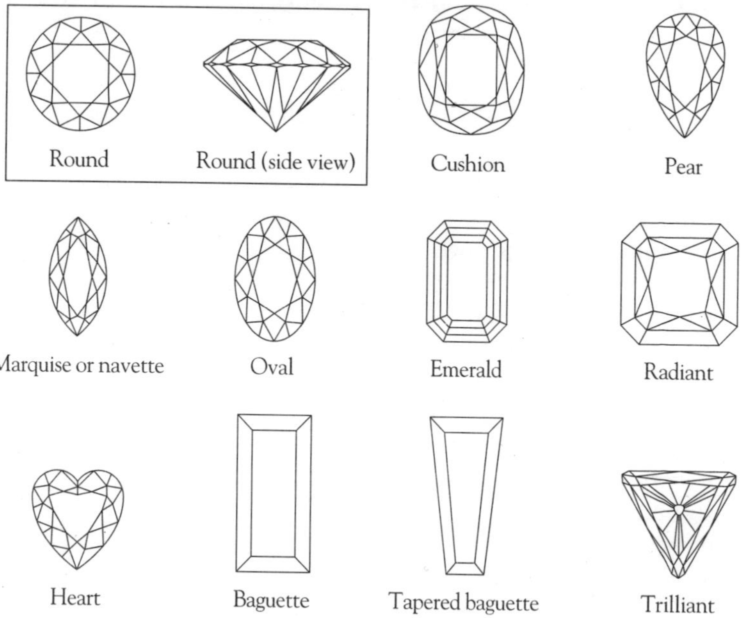

Make Makes a Big Difference

The shape of the stone may affect the personality it displays, but it is the overall cutting that releases its full beauty. A term used by professionals to describe the overall quality of the cutting is *make*. Having a "good make" is especially important in diamonds. A diamond with an "excellent make" will sell for much more than one with a "fair make." The difference in price between a well-cut diamond and one that is poorly cut can be as much as 50 percent or more. Even more important, careless cutting, or cutting to get the largest possible stone from the rough, can sometimes result in faults that may make a stone more fragile and vulnerable to breakage. Such stones should sell for much less, although the fault may not be visible without careful examination by an expert. Here we will discuss cutting in a general way. It will be discussed in greater detail later.

How to Know Whether a Stone Is Well Cut

The precision of the cutting dramatically affects the beauty and value of any gemstone. This is especially true in *faceted* stones, those on which a series of tiny flat planes (facets or faces) have been cut and polished. (Nonfaceted stones are called *cabochons*.) You should also keep in mind that there are several cutting styles used for faceted stones: brilliant cut, as seen in round diamonds (using many triangular and kite-shaped facets); step cut, as seen in emerald-cut stones (using trapezoidal or rectangular facets); and mixed cut, which combines both styles.

Whichever faceting style is used, by following some general guidelines for looking at faceted gemstones, you can better determine both the quality of the stone and the quality of the cut. The first thing to keep in mind is that if the basic material is of good quality, the way it is cut will make the difference between a dull, lifeless stone and a beautiful, brilliant one. In diamonds, the cutting and proportioning have the greatest influence on the stone's brilliance and fire.

Look at the stone face up, as you see any stone set in jewelry, from the top. This is the most critical area to view, since this is the one most often noticed. As you look at a diamond, does it seem to sparkle and dance across the whole stone, or are there dead spots?

A quick way to check the symmetry of a round diamond is to look at the table edges. The lines should be straight, regular, and parallel to one another. The table edges should form a regular octagon, with the edges meeting in sharp points. If the lines of the table are wavy, the overall symmetry is not good, and the symmetry of the adjoining facets will also be affected.

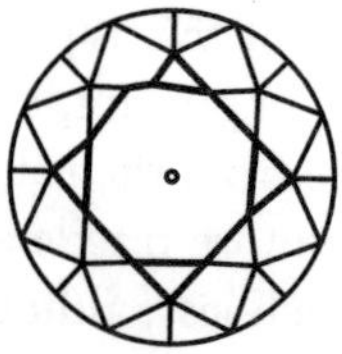

Table centered but not symmetrical

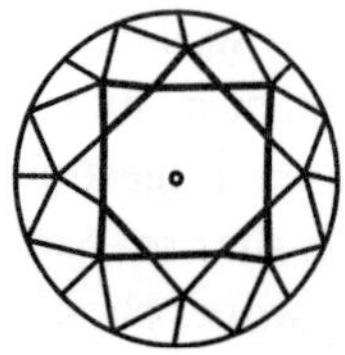

Table off-center and asymmetrical

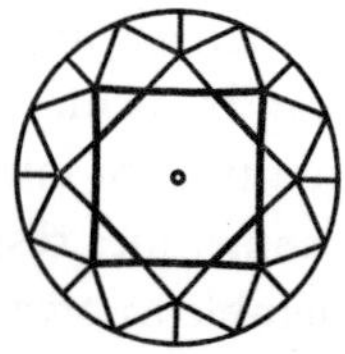

Table centered and symmetrical—the ideal

Next, look at the stone from the side. Note the proportion of the stone both above and below the girdle.

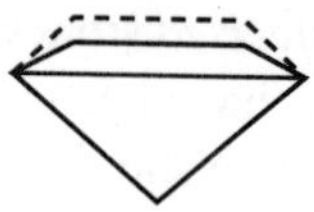

Crown too shallow (thin)

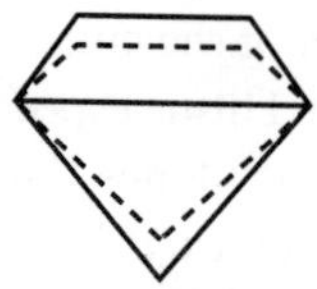

Crown and pavilion too heavy (thick)

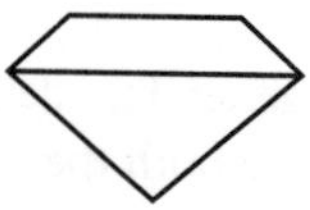

Ideal stone

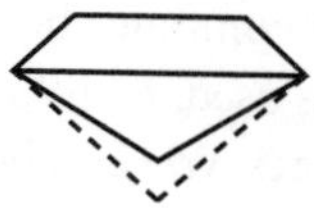

Pavilion too shallow

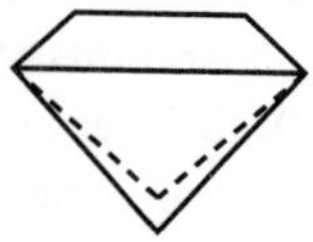

Pavilion too deep (heavy)

The stone's proportion—whether it is too thin or too thick—will have a marked effect on its overall beauty. The effects of cut and proportioning will be discussed in greater detail in chapter 5, but it is an important first step to become aware of general views and to begin to have a feeling about what looks "right."

Before Beginning

As you shop for any fine gem or piece of jewelry, keep in mind the importance of visiting fine jewelry stores to look at stones and compare them. Many of the factors discussed in the following chapters will become clearer when you have actual stones before you to examine, and you will gain a deeper understanding and appreciation for the gem you are considering. Knowledgeable jewelers will also be happy to take time to help you understand differences in quality and cost.

Also keep in mind the importance of buying only from a well-trained, reputable jeweler. Remember, you are not an expert. The information provided here should help you begin your search more confidently and gain insights that will make the experience more fun, more challenging, and more fulfilling. But perhaps just as important, I hope it will help you make a wiser decision about the jeweler with whom you decide to do business, and about his or her knowledge, professionalism, and integrity. If so, this book will have provided a valuable service and perhaps saved you from a costly mistake.

PART TWO

Diamonds

CHAPTER FOUR

What Is a Diamond?

Chemically speaking, diamond is the simplest of all gemstones. It is plain, crystallized carbon—the same substance, chemically, as the soot left on the inside of a glass globe after the burning of a candle; it is the same substance used in "lead" pencils.

The diamond differs from these in its crystal form, which gives it the desirable properties that have made it so highly prized—its hardness, its ability to withstand heat and pressure, its brilliance, and its fire. (But note that while diamond is the hardest natural substance known, it *can* be chipped or broken if hit from certain angles, and if the "girdle"—the edge of the diamond that forms the perimeter—has been cut too thin, it can be chipped with even a modest blow.)

The transparent white—or, more correctly, *colorless*—diamond is the most popular variety, but diamond also occurs in colors. When the color is prominent it is called a *fancy-color* diamond. Diamond is frequently found in nice yellow and brown shades. Colors such as pink, light blue, light green, and lavender occur much more rarely. In diamonds, the colors seen are usually pastel. Deep colors in hues of red, green, and blue are extremely rare. Historically, most colored diamonds have sold for more than their colorless counterparts, except for light yellow or brown varieties. Yellow or brown in *very* pale shades may not be fancy diamonds but *off-color* stones that are very common and much less valuable than colorless diamonds or those with a true "fancy" color. Since fancy-color diamonds are graded and valued differently from colorless diamonds, we cover them separately in chapter 12.

India was one of the earliest known sources of diamond, and the most important, until the eighteenth-century discovery of diamonds in Brazil. In the nineteenth century, a major diamond discovery was made in South Africa, and the twentieth century saw diamond discoveries in other African nations such as Botswana and Angola, and in Russia, Australia, and, most recently, Canada. Commercial diamond mining is also taking place in the United States.

Many diamonds mined today have no "jewelry" value because they are too tinted and heavily flawed, but they are used for many industrial purposes. Colorless and fancy-color diamonds remain rare, with red diamond being the rarest and most valuable of all gems.

The Four Factors That Determine Diamond Value

Diamond quality and value are determined by four factors, which are called the "four Cs." They are often listed as follows:

1. Color (body color or *absence* of color)
2. Clarity (degree of flawlessness)
3. Cutting and proportioning (often referred to as the *make*)
4. Carat weight (which affects the size)

In terms of determining beauty, however, we would rank them in a different order:

1. Cutting and proportioning
2. Color
3. Clarity
4. Carat weight

Finding the Right Combination

Keep in mind, however, that the key to being happy with your diamond purchase is understanding how each of these four Cs affects beauty and durability, cost, and the stone *as a whole*. It may sound complicated at first, but when you begin looking at stones you'll see it really isn't. With a little experience, you'll decide which Cs are most important to you, and you'll know what to look for to get the right combination—one that meets your *emotional* and *financial* needs.

Because each factor is a lesson in itself, I have devoted a chapter to each. I will begin with a discussion of diamond cutting and proportioning because it is the least understood and because I think it's the most important factor in terms of the stone's beauty.

CHAPTER FIVE

The Importance of Cut & Proportion

The cutting of a diamond is the least understood of the four Cs, and yet it has a significant impact on cost. A well-cut diamond can easily cost 40 to 50 percent more than one that is poorly cut, so let's be sure you understand what it's all about.

It is important to distinguish exactly what *cut* means in reference to diamonds and other stones. *Cut* does *not* mean *shape*. Shape pertains to the outline of the diamond's perimeter. The selection of shape is a matter of individual preference. No matter which shape is selected, its *cutting* must be evaluated.

There are several different cutting styles: *brilliant* cut, *step* cut, or *mixed* cut. A brilliant cut uses many facets, usually triangular and kite-shaped, arranged in a particular way to create maximum brilliance. A step cut uses fewer facets, usually trapezoidal or rectangular in shape, arranged in a more linear pattern, as you see in the emerald cut (see the "Classic Shapes" chart on page 14). Although usually less brilliant than those cut in a brilliant style, step-cut diamonds can produce a lively, fiery stone with a very elegant and understated personality. You often see step-cut triangle, square, and trapezoid shapes in art deco–period jewelry. A mixed-cut style incorporates elements from both the step-cut and brilliant-cut styles.

The term *cut*—also referred to as the stone's *make*—is especially important because of its effect on the beauty and personality of the diamond. When we evaluate the cut, we are really judging many factors, including the stone's proportioning and finish, and their impact on producing the *fire* (the lovely rainbow colors that flash from within) and *brilliance* (the liveliness, the sparkle) that sets diamond apart from all other gems. Regardless of the shape or cutting style, a stone with an excellent make will be exciting, while a stone with a poor make will look lifeless; it will lack the sparkle and personality we identify with diamond. In addition, diamonds are often cut to make them *appear* larger. But a stone that looks much larger than another of the same weight will not be as beautiful as a smaller stone that is properly cut.

Differences in cutting can also affect the *durability* of a diamond. Some cutting faults weaken the stone and make it more susceptible to breaking or chipping.

Fine cutting requires skill and experience, takes more time, and results in greater loss of the "rough" from which the stone is being cut, resulting in a stone that yields less weight when finished. For all these reasons, a well-cut diamond commands a premium and will cost much more than one that is cut poorly.

There are many popular shapes for diamonds. Each shape affects the overall look of the stone, but if the stone is cut well, beauty and value endure no matter which shape you choose. I will begin the discussion of diamond cutting with the round brilliant cut, since this is the most popular shape.

A traditional round brilliant-cut diamond has fifty-eight facets. There are thirty-three on the top, twenty-four on the bottom, plus the culet—the "point" at the bottom, which normally is another tiny facet (although many diamonds today are cut without a culet). Round brilliant-cut stones that are small in size are referred to as "full-cut" to distinguish them from "single-cut" stones that have only seventeen facets, or "Swiss-cut" with only thirty-three facets. Older pieces of jewelry such as heirloom diamond bands, or inexpensive pieces containing numerous stones, often contain these cuts instead of full-cut stones. They have less brilliance and liveliness than full-cuts, but with fewer facets they are easier and less expensive to cut. Rings containing single- or Swiss-cut stones should sell for less than rings with full-cut stones. Today there are also an increasing number of specialty cuts that have more than fifty-eight facets.

When a round brilliant-cut diamond is cut well, its shape displays the most liveliness because it enables the most light to be reflected back up through the top. This means that round brilliant-cut diamonds will have greater brilliance, overall, than other shapes, but other shapes can also be very lively. New shapes are also appearing, some of which compare very favorably to round stones for overall brilliance and liveliness.

As a rule of thumb when looking at round diamonds, if the top portion of the stone (the crown) appears to be roughly one-third of the pavilion depth (distance from girdle to culet), the proportioning is probably acceptable.

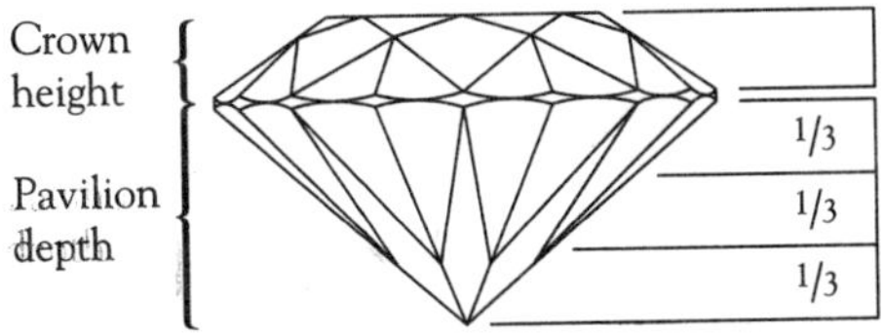

Crown height about ⅓ of pavilion depth.

A well-proportioned stone

Types of Diamond Proportioning

The proportioning—especially the height of the crown in relation to the depth of the pavilion, and the width of the table facet in relation to the width of the stone—is what determines how much brilliance and fire the stone will have. Over the years, several formulas for correct proportioning have been developed for round diamonds. Until recently it was believed that stones cut to these very precise formulas were "ideal" and would be more beautiful than other diamonds. These "ideal" cut stones

How Cutting Affects Brilliance

Light Reflection in a Well-Proportioned Diamond
Correct proportions ensure the maximum brilliance. When light enters a properly cut diamond, it is reflected from facet to facet, and then back up through the top, exhibiting maximum fire and sparkle.

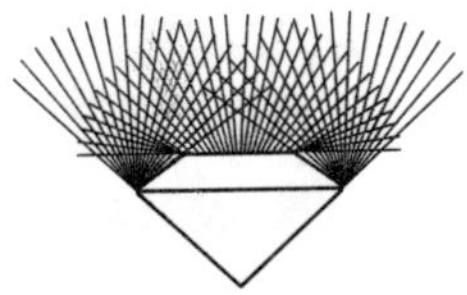

Light Reflection in a Diamond Cut Too Deep
In a diamond that is cut too deep, much of the light is reflected to opposite facets at the wrong angle and is lost through the sides. The diamond appears dark in the center.

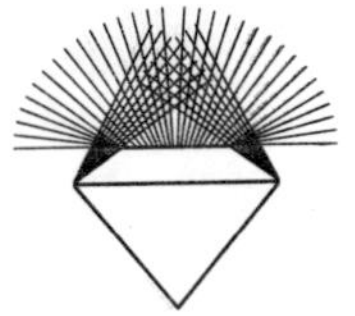

Light Reflection in a Diamond Cut Too Shallow
A diamond cut too shallow (to make it look larger) loses brilliance. The eye sees a ring of dull reflection instead of the great brilliance of a well-cut diamond.

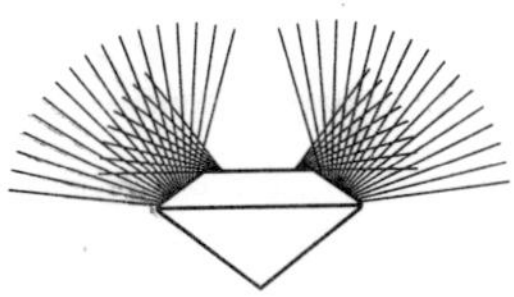

also cost more than other diamonds because of the extra time and skill required to cut them, and because more diamond "rough" is lost in the cutting. However, advanced research and technology have shown us that a wider range of proportioning, combined with other factors, can create equally beautiful diamonds. Today the use of the term "ideal" is discouraged. Nonetheless, no one can deny that precision cutting is essential to releasing maximum beauty in a diamond.

What Is Ideal?

Diamond cutting is an art form that is still evolving, and technological advances continue to shed new insights on how cutting affects the way light travels through diamond to create a scintillating stone. Today there are several slightly differing formulas for cutting an "ideal" stone, and there is no consensus as to what is "best," but each results in an exceptionally beautiful stone. Generally speaking, diamonds that are cut with smaller tables exhibit more fire; those with larger tables exhibit more brilliance. Larger tables seem to be more in fashion today. But, as common sense may tell you here, both can't excel in the same stone. A larger table can create greater brilliance but may cause some reduction in fire; a smaller table area can increase fire but may reduce brilliance. The ideal would be a compromise that would allow the greatest brilliance and fire simultaneously. No one has come to agreement, however, on what the percentages should be, since some people prefer fire to brilliance, and vice versa. This is one reason why there are several different types of proportioning found in dia-

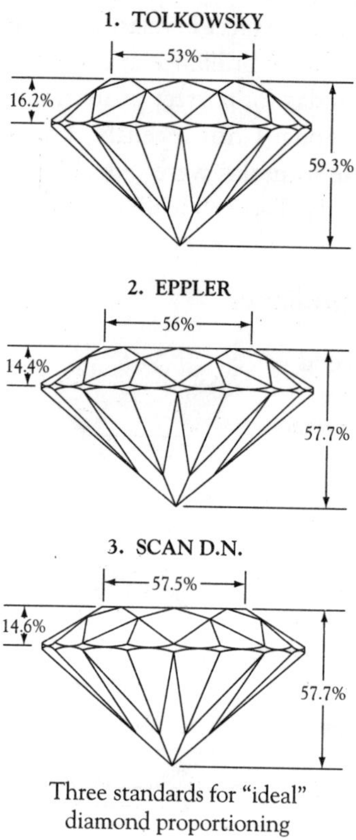

Three standards for "ideal" diamond proportioning

monds, and "best" is usually a matter of personal preference.

EightStar® Diamond

In 1919, Marcel Tolkowsky developed what he thought would be the best combination of angles to allow light to enter the stone and be reflected back in such a way as to create the most vivid fire combined with intense brilliance. The Tolkowsky cut provided the basis for the modern American ideal make, but today there are several variations of Tolkowsky's formula, some with brand names, such as the *Lazare Kaplan Ideal®*, the *EightStar®* (which exhibits eight perfectly aligned arrows that can be seen with a special viewer), and the *Hearts on Fire®* (which produces a hearts-and-arrows pattern that can be seen with a special viewer). Whatever "ideal" you choose, each results in a very beautiful diamond, but you must compare them for yourself to discover which "ideal" you prefer.

The "Ideal" May Not Always Be Ideal

We should also caution you against diamonds that are described as "ideal" but really are not. Such diamonds are graded "ideal" because they have a depth percentage and a table percentage that are in the "ideal" range, but the *particular* table percentage is not correct for the *particular* depth percentage. These stones may sell for a premium because of their "ideal" grade, but will lack the beauty of other "ideal" cut stones, and are often less beautiful than stones that have been cut with proportions and percentages not currently considered "ideal." We've seen diamonds cut to "ideal" proportions that are not as brilliant and fiery as diamonds cut to non-ideal proportions and vice versa. And to compound matters further, some people simply like the look of diamonds that have tables that are wider than what is currently considered "ideal." We've even seen diamonds with tables exceeding 64 percent that were surprisingly beautiful and very desirable.

What Is "Ideal" Today May Not Be Called "Ideal" Tomorrow

While no one questions the importance of cutting on the beauty of a diamond, the term "ideal" may soon become obsolete. Years of research by major laboratories, and the development of advanced technology, has changed our prior understanding of the factors affecting brilliance, fire, and scintillation in diamonds. Using new instrumentation that actually measures the performance of light within the stone—how much brilliance and fire is produced—researchers have learned that proportioning is only *one* of *numerous* factors that can affect the stone's beauty and liveliness. For example, altering the length of certain facets on the top and bottom of a diamond can result in a stone with a table or depth percentage outside of today's "ideal" parameters but in which there is even greater brilliance and fire than one cut *within* the "ideal" parameters.

The most important outcome of the research is that we are seeing changes that allow for a broader range of proportioning for top cut grades. Cut grades at respected laboratories today are moving toward "performance-based" rather than "proportion-based" evaluation and are using state-of-the-art ray-tracing software to measure the light *performance*—the quality and quantity of light being returned to the viewer—in addition to proportions, symmetry, polish, and other factors. The Gemological Institute of America (GIA) has also developed new software based on years of research that incorporates light performance with other important factors, and with which they have recently begun to evaluate and assign cut grades on reports.

As a result of these changes, even the term "ideal" itself has come under scrutiny. Most American labs no longer use this term, nor does GIA; GIA uses the terms "Excellent," "Very Good," "Good," "Fair," and "Poor" to indicate the quality of the cutting.

New Technology Provides *Ideal* Solution

Rather than relying rigidly on formulas or subjective perceptions, new technology has provided the "ideal" solution to the dilemma of judging the overall make of a diamond. Increasingly we are finding new tools on the jewelry store counter—including the *FireScope®*, introduced by EightStar® Diamond Company, the *BrillianceScope™ Analyzer,* and the *BrillianceScope™ Viewer,* developed by GemEx, and the *Gilbertson Scope*—to make it easier for you to know whether or not a diamond is cut to exceptional standards. These tools provide information regarding the *light activity within a diamond.*

One of the first to be developed was the FireScope®. With it, you can compare the cutting of several diamonds side by side very quickly.

When a precisely cut diamond—one in which each of the fifty-eight facets has been properly shaped, angled, and aligned—is viewed through the scope, the diamond will produce a pattern showing eight black arrows against a red background. When you see this, you know the diamond exhibits high brilliance, fire, and scintillation.

The BrillianceScope™ Analyzer and the BrillianceScope™ Viewer also enable you to compare several diamonds, but rather than relying on patterns they actually *measure* how much brilliance, fire, and scintillation is seen in the diamond. The latest viewer, the Gilbertson Scope, is similar to the FireScope® but produces a pattern in three colors for a more precise impression of the fire and scintillation.

What is most exciting about these new technologies is that they are providing information about what is really important; that is, what the diamond is *doing* with the light that enters it. With viewers such as those mentioned here, even the most inexperienced consumers will be able to see how light is performing in a specific stone, compare the brilliance and the fire—the overall personality—of different stones, and pick what they really like best. As more jewelers acquire such diamond viewers, it will become much easier for consumers to judge not only the cutting of a diamond, but the final result: its beauty.

Six diamonds, as seen with the FireScope®, showing the progression of cutting perfection. The diamond on the far right is not very well cut, while the diamond on the far left, one of the "super ideal" cuts known as an EightStar® diamond, shows eight perfect arrows, telling you the diamond is precision-cut; that is, each of the fifty-eight facets is perfectly shaped, angled, and aligned.

Beauty Is in the Eye of the Beholder

Despite the debate over what is really "ideal," or what terminology will be used in the future to communicate the quality of the cutting, no one will argue that a diamond that is really beautiful, one that exhibits a brilliant, fiery character, *is* well cut, regardless of what it is called.

But what one person might consider the most beautiful stone may not be the choice of another. Diamonds exhibit different personalities depending on the make. Stones with what has come to be known as an "ideal" make will exhibit one personality, while another diamond with different proportioning will exhibit a different personality. Some stones throw out much more white light than others, while some seem more fiery because of the way they break up the white light into pinpoint flashes of its component rainbow colors. Some seem to have more contrast within the stone, and exhibit an interesting pattern within the stone, while others do not. Today a diamond cut with an "ideal" make may cost more, but that doesn't mean everyone will prefer the appearance of that stone to another that is cut to different proportions. *You* must decide what you really like the best, not the salesperson. More importantly, today some stones that do *not* have "ideal proportions" are receiving GIA's *highest* cut grade, while some stones that *do* have "ideal proportions" are *not* getting the highest grade.

Experienced professionals know when they look at a diamond, regardless of its proportioning, whether or not it has a fine make. If you take the time to focus on a stone's personality and overall character, to focus on how it really looks to your unaided eye, you can also learn to see differences and recognize whether or not a stone is well cut. Let your eye be responsible for making the final determination. In general, when you look at a diamond that has a lot of brilliance and fire, the cutting and proportioning will be good. A stone that appears lifeless or dead, or seems dark across the center, probably suffers from poor cutting and proportioning. The more time you take to look at and compare diamonds of different qualities and prices, the better trained your eye will become to detect differences in brilliance and fire, lifelessness and dullness.

Since well-cut stones cost more, when purchasing a diamond, always ask about its "make." Ask the seller how they would describe it: Excellent or Exceptional ("ideal"), Very Good, Good, Fair, or Poor.

Gem Testing Laboratories That Provide Diamond Cut Grades or Information on the Cut of a Diamond

Since cutting has such an effect on a diamond's beauty, durability, and cost, an increasing number of American laboratories now assign a cut grade on reports or provide information indicating how well or poorly cut the stone may be. European laboratories do not yet provide cut grades because they think research findings are incomplete and still do not reflect the whole story. This is also the case among laboratories in most other parts of the world, including South America, Asia, the Middle East, and Africa.

For those who want to have information about the cut of a particular diamond or a cut "grade," American laboratories that currently provide this information include: American Gem Society Laboratories (AGSL) in Las Vegas; Gem Certification and Assurance Lab (GCAL) in New York City; and Professional Gem Sciences Laboratory (PGS) in Chicago. In addition, in January 2006, GIA began to show cut grades on diamond reports (for round diamonds only).

Given the prevalence of GIA diamond grading reports and the reliance of so many buyers on the information they provide, we must take a moment here to explain the GIA cut grade. The cut grade shown on GIA reports is computer generated, based on input from the grader. The computer program was developed based on data compiled from years of research on thousands of diamonds, using sophisticated ray-tracing technology to evaluate the actual movement of light within the diamond, along with other data affecting weight retention and durability factors. The grade shown for a particular diamond on a GIA report, however, is not based on its actual light performance. As a result, while any diamond having a cut grade of good, very good, or excellent will be a lovely diamond, the computer program cannot replicate the actual light performance within a particular diamond. What we have been seeing since the introduction of cut grades on GIA reports is that there are some stones that are more beautiful than their grade indicates, and others that are less beautiful. This is important for any diamond buyer to understand, since you pay more for a higher cut grade, so you will want to look carefully at any stone you're considering to make sure the diamond's beauty merits the additional cost. In some cases, it might be wise to submit the stone to another lab that uses ray-tracing technology to confirm that the cut grade reflects the maximum light performance.

Don't rely entirely on the cut grade as an indicator of beauty and value! If your goal in seeking a diamond with a fine cut grade is to ensure you get a beautiful stone, you must compare stones having different cut grades side by side, paying attention to their sparkle and fire. Differences really can be seen when you pay attention to the "personality" of the stone. I see this with my own clients, who often tell me they are interested only in diamonds with "excellent" cut grades, but sometimes I come across an exceptionally beautiful diamond that for some unknown reason has been graded "very good" rather than excellent, and I add it to the stones I show the client. When it turns out that the "most beautiful" stone among all those under consideration is the one with the "very good" cut grade rather than an "excellent" grade, the client is always very surprised ... but also delighted to pay *less*, and get *more*!

Whether or not your diamond has a diamond grading report or a "cut grade," no matter what the proportions are, let your eye be the judge. Before making a final decision, ask yourself whether or not you think the stone is beautiful. If you like it, don't allow yourself to be overly influenced by formulas, terms, or numbers on a report.

Faulty Cuts

Many errors that affect the appearance and value of a diamond can occur in the cutting. Remember that some cutting faults will make a stone more vulnerable to breakage. I recommend avoiding such stones unless they can be protected by the setting.

There are several cutting faults to watch for in round diamonds. First, look carefully for a *sloping table* or a table that is not almost perfectly perpendicular to the point of the culet.

Second, the culet can frequently be the source of a problem. It can be chipped or broken, open or large (almost all modern cut stones have culets that come nearly to a point), off-center, or it can be missing altogether.

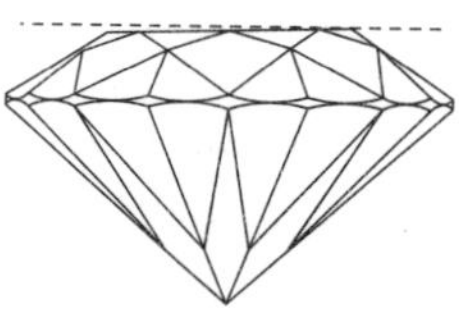

A brilliant-cut stone with a sloping table

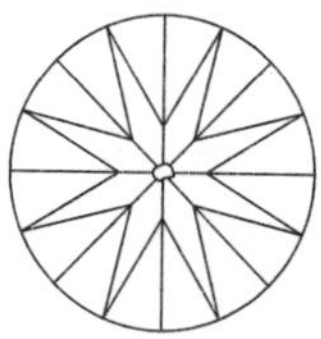

Chipped and "open" culet (viewed from the bottom)

Off-center culet

Third, repairs to chipped areas can result in *misaligned facets,* which destroy the stone's symmetry.

Sometimes, too, as a result of repair, an *extra facet* will be formed, often in the crown facets, but also on or just below the girdle. These extra facets may slightly affect the stone's brilliance.

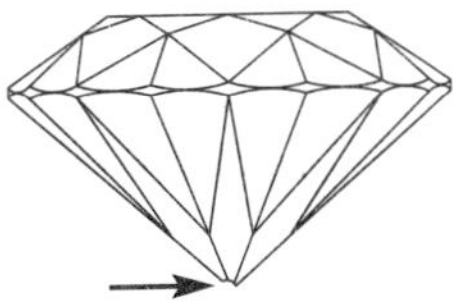

Broken or chipped culet

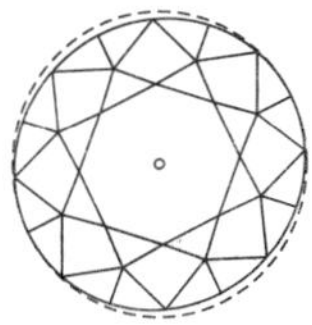

Poor symmetry

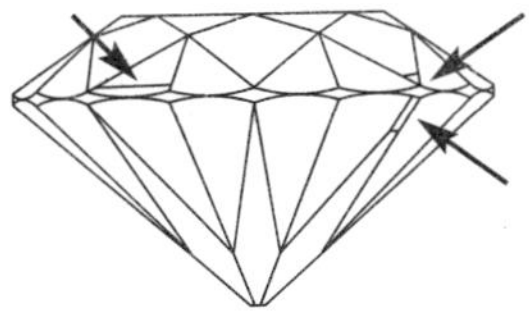

Stone with extra facets

Girdle Faults

The girdle is often the source of faults. *Bearded* or *fringed girdles* are common. A fringed girdle exhibits small radial cracks penetrating into the stone; these can result from a careless or inexperienced cutter. A bearded girdle is similar but not as pronounced a fault and can be easily repaired by repolishing, with minor loss in diamond weight.

The relative thickness of the girdle is very important because it can affect the durability as well as the beauty of the stone. Any girdle can be nicked or chipped in the course of wear, or by careless handling, but if the girdle is too thin it will chip more easily. Some chips can be easily removed by repolishing, with minimal diamond weight loss. If there are numerous chips, the entire girdle can be repolished. Chips or nicks in the girdle are often hidden under the prongs or concealed by the setting.

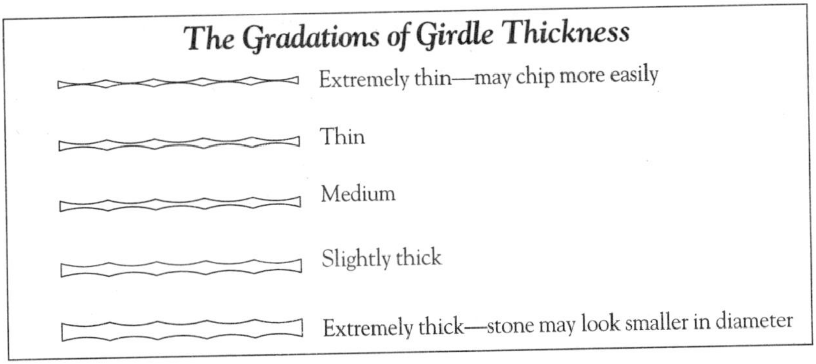

If the girdle is too thick, the stone may look smaller because a disproportionate amount of its weight will be in the girdle itself; such stones, for their weight, will be smaller in diameter than other stones of comparable weight. The girdle can also be *wavy, rough,* or *entirely out-of-round.*

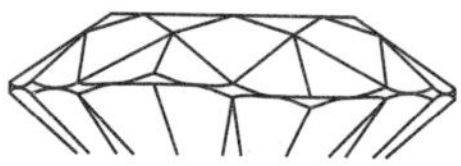

Wavy girdle

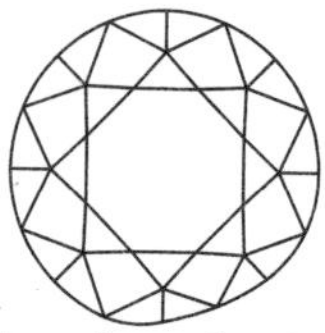

Out-of-round girdle

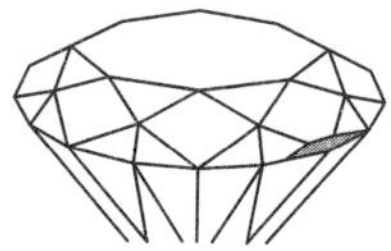

A natural at the girdle

A *natural* may not be a fault. It's actually a piece of the natural surface of the diamond crystal. In cutting, a cutter may decide to leave part of the "natural" rough surface in order to get as large a diamond as possible from the rough stone. If this natural is no thicker than the thickness of the girdle and does not distort the circumference of the stone, most dealers consider it a minor defect at worst; if it extends into the crown or pavilion of the stone, it is a more serious fault.

Sometimes if the natural is somewhat large but slightly below the girdle, it will be polished off. This produces an extra facet.

Other Popular Shapes

Unlike round diamonds, "fancy" shapes—all shapes other than round—have no set formulas, so evaluating the make of a fancy is more subjective. Table and depth percentage can vary widely among individual stones of the same shape, each producing a beautiful stone. Personal taste also varies with regard to what constitutes the "ideal" for shapes other than round. Nonetheless, there are certain visual indicators of good or poor proportioning—such as the bow tie effect—which even the amateur can learn to spot. There are recommended ratios for overall shape and symmetry, but a preferred shape is largely a personal matter. Ranges for what is acceptable or unacceptable have been developed (see chapter 9). As you gain experience looking at specific shapes, you will be able to spot faults and begin to determine what is within an acceptable range. Moderate deviations will not significantly affect the beauty or value of a stone; however, extreme deviations can seriously reduce a stone's beauty and value.

Cutting Faults in Popular Fancy Shapes

One of the most obvious indicators of poor proportioning in fancy shapes is the *bow tie* or *butterfly* effect: a darkened area across the center or widest part of the stone, depending on the cut. The bow tie is most commonly seen in the pear shape or marquise, but it may exist in any fancy shape. Virtually all fancy shapes cut today will exhibit some minimal bow-tie effect. Nonetheless, the presence or absence of a bow tie is an indicator of proportioning. In poorly proportioned stones there is a pronounced bow tie; the more pronounced, the poorer the proportioning. The less pronounced the bow tie, the better the proportioning. The degree to which the bow tie is evident is the first indicator of a good or a poor make. A diamond with a pronounced bow tie should sell for much less than one without.

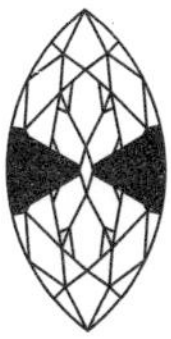

Marquise with a pronounced bow tie, or butterfly

As with the brilliant-cut diamond, fancy shapes can also be cut too *broad* or too *narrow,* and the pavilion can be too *deep* or too *shallow.*

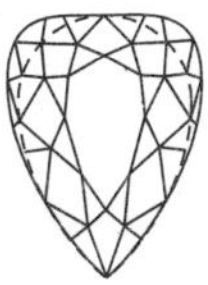

Too broad

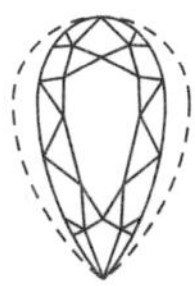

Too narrow

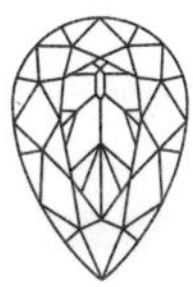

Culet too high

Culet too low

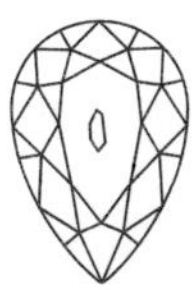

Open or misshapen culet

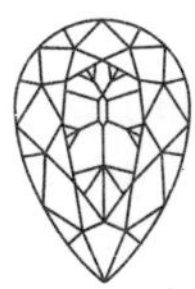

Pear-shaped stone, cut correctly

Personal taste will always play a role in fancy shapes—some prefer a narrow pear shape, for example, while others might prefer a fatter pear. Whatever the shape you are considering, you must ask yourself whether or not you find the stone exciting. Does it have a pleasing personality? Does it exhibit good brilliance and fire? Is the entire stone brilliant, or are there "dead" spots? Are there any cutting faults that might make it more susceptible to chipping? Then you must make the choice.

New Shapes Create Excitement

Today we can choose from many shapes and cuts, ranging from the classics—round, oval, pear, marquise, emerald cut, and heart shape—to new shapes that appear as cutters continue to experiment with novel looks. Here are some of the most popular:

The *radiant cut* is perfect for the person who likes the shape of an emerald cut—square or rectangular—but wants more sparkle and brilliance, a personality closer to a round diamond. The *Crisscut®* is a wonderful blend between the two, more understated than the radiant but livelier than an emerald cut.

Radiant

Crisscut®

The *princess cut,* a square brilliant cut, is ideal for bezel and channel settings (see chapter 16) or any setting in which you want the stone to be flush with the mounting. The *Quadrillion™* was the first trademarked "princess," cut to unique specifications for maximum brilliance and fire.

Standard princess

Quadrillion™

The *Biro 88™* with its 88 facets, and the *Gabrielle®* cut with its 105 facets, create more scintillation and more sparkle than is seen in traditional cuts. The Gabrielle® comes in all the classic shapes. The *Spirit Sun®,* a revolutionary new cut with only 16 facets and a pointed crown, represents an entirely new cutting approach. It achieves exceptional brilliance and reflectivity.

Biro 88™

Gabrielle®

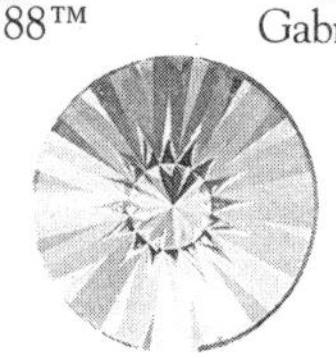
Spirit Sun®

Lucida™

Tiana™

Context®

Trilliant

Lily Cut®

Noble Cut™

A cut patented by Tiffany, the *Lucida*™ blends a modern, square brilliant cut with the high crown and small tables of an antique old-mine cut (cushion). This cut is available only from Tiffany, but similar cuts, such as the *Tiana*™, are also available. Another of the new "square" cuts, the *Context*®, creates a wholly new look with amazing luminosity. The epitome of simplicity, it can be fashioned only from rare, perfectly formed diamond crystals—one in one hundred thousand—and maintains the inherent shape of the natural crystal.

The *trilliant cut* is a popular shape for center stones or side stones. This brilliant cut is also a thin cut, giving a large appearance for its weight. Extra facets and precision cutting produce high brilliance. The *Lily Cut*® is a brilliant new cut shaped like a four-leaf clover, and is great in pendants and earrings, and the *Noble Cut*™ is a newly branded elongated "kite" shape with 29 facets, ideally suited for classic, linear designs.

As we learn more and more about diamond cutting and how various facet arrangements and angles affect the way light performs in a diamond, new cuts continue to emerge. These include the *New Century*®, a patented 102-facet, round, super-brilliant cut; the Zoë, a scintillating 100-facet cut; the extra-fiery 82-facet *Royal 82*; the 80-facet *Spirit of Flanders*™; the 66-facet *Leo Diamond*™; and the new 97-facet, 12-sided *Escada*® that was created exclusively for the great fashion house.

In addition to the new cuts above, we are also seeing cutting innovations in baguettes, with new brilliant-cut baguettes, such as the *Princette*™ and the *Bagillion*™. They occur in straight and tapered shapes. There are also Crisscut® baguettes and tapered baguettes. These are gaining in popularity because they have greater brilliance than traditional baguettes. They can be used to flank diamonds or other stones in traditional settings, or in very contemporary jewelry designs with straight, clean lines.

Early Cuts Enjoy Renewed Popularity

Interest in antique and period jewelry is growing rapidly. As it does, the diamonds that adorn them are arousing renewed attention and gaining new respect. The way a diamond is cut is often one of the clues to the age of a piece. Older diamonds can be replaced or recut to modern proportions, but replacing or recutting stones mounted in antique or period pieces could adversely affect the value of the jewelry. To preserve the integrity of the piece, antique and period jewelry connoisseurs want original stones, or, if stones have been replaced, at least stones cut in the manner typical of the period. The market is becoming increasingly strong for diamonds with older cuts, and prices are also strengthening.

As these early cut diamonds receive more and more attention, a growing number of people are beginning to appreciate them for their distinctive beauty and personality and for the romance that accompanies them. The romantic element—combined with a cost that is more attractive than that of new diamonds—is also making them an increasingly popular choice for engagement rings.

Some of the earlier cuts are the *table cut,* the *rose cut,* the *old-mine cut,* and the *old-European cut.* (Before 1919, when America began to emerge as an important diamond cutting center, most diamonds were cut in Europe. Thus most "old European" diamonds were cut before the first quarter of the twentieth century.)

The *table cut* illustrates history's earliest cutting effort. By placing the point of a diamond crystal against a turning wheel that held another diamond, the point could be worn down, creating a squarish, flat surface that resembled a *tabletop.* Today we still call the flat facet on the very top of the stone the *table* facet.

Table Cut

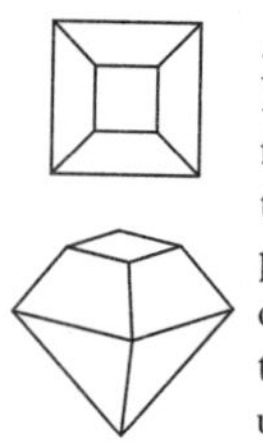

A table-cut diamond. Note the tablelike flat surface on the top, where the crystal point was polished off. The remainder of the crystal is left unchanged.

Rose Cut

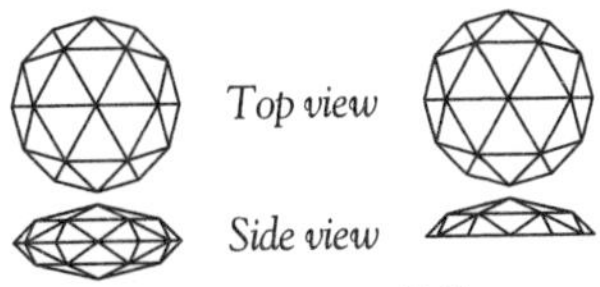

Double rose cut — Full rose cut

Old-Mine Cut

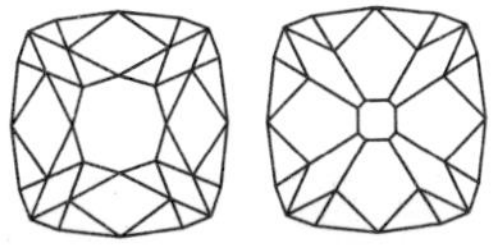

Crown (top) — Pavilion (bottom)

In both cuts, the crown is higher and pavilion deeper than in modern cuts.

An open culet can also be seen in both from top.

Old-European Cut

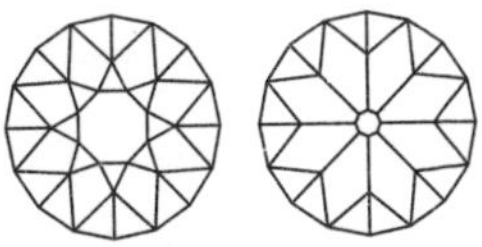

Crown (top) — Pavilion (bottom)

Asscher cut in a modern setting

Cushion cut

The *rose cut* is a sixteenth-century cut, usually with a flat base and facets radiating from the center in multiples of six, creating the appearance of an opening rosebud. The rose cut appears in round, pear, and oval shapes.

The *old-mine* is a precursor to the modern round. This cut has a squarish or "cushion" shape (a rounded square). Proportions follow the diamond crystal, so the crown is higher and the pavilion is deeper than in modern stones. The table is very small, and the culet is very large and is easily seen from the top (resembling a "hole" in the diamond). These lack the brilliance of modern stones but often exhibit tremendous fire. The old-mine is enjoying a resurgence in popularity today.

Appearing in the mid-1800s, the *old-European* is similar to the old-mine cut but is *round* rather than squarish, with fifty-eight facets. The crown is higher than in modern cuts but not as high as in the old-mine cut; it has a deep pavilion, but not as deep as in old-mines. The culet is still "open" but smaller than in old-mines.

In addition to the early cuts described above, there are two other older cuts that are enjoying renewed popularity: the *cushion cut,* with a small table, high crown, and large culet, which resembles the old-mine but usually has somewhat straighter sides and may be more elongated; and the *Asscher cut,* a more or less square emerald cut that, like old-European and old-mine cut diamonds, is characterized by a very high crown, deep pavilion, small table, large culet, and very canted corners (in some cases the angles formed at the corners are so pronounced that the stone resembles an octagon). Although exhibiting less brilliance than modern-cut diamonds, the cushion and Asscher both exhibit very fiery personalities, and offer a distinctive look with a classic character.

Older cutting styles once popular for use in side stones, or to create interesting design elements, are also enjoying renewed popularity. Among the most popular are two *step-cut* shapes—the trapezoid and the half-moon—and the briolette.

The *trapezoid* and *half-moon* are often seen in art deco–period jewelry (1910 into the 1920s) and make especially elegant choices to use with emerald-cut diamonds (which are also step cut) and colored gemstones. Here the understated character of the trapezoid or half-moon is very complementary; while lively, their brilliance is not as overpowering as modern brilliant cuts often are.

Trapezoid

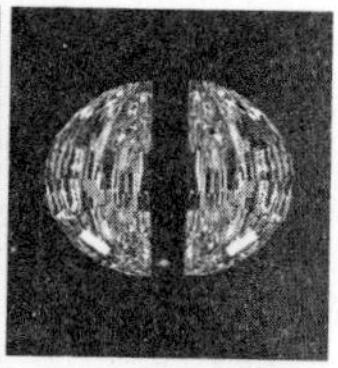

Half-moon

The *briolette* is fashioned into a "drop," completely encircled with tiny triangular facets. A single briolette can be worn as a pendant, or multiple briolettes can be suspended from almost any piece of jewelry. We are again seeing briolettes used in earrings and brooches and suspended in multiples, like a fringe, from necklaces.

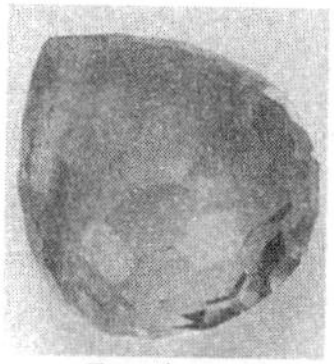

Briolette

Are Diamonds with Old Cuts Valuable?

Old cuts can be very beautiful. The finest examples of these earlier cutting styles exhibit intense fire and have tremendous allure, especially among collectors and those who appreciate authentic jewelry from these earlier periods. By today's standards, however, they lack brilliance, and a very large culet may detract from the stone's beauty.

Until recently, old-mine cut and old-European cut diamonds have been evaluated by comparison with modern-cut stones. Value has been determined by estimating the color, the clarity, and the weight the stone would *retain* if it were recut to modern proportions. However, this practice is changing because of the increasing demand for old cuts, and while still valued lower than modern cuts, they are priced higher today than previously.

I don't suggest recutting old diamonds if they are in their original mountings. The overall integrity of the piece—and its value—would be adversely affected.

If the setting has no special merit, the decision must be an individual one, based on whether or not the stone appeals to you. As I have said, some older cuts are very lovely, while others may look heavy, dull, or lifeless. An unattractive older cut may benefit from recutting, and although it will lose weight, it may have equal or greater value because of the improved make. In addition, recutting can sometimes improve the clarity grade of an older stone. Finally, before deciding whether or not to recut, you should note that the increasing popularity of older cuts is driving prices higher since they are difficult to find. In addition to their unique personalities, old cuts can have a distinctive character that sets them apart from more modern cuts.

A Word about Recutting Diamonds

There are many fine diamond cutters in the United States—New York City is one of the most important diamond cutting centers in the world for top-quality diamonds—and many diamonds can be greatly improved by recutting.

If you have an old-cut diamond that you don't care for, or a damaged diamond, your jeweler can consult with a diamond cutter—or refer you to one—to determine whether or not your stone can be improved by recutting and, if so, what risks and costs might be involved. Keep in mind that there is *always* some degree of risk whenever a stone is recut.

Normally, the cost to recut a diamond ranges from approximately \$350 *per carat* to as much as \$500 *per carat*, depending on the skill required and the labor involved. In rare instances, the cost might be more. Thus, if the labor estimate to recut a stone is \$350 per carat, recutting a two-carat diamond will cost \$700.

A knowledgeable jeweler can help you decide whether or not a diamond should be recut, make arrangements for you, and help assure you that you've received the same stone back. For your own comfort and security, as well as the cutter's, I recommend that you obtain a diamond grading report or a thorough appraisal before having a stone recut, so that you have a point of reference when the stone is returned.

To What Extent Do Cutting & Proportioning Affect Value in Modern Diamonds?

Excellently cut and proportioned stones cost significantly more per carat than those that are not cut well. The following will give a very basic idea of how some of the most frequently encountered defects can affect a diamond's price.

- Table is not a reasonably accurate octagon—2 to 15 percent off
- Girdle is too thick—5 to 10 percent off
- Girdle is too thin—5 to 25 percent off
- Symmetry of crown facets off—5 to 15 percent on round, less on fancy cuts since defect is not as easily seen
- Asymmetrical culet—2 to 5 percent off
- Misaligned culet—5 to 25 percent off
- Stone too shallow—15 to 50 percent off
- Stone too thick—10 to 30 percent off
- Thin crown—5 to 20 percent off
- Thick crown—5 to 15 percent off

As you can see, there is a fairly wide range here, depending on the severity of the error, and only an experienced professional can determine the extent to which the value of a given stone may be lessened. But a quick computation shows that a stone suffering from several errors (which is fairly common) could certainly have a significantly reduced price per carat.

Remember: The value of two diamonds with the same weight, color, and clarity can differ dramatically because of differences in cutting.

CHAPTER SIX

Body Color

Color is one of the most important factors to consider when selecting a diamond because it is one of the first things people notice—whether or not the diamond is white, or, more accurately, *colorless* (there actually are *white* diamonds, usually milky white in color and translucent, but they are very rare and most people do not find them attractive) or the exotic, rare *fancy* color. The color grade of a diamond is also one of the most significant factors affecting value.

Color refers to the natural body color of a diamond. The finest and most expensive "white" diamonds are absolutely colorless, like pure springwater. Most diamonds show some trace of yellowish or brownish tint. Diamonds also occur in every color of the rainbow. Natural colored diamonds are called *fancy-color* diamonds. The grading of fancy-color diamonds is covered in chapter 12.

How to Look at a Colorless Diamond to Evaluate Color

In colorless diamonds, color differences from one grade to the next can be very subtle, and a difference of several grades is difficult to see when a diamond is mounted. Keep in mind that it is impossible to accurately grade color in a mounted diamond. When looking at an unmounted stone, however, even an amateur can learn to see color differences if the stone is viewed properly.

Because of the diamond's high brilliance and dispersion (fire), the color grade cannot be accurately determined by looking at the stone from the top, or face-up, position. It is best to observe color by examining the stone through the *pavilion*, with the table down. Use a flat white surface

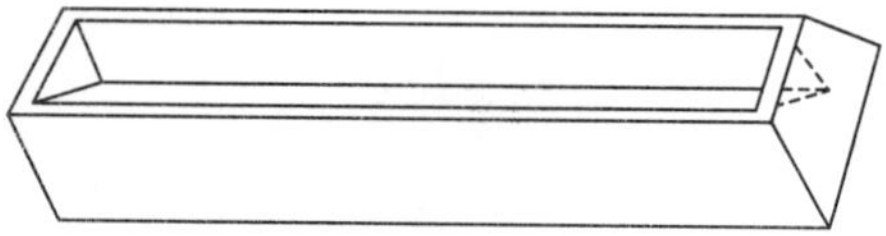

A grading trough, available in plastic or in disposable white cardboard stand-up packs. Be sure to use a *clean* trough.

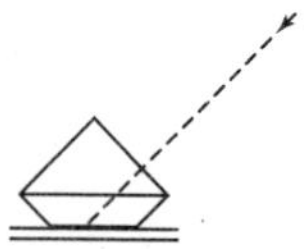

Position 1. Place table-side down and view the stone through the pavilion facets.

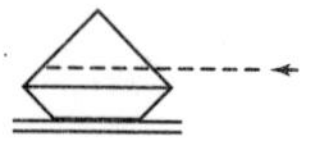

Position 2. Table-side down, view the stone through the plane of the girdle.

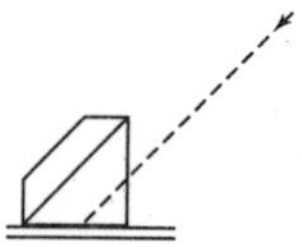

Position 3. Place the pavilion down with the culet pointing toward you. View the stone through the girdle plane.

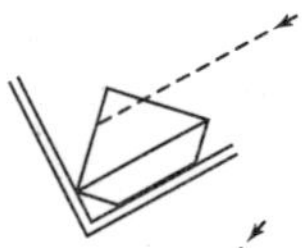

Position 4. Place table-down in a grading trough and view the stone through the girdle plane.

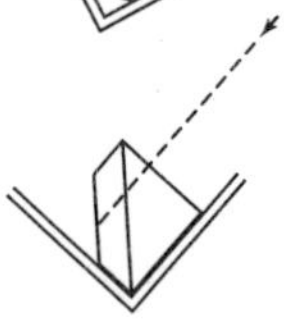

Position 5. Place pavilion-down in a grading trough, with the culet pointing toward you. View the stone through the pavilion facets.

such as a folded white business card or a grading trough, which can be purchased from a jewelry supplier.

What Is Body Color?

When we discuss body color in colorless diamonds, we mean how much yellow or brown tint can be seen. We are not referring to rare natural-color diamonds.

Today, most colorless diamonds in the United States and other countries are graded on an alphabetical scale beginning with the letter *D*. This letter designation is part of a color grading system introduced by the Gemological Institute of America (GIA) and is used extensively in the diamond trade worldwide. The GIA classification progresses from D, the rarest classification on this scale (colorless), through the alphabet to Z, getting progressively more tinted. The grades D, E, and F are exceptionally rare and are the only grades that should be referred to as colorless. (Technically, E and F are not colorless, since they possess a trace of yellow or brown, but the tint is so slight that referring to them as colorless is acceptable.)

A diamond with the color grade D exhibits the most prized color. It is essentially colorless—like crystal-clear springwater—and is considered the most desirable. Diamonds with D-color are very rare, and a significant premium is paid for them. A diamond with the color grade E is also exceptionally rare and is almost indistinguishable from D except to the very experienced. Nonetheless, diamonds graded E in color cost significantly less per carat than those graded D, despite the difficulty in seeing the difference. The next color grade is F, and it is close to E, but there is more gradation in color than the difference observed between D and E.

What Color Grade Is Most Desirable?

The colors D, E, and F can all be grouped as exceptionally fine, rare colors and may be referred to as *colorless, exceptional white,* or *rare white,* as they are often described by diamond dealers. The colors G and H may be referred to as *fine white* or *rare white*. These grades are also rare and considered very fine. The I and J colors are slightly more tinted than G and H, and sell for less, but diamonds possessing color grades G through J are all fine colors and can be classified as *near colorless*. The colors K to M show a stronger tint of yellow or brown, but settings can often mask the tint. Grades N through Z will show progressively more and more tint of yellowish or brownish color. Grades D through J seem to have better resale potential than grades K through Z. This does not mean, however, that diamonds having less rare color grades are less beautiful or desirable. Sometimes a more tinted diamond can exhibit a warmth not shown by other diamonds and create a very beautiful ring with a unique appeal.

To What Extent Does the Color Grade Affect Value?

To an untrained eye, discerning the difference in color from D down to H in a mounted stone, without direct comparison, is almost impossible. Nevertheless, the difference in color greatly affects the value of the diamond. A one-carat flawless, excellently proportioned D-color diamond might retail for $30,000, while the same stone with H-color might sell for only $12,000, and the same stone with K-color might sell for only $7,500. And, of course, if the stone were not flawless, it could sell for much less (see the next chapter). This sounds complicated, but color differences and their effect on price will become clear to you the moment you begin looking at stones. It is important to understand your options and to be watchful when you go to purchase a stone.

Diamond Color Grades		
COLORLESS	D	Loose diamonds appear colorless.
	E	
	F	
NEAR COLORLESS	G	When mounted in a setting, these diamonds may appear colorless to the untrained eye.
	H	
	I	
	J	
FAINT YELLOWISH* TINT	K	Smaller diamonds look colorless when mounted. Diamonds of ½ carat or more show traces of color.
	L	
	M	
VERY LIGHT YELLOWISH* TINT	N	These diamonds show increasingly yellow tints to even the untrained eye, and appear very "off-white."
	O	
	P	
	Q	
	R	
TINTED LIGHT YELLOWISH*	S	
	T	
	U	
	V	
	W	
	X	
	Y	
	Z	
* Usually yellow, but can be brown or gray		

Commonly Used Diamond Color Grading Systems

The GIA and American Gem Society (AGS) grading systems are the most commonly used in the United States. The GIA system is the most widely used in the world. Scandinavian Diamond Nomenclature (Scan D.N.) is often used in Scandinavian countries, as well as a system developed by CIBJO (the World Jewellery Confederation). Participating member nations include most European nations, Japan, and the United States. Another system, HRD, is applied by the Belgian Diamond High Council.

<table>
<tr><th></th><th></th><th>GIA</th><th>AGS</th><th>SCAN D.N. UNDER 0.50 CARAT</th><th>SCAN D.N. 0.50 CARAT AND OVER</th><th>CIBJO UNDER 0.47 CARAT</th><th>CIBJO 0.47 CARAT AND OVER</th><th>HRD</th></tr>
<tr><td rowspan="7">Small mounted stones appear colorless</td><td rowspan="6">Mounted stones appear colorless</td><td>D</td><td>0</td><td rowspan="5">White</td><td rowspan="2">River</td><td rowspan="2">Exceptional white</td><td>Exceptional white</td><td>Exceptional white</td></tr>
<tr><td>E</td><td>.5</td><td>Exceptional white</td><td>Exceptional white</td></tr>
<tr><td>F</td><td>1</td><td rowspan="2">Top wesselton</td><td rowspan="2">Rare white</td><td>Rare white</td><td>Rare white</td></tr>
<tr><td>G</td><td>1.5</td><td>Rare white</td><td>Rare white</td></tr>
<tr><td>H</td><td>2</td><td>Wesselton</td><td>White</td><td>White</td><td>White</td></tr>
<tr><td>I</td><td>2.5</td><td rowspan="2">Slightly tinted white</td><td>Top Crystal</td><td rowspan="2">Slightly tinted white</td><td>Slightly tinted white (I)</td><td rowspan="2">Slightly tinted white</td></tr>
<tr><td rowspan="8">Mounted stones appear increasingly tinted</td><td>J</td><td>3</td><td>Crystal</td><td>Slightly tinted white (J)</td></tr>
<tr><td rowspan="16"></td><td>K</td><td>3.5</td><td rowspan="2">Tinted white</td><td rowspan="2">Top cape</td><td rowspan="2">Tinted white</td><td>Tinted white (K)</td><td rowspan="2">Tinted white</td></tr>
<tr><td>L</td><td>4</td><td>Tinted white (L)</td></tr>
<tr><td>M</td><td>4.5</td><td rowspan="12">Tinted color</td><td rowspan="2">Cape</td><td rowspan="12">Tinted color</td><td rowspan="12">Tinted color</td><td rowspan="12">Tinted color</td></tr>
<tr><td>N</td><td>5</td></tr>
<tr><td>O</td><td>5.5</td><td rowspan="4">Light Yellow</td></tr>
<tr><td>P</td><td>6</td></tr>
<tr><td>Q</td><td>6.5</td></tr>
<tr><td rowspan="9">Mounted stones appear yellow</td><td>R</td><td>7</td></tr>
<tr><td>S</td><td>7.5</td><td rowspan="6">Yellow</td></tr>
<tr><td>T</td><td>8</td></tr>
<tr><td>U</td><td>8.5</td></tr>
<tr><td>V</td><td>9</td></tr>
<tr><td>W</td><td>9.5</td></tr>
<tr><td>XYZ</td><td>10</td></tr>
</table>

In diamonds over one carat, the whiter the stone, the more critical it becomes to know the exact color grade because of its effect on value. On the other hand, as long as you know for sure what color the stone is and are paying the right price, choosing one that is a grade or two lower than another will reduce the cost per carat but there will be little, if any, visible difference when the stone is mounted. Therefore, for the difference in cost, you might be able to get a larger diamond, or one with better cutting or a better clarity grade, depending on what is most important to you.

Natural Color or HPHT Processed

Color differences can be subtle, but the difference in cost can be extreme. It is important to know the precise color grade, but it is even more important to know whether the color is natural or the result of some type of treatment. In chapter 10, I discuss several fraudulent techniques that have been used for many years to "whiten" tinted diamonds. Until recently, these treatments produced results that were only temporary, and any competent gemologist could detect the treatment. This has changed rapidly in the past few years, however, and new techniques are creating permanent results. Perhaps more important, detection often requires very sophisticated testing. On the one hand, what has been developed is very exciting, but on the other hand it provides yet another reason to take precautions to ensure you are buying what you think you are buying.

A new product entered the market in the 1990s, resulting from years of research conducted in a joint venture between a diamond manufacturer and General Electric. The product was created by a new process involving the use of high-pressure/high-temperature annealing (often referred to as the *HPHT process*). With it, very tinted, off-white diamonds can be transformed into colorless and near-colorless stones ranging from D through H in color. In addition to using this process to create colorless and near-colorless stones, the process can also be used to produce "fancy" colors, including yellow, yellowish green, pink, and blue (see chapters 10 and 12).The innovators of this process believe they have created a new diamond category that will provide new alternatives to consumers. The color of these stones, originally referred to as *GE-POL* diamonds, is permanent and irreversible.

Not all tinted diamonds can be transformed into colorless or near-colorless diamonds. Only very rare diamond types respond to HPHT whitening techniques. Of all the diamonds mined, reports estimate that fewer than 2 percent produce the desired effect, but a higher percentage of *larger* diamonds can be improved by HPHT methods.

The color-enhanced "colorless" diamonds produced by GE are now sold under the name *Bellataire*™ through exclusive arrangements with selected retailers. They are usually cut in fancy shapes (approximately 85 percent) and are available in color grades from D through H, with clarity grades of VS_2 or better (see chapter 7 for a discussion on clarity grades). In an effort to communicate clearly and honestly, each diamond is laser inscribed on the girdle with the Bellataire™ logo and a registered number, but there have been cases where the laser inscription has been polished off.

In terms of cost, it is unclear how they will be priced. Some retailers are charging a small premium because of the rarity of these diamonds, while others are providing an incentive to customers by pricing them at 15 to 20 percent below their natural-color counterparts. For many, these newcomers are a beautiful and exciting "high-tech" alternative. Ultimately, however, it will be consumer acceptance and demand that will determine their pricing.

In addition to Bellataire™ colorless and fancy yellow, blue, and pink diamonds, other companies are using HPHT annealing techniques to whiten diamonds and to produce a range of colors. Lucent Diamonds™ *Luminari* brand offers a wide range of yellow, deep yellow, orange-yellow, and yellow-green diamonds, and recently introduced an exciting new color, *Imperial Red.* Nova™ and Sundance Corp. are offering a range of colors in HPHT-treated stones, and Sundance offers a service to provide treatment to improve off-color stones. Diamonds are even being transformed into mysterious *black* diamonds through HPHT methods, and who knows what alluring colors await us in the future. In fancy colors, these treated diamonds should sell for significantly less than natural-color fancy diamonds.

Many people are intrigued by these stones and find them a very attractive alternative to other diamonds. Labs such as the GIA, the Swiss Gemmological Institute (SSEF), and the European Gemological Laboratory (EGL) will grade diamonds treated in this manner, indicating the use of this process on the report, usually under "Comments" (see chapter 9). GIA also requires that the words "HPHT Processed" be laser inscribed on the stone's girdle before issuing the grading report. However, caution needs to be taken. Once again, the availability of this new product in the marketplace provides yet another reason to obtain laboratory verification prior to the purchase of any important diamond. There have already been incidents of HPHT-treated diamonds having been sold without disclosure of the treatment. More important, before becoming aware of the use of this technology on diamonds, gem-testing laboratories were not checking for it, nor did they have the data to understand how to detect it. Today most diamonds treated in this manner can be identified, but prior to the year 2000, HPHT-treated stones may have slipped through the world's labs undetected. See chapter 10 for more advice on how to protect yourself from buying an HPHT diamond unknowingly.

What Is Fluorescence and How Does It Affect Your Diamond Choice?

If you have ever visited gem and mineral exhibits at a natural science museum such as the American Museum of Natural History in New York City, the Smithsonian in Washington, D.C., or the Houston Museum of Natural Science, you will probably remember seeing a display of common-looking rocks in various shades of white, gray, black, and so on, which suddenly—and magically—change into intense, psychedelic hues of red, orange, yellow, green, blue, and violet, with just the touch of a switch! People are amazed by this transformation and wonder how it happens; it is really quite fascinating.

When people "see" color, we are seeing certain wavelengths of light that are in our "visible spectrum"—which includes red, orange, yellow, green, blue, and violet. There are also wavelengths of light that go *beyond* our visible spectrum, and are invisible to us. For example, beyond the violet end of the spectrum there are *ultraviolet* wavelengths; they exist, but we can't see them. When some rocks—such as the "magical rocks" you may have seen in these museum exhibits—are viewed under these invisible *ultraviolet* wavelengths, we suddenly see colors that were previously invisible to us. The reaction we see is the result of switching the wavelengths of the lighting in which we are seeing them. As soon as we switch the lighting to a "black light" (*ultraviolet radiation*), invisible wavelengths are changed into *visible* wavelengths, and thus the startling colors we suddenly see! This color-change behavior is referred to as *fluorescence.*

The ultraviolet radiation produced when the black light is turned on causes the rock's fluorescence to become *excited* and you see those fabulous colors; when you turn it off, the fluorescence is no longer excited, and the rocks return to their *stable* state (the ordinary colors you see in normal lighting). In some rare cases, a few of the rocks will continue to glow for a short time; we call this continuous glow *phosphorescence* (some watches have phosphorescent dials, which "glow in the dark" for a brief time when you go from light into dark). But the fluorescent colors are seen *only* when exposed to ultraviolet radiation.

Some diamonds and other gems also show fluorescence when exposed directly to ultraviolet wavelengths. If the diamond you are considering is accompanied by a diamond grading report issued by a respected gem-testing laboratory such as the Gemological Institute of America (GIA), the report will indicate whether or not the diamond shows any fluorescence; it will also indicate the strength of its fluorescent color reaction (faint, weak, moderate, strong, very strong). Here again, whatever fluorescent color the diamond may show, it will only be seen when the stone is exposed to strong ultraviolet emissions that excite the fluorescense.

Whether or not a diamond fluoresces, what color it fluoresces, and the strength of its fluorescence is determined by viewing the diamond with a special lamp known as an *ultraviolet lamp* (UV lamp), which emits only ultraviolet radiation; the black light used by museums to show the fluorescent colors of the rocks in their fluorescent mineral collections is a type of UV lamp. A UV lamp is a standard piece of equipment used in gem-testing laboratories and by diamond dealers and knowledgeable jewelers.

My own engagement ring, which dates from the mid-1800s, contains a natural pearl at the center and is flanked on each side by an antique old-mine cut diamond. When I lecture, I love to turn off the lights, turn on my ultraviolet lamp, hold it over my ring, and listen to the audience gasp as they observe the strong blue glow from *one* of my diamonds; one fluoresces and the other does not! Should my ring ever be stolen and recovered by police, the fact that one diamond fluoresces a strong blue while the other does not, in conjunction with their antique cuts, should be sufficient proof of ownership to be able to reclaim my ring.

It is estimated that over 40 percent of all diamonds fluoresce, and that approximately 15 percent of those that do will have a strong or very-strong fluorescent reaction to ultraviolet radiation. A diamond can fluoresce any color, but the overwhelming majority of colorless diamonds fluoresce *blue* (approximately 98 percent). An extremely small percentage fluoresce other colors, but normally if the color is not blue, it is yellow. Notably, fluorescent colors other than blue or yellow are so rare in diamonds that this can be a *very important "identifier"* should you ever need to prove ownership or leave your diamond anywhere for any period of time. Its distinctive fluorescent color will provide you with immediate reassurance when you are reunited with the stone.

Whatever color a diamond fluoresces, remember that it will only be seen when viewed directly beneath a UV lamp. In the case of colorless (white) diamonds, the stone is really colorless, and it will look colorless in normal light. Nonetheless, if the diamond has an adequately strong reaction to UV radiation—"medium," "strong," or "very strong"—this property can affect the degree of "whiteness" you see, depending on the type of lighting in which it is seen.

It is important to note whether or not a diamond fluoresces and what color it fluoresces, because there are varying wavelengths of ultraviolet radiation in the lighting around us that can trigger a diamond's fluorescence and make the color appear whiter, or less white. We are exposed to strong ultraviolet radiation outdoors during daylight, and there are weaker emissions of ultraviolet radiation produced by some indoor lighting, such as daylight-type fluorescent lights. Fluorescence can also be triggered by emissions from some very strong incandescent lights. Where indoor lighting is concerned, however, the emissions are not strong enough to excite any fluorescence, except when held within a few inches of the light source itself; as the diamond is moved away from the light, any fluorescence is diminished and the stone quickly returns to its stable, normal color.

The strongest impact of fluorescence on color will be seen primarily outdoors, during daylight hours. A diamond that fluoresces strong or very strong *blue*, for example, *will appear whiter when seen outdoors during daylight hours*—sometimes several grades whiter—because the UV wavelengths present outdoors in daylight hours are strong enough to excite a strong fluorescent reaction. If the stone fluoresces blue when excited, this will cause the stone to produce enough blue to mask any faint yellow tint that might be present, thus creating a whiter appearance. Note that the degree of blue produced outside is not as intense as what you would see if it were directly beneath a UV lamp, nor, generally speaking, is it enough for you to even notice. However, some colorless diamonds in the D–F color range, with strong or very-strong blue fluorescence, do actually look "light blue" in outdoor light! At one time, these diamonds were called "blue-white" diamonds, but this term should not be used today except in such cases when the stone actually has a blue hue outdoors.

Whatever fluorescent color a diamond may show in outdoor daylight, it is rarely seen when viewed indoors. Unless held within a few inches of a pane of glass through which daylight is pouring in, or within a few inches of a certain type of fluorescent light (and in rare cases, very close to some types of incandescent lighting), there is insufficient UV to excite a diamond's fluorescence. This means that the color seen will be the stone's inherent body color, the "normal" color you see when the diamond is in its "steady" state.

Understanding the Effect of Fluorescence on the Color of Diamonds

To better understand the effect of fluorescence on the color you see in diamonds, imagine you are looking at three diamonds that all have a G color grade when graded with a light that has no UV emission (so even if it is a fluorescent diamond, its color will be its "normal" color, the color seen when it is *not* fluorescing). Let's imagine that one of these stones has no fluorescence, one has strong blue fluorescence, and one has strong yellow fluorescence. The stone with no fluorescence will look the same color indoors or outdoors. The blue-fluorescent diamond will appear G-color indoors, but will *look whiter outdoors during daylight hours*—it could appear F or even E or D! The yellow-fluorescent diamond will be G-color indoors, but will *look more yellow outdoors during daylight.* How much whiter or yellower a fluorescent diamond will appear outdoors depends not only on the strength of its fluorescence, but also on such factors as time of day, altitude, the hemisphere you're in, smog, and so on. The important thing to understand is that although the color may appear whiter or more yellow when viewed outdoors during daylight hours, *all three diamonds will be the same color when seen indoors or in evening light.* This is very important to understand, since most diamonds are seen, most of the time, indoors.

Just like the fluorescent rocks in the museum, which go back to their ordinary colors when the black light is switched back to normal light, so it is with fluorescent diamonds; when worn outdoors, the effect is the same as switching on the black light; when indoors, it's as though you turned off the black light, and returned to normal light.

Is Fluorescence Desirable or Undesirable?

When it comes to fluorescence, as long as the inherent body color is indicated on the diamond report or by the seller, and you are paying an appropriate price for the diamond's *true body color—when no fluorescence is being excited by exposure to UV radiation*—it is neither a good thing nor a bad thing, but a matter of personal preference. Many people are fascinated by fluorescence and search for a fluorescent diamond. For some, the idea that a blue-fluorescent diamond will look whiter in outdoor daylight is seen as an extra benefit. For others, yellow fluorescence is preferred because they are usually discounted as a result of a trade bias against them (often unmerited), and they'd rather pay less, knowing that any tint of yellow will only appear when seen outdoors during daylight, and that most of the time the diamond will be seen indoors or at night and be comparable in color to more expensive stones!

To ensure that the stone's true body color is the grade shown on any diamond grading report, the stone should always be tested for fluorescence with an ultraviolet lamp prior to color grading. If a diamond fluoresces, the grader should use a UV-free light to color grade it, or use a UV filter to screen out any UV emission. This is necessary to avoid "exciting" a fluorescent reaction, which may result in an erroneous grade.

Blue Fluorescence Provides Confirmation That a Diamond Is Not Lab-Created

Now that colorless laboratory-created diamonds (see chapter 10) have entered the marketplace, it is worth noting that *blue fluorescence in a diamond is confirmation that the diamond is* ***not lab-grown, but natural!*** While a laboratory-created diamond is difficult to distinguish from a natural diamond because, like any laboratory-created stone (the words "laboratory-created" and "synthetic" are synonymous), it *is* a diamond, with the same physical, chemical, and optical properties of diamond. Gem-testing laboratories can separate one from the other, but in the case of a diamond with blue fluorescence, you don't need a lab to rest assured the diamond is natural!

Does Fluorescence Affect Value?

If the color grade represents the inherent body color of the diamond, its true body color, then fluorescence will have little, if any, impact on value. Historically, diamonds were color graded under lighting conditions in which the UV emissions were filtered out so that the grade did, in fact, represent the diamond's true body color. In addition to the body color, the report would also indicate whether or not the diamond fluoresced and the intensity and color of the fluorescence. Thus, knowledgeable buyers often sought "blue fluorescent" diamonds, knowing that they would look whiter in certain environments. At that time, diamonds with blue fluorescence were very desirable, offering a little bonus since they looked whiter in daylight! A blue-fluorescent diamond could even command a small premium over a nonfluorescent diamond.

In recent years, however, for a variety of reasons we don't have space here to discuss (for more information on this important topic, visit www.antoinettematlins.com), the color grade now shown on many laboratory reports does *not* represent the stone's inherent body color. Instead, the grade often represents a color that is perceived *only* when the stone's fluorescence is excited. Today, if a diamond has sufficiently strong blue fluorescence ("medium," "strong," or "very strong"), the grade may indicate a whiter color than the color that will normally be seen; if yellow, the grade may represent a color lower than what will normally be seen. For this reason, one must take extra precaution when buying fluorescent diamonds. We suggest having *any* fluorescent diamond—with or without a diamond grading report from a respected lab—double-checked by a gemologist who uses a UV-*free* or UV-*filtered* light source to color grade the diamond in order to confirm its inherent body color and determine whether or not the price is appropriate (see appendix for a selected list of laboratories).

If this is not possible, we recommend looking at any fluorescent diamond in several different lighting environments to see if you can detect any change in its whiteness. Check it in direct daylight (not through the glass, but either outside or through an *open* door or window) or directly beneath a fluorescent light, and then try to compare the color you see to the color the stone appears when you move it to the middle of a room or somewhere several feet from any light source. If the stone appears the same color in all lights, then its grade is probably accurate; if the stone looks less white when away from daylight or the fluorescent lamp, then it may be overgraded—and possibly overpriced. The best way to make this comparison is to take another diamond, *a nonfluorescent diamond*, with the same color grade (and about the same size) and compare them side by side in these different lighting environments, noting whether or not they *both* appear the same color wherever you view them.

By How Much Can Fluorescence Affect Value If Overgraded?

Generally speaking, if the strength of a diamond's fluorescent reaction is "negligible," "faint," or "weak" it will have no effect on the diamond's color or value. If more intense, it can affect value, sometimes significantly. In rare instances, diamonds with "strong" and "very strong" fluorescence (especially if they show a bluish tint outdoors) may offer a very *good* value, because even though the color may be positively impacted, their true body color may still be exceptionally high.

Depending on the kind of lighting used to color grade the stone, a diamond with "medium" fluorescence can have a color grade that differs by ½–1 grade from its inherent body color; if "strong," by 1–2 grades; if "very strong," by 3–4 grades. If the color grade on the report represents a temporarily improved color resulting from *blue* fluorescence, you may be overpaying; but if it reflects a temporarily lower color resulting from *yellow* fluorescence, you may be paying *less* than what its true body color should sell for. In the latter case, as long as the stone is beautiful indoors, you may pay less and have a stone that is comparable in color to other stones that sell for more. The important thing is to take steps to get what you pay for.

In the case of diamonds that have "medium," "strong," or "very strong" fluorescence, as we mentioned earlier, we stress the importance of seeking a gemologist who uses UV-free lighting for color grading, to confirm the stone's inherent body color. This way you will not only know its inherent body color, but whether or not the price is appropriate. If the jeweler is not comfortable permitting you to take the stone prior to the sale, make the sale contingent on the gemologist's report and confirmation that the price is appropriate for the stone's inherent body color.

If you are unable to take the stone to a gemologist-appraiser, and you are not sure whether or not you can see any color difference with your own eyes when you view the stone in various lighting conditions, we recommend continuing your diamond search until you find another beautiful stone that is nonfluorescent. Another approach would be to apply a "worst-case scenario" to determine whether or not the stone is appropriately priced. Here is how the "worst-case scenario" would work. Let's say, for example, that you're considering a one-carat diamond with "very strong" blue fluorescence, and the report indicates E color. Calculate its value on the assumption that the inherent body color is probably 3–4 grades lower, which would be H–I color. In such a case, the cost difference is considerable. A nonfluorescent diamond with an inherent body color of E might cost $20,000; a comparable nonfluorescent diamond of I color would be $11,000. If the stone is beautiful, and it will look a lot whiter in some lighting environments, it may be worth a little bonus, so figure a value of around $12,000–$13,000. If this is close to the price being asked, the stone is probably priced appropriately. If the seller wants a lot more, our advice is to find another diamond!

We want to stress that if a diamond is properly priced, there is nothing wrong with buying a fluorescent diamond, whether it fluoresces blue, yellow, or any other color. Fluorescent diamonds are fascinating, distinctive, and have an allure all their own!

What Is a "Premier"?

At this point I should mention a type of fluorescent diamond that is not encountered often, but which occurs frequently enough to warrant a brief discussion. It is called a *premier.* This does not mean the diamond is better than others. In fact, it should sell for much less than other white diamonds.

The true color of any premier diamond will be yellowish (referred to in the trade as *cape*), but the yellow color is masked by strong blue fluorescence. As with other diamonds that fluoresce blue, the premier will appear whiter than it really is in certain light. It may actually have a bluish tint, sometimes with a greenish cast. However, a premier will *always* have a murky or oily appearance in daylight or fluorescent light, resulting from the coupling of the yellow with the blue. The murkiness detracts from its beauty and causes a deep reduction in value. The price of the premier varies depending on the degree of yellow present and the degree of murkiness.

Do not confuse a premier diamond with one that exhibits normal blue fluorescence. Many diamonds exhibit some degree of fluorescence. Many have a very fine white body color to begin with. But most important, they differ from the premier because they will not appear oily or murky in daylight-type light.

What Is a Chameleon Diamond?

A true chameleon diamond is one that normally has a greenish color (with a grayish or yellowish undertone) that undergoes a prominent but temporary color *change* to a more *yellow* color when heated (thermochromism) and when kept in the dark (photochromism). The change will be evident after just a few hours in the dark, and, when heated, within a few seconds at just 300 degrees Fahrenheit (approximately 150 degrees Celsius).

True chameleons change from greenish to yellowish when exposed to heat *and* dark. There is another color-change phenomenon shown by some diamonds known as the "reverse chameleon effect," in which a yellow diamond changes to greenish, but only after being kept in the dark, not when heated.

True chameleons are rare and highly sought by collectors and connoisseurs. They are usually small, rarely over 5 carats. They can command very high prices. A 2–3 carat stone can easily bring $75,000, and a stone over 4 carats fetched approximately $240,000 several years ago. The auction market is the primary source of such stones, but they seldom have more than one or two per year.

There are other "color-change" diamonds that change color depending on the type of light in which they are seen. Strongly fluorescent fancy-color diamonds can appear one color in incandescent light and an entirely different color or distinctly different shade of color in daylight or fluorescent light. However, these are not considered "chameleon" diamonds and should not be referred to as such.

Keep It Clean if You Want the Color to Look Its Best

A dirty diamond will not look white, nor will it sparkle. An accumulation of dirt, especially greasy dirt, will give a diamond a yellowish cast, so if you want to see and enjoy its full beauty, keep your diamond clean.

This principle applies especially when you are looking at old jewelry for possible purchase. When you are considering old diamond pieces, pay particular attention to whether or not it is impacted with dirt accumulated by years of use. If it is, there is a possibility that the diamond will have a better color grade than it may appear to have at first glance. This is because the dirt may contain varying amounts of fatty deposits (from dishwashing, cosmetics, etc.), which yellow with age. When this type of dirt builds up and is in contact with the diamond, it will also make the diamond appear more yellow.

CHAPTER SEVEN

Clarifying Clarity

How Flaws Affect Diamonds

Flaw classification—also called *clarity* grade—is one of the criteria used to determine the value of a diamond. As with all things in nature, however, there is really no such thing as "flawless." Even though some very rare diamonds are classified "flawless," the term is somewhat misleading, and you must be sure you understand what it really means.

When we talk about this classification, we are referring to the presence of tiny, usually microscopic, characteristics. The word *flaw* suggests something bad, but this is not really the case; rather, the flaw grade simply provides part of the complete description of the stone. It is important to understand that as diamonds form in nature, *every* diamond develops certain types of internal characteristics. They might be microscopic cracks shaped like feathers—some are quite lovely when viewed with the microscope—or microscopic diamond crystals, or even crystals of some other gemstone!

Every diamond contains distinctive internal characteristics. In the jewelry trade, these internal characteristics are called *inclusions*, something *included* within the stone as it was forming in nature. Each diamond's internal picture—its internal character—is unique. No two are alike, so the clarity picture can be an important factor in identifying a specific diamond.

To What Extent Does Clarity Affect the Beauty of a Diamond?

It is very important to understand that clarity may have little or no effect on the beauty of a diamond if it falls within the first eight clarity grades discussed later in this chapter (FL through SI). Few people can discern any visible difference between stones until they reach the imperfect grades, and even then it is sometimes difficult to see anything in the stone without magnification.

Many people mistakenly believe that the clarity grade affects a diamond's brilliance and sparkle. This is not true; the clarity grade has little effect on a diamond's visible appearance except in the very lowest grades. Many people think that the better the clarity, the more brilliant and sparkling the diamond. Perhaps it is the term itself, *clarity,* that leads to the confusion (and the reason I don't like the term *clarity grade*). Whatever the case, as discussed in chapter 5, it is the precision of the *cutting* that determines how brilliant and sparkling a diamond will be.

To the buyer, the flaw grade, or clarity grade, is important because it indicates, on a relative basis, how "clean" the diamond is, and this ranking has a significant effect on cost. The cleaner the stone, the rarer; the rarer the stone, the costlier. But diamonds don't have to be flawless to be beautiful and sparkling.

As you will see when you shop and compare, you can find very beautiful, sparkling diamonds in a wide range of clarity grades. Juggling the clarity grade can give you tremendous flexibility in getting a whiter or larger diamond for your money. Just keep in mind that you won't see differences with the eye alone, so you must take care to know for sure what the specific clarity grade is.

How Is the Clarity Grade Determined?

Diamonds used in jewelry are usually very clean, and little if anything can be seen without magnification. This is starting to change as an increasing number of diamonds with visible cracks or other inclusions enter the market—stones in the I_1 through I_3 range and below—but for the most part, differences in clarity cannot normally be seen simply by looking at the stone with the naked eye. The clarity grade is based on what can be seen *when the diamond is examined with 10x magnification* under a loupe (see chapter 2). The clarity grade is based on the number, size, color, and location of inclusions or blemishes in the stone. The flawless grade is given to a stone in which no imperfections can be seen internally (inclusions) or externally (blemishes) when examined with 10x magnification, although at higher powers inclusions will be visible even in a flawless diamond. For clarity grading purposes, if an inclusion can't be seen at 10x, it doesn't exist.

Clarity grading requires extensive training and practice, and proper grading can be done only by an experienced jeweler, dealer, or gemologist. If you want to examine a diamond with the loupe, remember that only in the lowest grades will an inexperienced person be able to see inclusions or blemishes easily, and even with the loupe it will be difficult to see what a professional will see easily. Few amateurs will see anything at all in the highest clarity grades.

Today, a jeweler might use a microscope with a video monitor to help you see what is inside a diamond you are considering. Be sure that the jeweler focuses at different depths into the stone and that the microscope is set at 10x (higher power may actually conceal something in the diamond because of the difficulty in focusing properly at higher powers). And remember: Don't panic—what you are seeing is magnified ten times!

I recommend that you first examine the stone carefully with your eyes alone, then with a simple loupe, saving the microscope, when offered, for last. Examining a diamond in this way will help you become familiar with the particular characteristics of the stone you purchase, and may give you information that will enable you to always recognize your diamond should it be necessary at some future time (after having it mounted in the ring, for example).

Types of Internal and External Characteristics

Basically, clarity grading systems grade the stone according to the presence or absence of internal and external characteristics, generally referred to as "flaws." They are called *inclusions* when internal, *blemishes* when external. Flaws can be white, black, colorless, or even red or green in rare instances.

I will discuss some of these flaws here, so that you have a working vocabulary of diamond imperfections.

Internal Flaws or Inclusions

Pinpoint. This is a small, usually whitish dot (although it can be dark) that is difficult to see. There can be a number of pinpoints (a cluster) or a "cloud" of pinpoints (usually very difficult to see with just a loupe).

Dark spot. This may be a small crystal inclusion or a thin, flat inclusion that reflects light like a mirror. It may also appear as a silvery, metallic reflector.

Colorless crystal. This is often a small crystal of diamond, although it may be another mineral. Sometimes it appears very small, sometimes large enough to substantially lower the flaw grade to SI, or even I. A small group of colorless crystals lowers the grade from a possible VS to I_3.

Cleavage. A cleavage is a particular type of crack that has a flat plane that, if struck, could cause the diamond to split, or cleave, as though it had been sliced cleanly with a saw. A large cleavage in the upper part of the diamond can be a serious flaw.

Feather. This is another name for a crack. A small feather is not dangerous and can be a very minor flaw if it does not break through the surface of the stone on the top portion where you might accidentally strike it; a large feather on the top can be a serious flaw.

Bearded girdle or girdle fringes. These are usually the result of hastiness on the part of the cutter while rounding out the diamond. The girdle portion becomes overheated and develops small radial hairlike cracks that resemble small whiskers going into the diamond from the girdle edge. Sometimes the bearding amounts to minimal "peach fuzz" and can be removed with slight repolishing. Sometimes the bearding must be removed by faceting the girdle. If the bearding is very minimal, a diamond can still be graded IF.

Growth or grain lines. These result from growth aberrations in the diamond's crystal structure as it is forming. They can be seen only when examining the diamond while slowly rocking or rotating it. They appear and disappear, usually instantaneously. They will appear in a group of two, three, or four pale whitish or beige lines. If they cannot be seen from the crown portion of the diamond and are small, they will not affect the grade adversely; if significant, they can affect the stone's transparency and result in a lower clarity grade.

Knaat or twin lines. These are part of a diamond-crystal inclusion left exposed on the surface. They are sometimes classified as external flaws because they appear as very small ridges, often with some type of geometrical outline; or as a small, slightly raised dot with a tail resembling a comet. They're difficult to see.

Laser lines. Laser techniques are used today to make black flaws less visible, and thus improve the stone aesthetically. Using laser technology, it is possible to "vaporize" black inclusions so they practically disappear. With the loupe, however, an experienced jeweler or gemologist can see the "path" cut into the diamond by the laser beam. This path looks like a fine, straight, white thread starting at the surface of the stone and penetrating into it. See the section "Clarity Enhancement" later in this chapter.

External Flaws or Blemishes

A natural. A natural is a remnant of the original skin of the diamond, and is often left on the girdle by the cutter in order to get the largest possible diameter from the rough. They are usually seen on the girdle and appear to be a rough, unpolished area. A natural may look like a scratch line or small triangle (called a trigon). If it is no wider than the normal width of the girdle or does not disrupt the circumference of the stone, it may not be considered a blemish. Often naturals are polished and become an extra facet, especially if they occur below the girdle edge.

Nick. This is a small chip, usually on the girdle, and can be caused by an accidental knock or blow in the course of wearing the diamond (especially if the girdle is on the thin side). Sometimes a nick or chip can be seen on the edge where the facets meet. If small, the bruised corner can be polished, creating an extra facet. This usually occurs on the crown.

Girdle roughness. This blemish appears as crisscrossed lines, brighter and duller finishing, and minute chipping. This can be remedied by faceting or repolishing.

Pits or cavities. Pits or holes on the facet. When on the table facet, especially if they are deep, the presence of pits or cavities will quickly lower the grade of the stone. Removing a pit may involve recutting the whole top of the stone and can also shrink the stone's diameter.

Scratch. A scratch is usually a minor defect that can be removed with simple repolishing. Remember, however, that in order to repolish the stone, you must remove it from its setting, and then reset it after it has been polished.

Polishing lines. Many diamonds exhibit polishing lines. If they appear on the pavilion side and are not too obvious, they do not lower the value. In some small diamonds these scratch lines can be obvious and are usually the result of a badly maintained polishing wheel.

Abraded or rough culet. The culet has been chipped or poorly finished. This is usually a minor flaw.

How Does the Clarity Grade Affect Diamond Value?

I will use the GIA system to explain clarity and its effect on value because it is the most widely used in the United States. As you can see from the comparison chart (on page 71), other systems now use similar classifications. Should you have a diamond with a report from one of these, you can use this chart to find the corresponding GIA grade.

On the GIA scale, *FL* is the grade given to a stone that has no visible flaws, internal or external, when examined under 10x magnification. Only a highly qualified person will be able to determine this grade. If you are using a loupe as you examine diamonds, remember that it is very difficult for the inexperienced viewer to see flaws that may be readily observable to the experienced jeweler, dealer, or gemologist, and you will not have the experience to determine whether or not a diamond is flawless. Often the novice is unable to see any flaws, even in SI grades, even with use of the loupe. A flawless, colorless, correctly proportioned stone, particularly in a one-carat size or larger, is *extremely* rare and is priced proportionately much higher than any other grade. Some jewelers insist there is no such thing available today.

IF is the grade given to a stone with no internal flaws and with only minor external blemishes that could be removed with polishing, such as nicks, small pits not on the table, and/or girdle roughness. These stones, when colorless and with well-proportioned makes, are also rare and are priced proportionately much higher than other grades.

VVS_1 and VVS_2 are grades given to stones with internal flaws that are very, very difficult for a qualified observer to see. These grades are also difficult to obtain and are priced at a premium.

VS_1 and VS_2 are grades given to stones with very small inclusions, difficult for a qualified observer to see. These stones are more readily available in good color and cut, and their flaws will not be visible except under magnification. These are excellent stones to purchase.

SI_1 and SI_2 grades are given to stones with flaws that a qualified observer will see fairly easily under 10x magnification. They are not as rare as the higher grades, so they are less costly; in these grades, flaws may sometimes be visible without magnification when examined from the back side or laterally. These grades are still highly desirable, and since they cannot normally be seen with the naked eye when mounted, they may enable one to select a stone with a higher color, or in a larger size, when working with a limited budget.

The *imperfect* grades are given to stones in which flaws may be seen by a qualified observer without magnification; they are readily available and are much less expensive. They are graded I_1, I_2, and I_3. (These grades

Flawless

SI_2

No difference can be seen between these two diamonds with the unaided eye, but accurate grading is important because it can dramatically affect price.

are called *first piqué* (pronounced pee-kay), *second piqué,* and *third piqué* in some classification systems.) I_1, I_2, and *some* I_3 grades may still be desirable if they are brilliant and lively, and if there are no inclusions that might make them more susceptible than normal to breaking. They should not be automatically eliminated by a prospective purchaser who desires lovely diamond jewelry. As a general rule, however, imperfect grades may be difficult to resell should you ever try to do so.

Exercise Care When Considering a Low Clarity Grade

For those considering a diamond with an I_3 clarity grade, I must issue a word of warning: *Some diamonds graded I_3 today are actually industrial quality and not suited for jewelry use.* Some cutters are cutting material that is lower than what is considered acceptable for jewelry. Since there is no grade lower than I_3 at this time, these stones are lumped in with other "better" (jewelry-quality) I_3 stones and are given an I_3 grade as well. But I_3 grade diamonds are *not* all comparable in terms of their clarity, and some should sell for much less than others. Be sure to shop around and compare I_3 diamonds to become familiar with what is acceptable for jewelry use.

Clarity Enhancement

Today, technological advances have made it possible to improve diamond clarity. Several clarity enhancement techniques are available; some are more or less permanent, and others are definitely not permanent. Unfortunately, clarity enhancement frequently is not disclosed, either to jewelers themselves or by jewelers to their customers. It is important to buy diamonds from knowledgeable, reputable jewelers who check for such treatments. In addition, before buying any diamond, you must *ask* whether or not the stone has been clarity enhanced. If the stone has been enhanced, ask what method was used, and be sure this is stated on the bill of sale. In addition, be sure to ask about special care requirements that might be necessitated by the process.

The two most widely used methods of clarity enhancement are lasering and fracture filling.

Lasering

Laser treatment is used today to make flaws less visible and thus improve the stone aesthetically. Laser technology makes it possible to "vaporize" black inclusions so they are much less visible; in some cases, they virtually disappear. With magnification, however, an experienced jeweler or gemologist can see telltale indicators of lasering. One such indicator (often seen with a simple 10x loupe) is a "path" that resembles a fine white thread starting at the surface of the stone and traveling into it. New lasering techniques do not show this path, but are detectable by other techniques used by gemologists. The effects of laser treatment are permanent. If a lasered diamond is accompanied by a diamond grading report issued by a respected lab, the report will state that the stone is lasered.

A lasered stone should cost less than another with the "same" clarity, so it may be an attractive choice for a piece of jewelry—as long as you *know* it's lasered and therefore pay a fair price for it (10 to 35 percent less, depending upon how many inclusions have been lasered within the stone). You must be sure to ask whether or not the diamond is lasered. Some countries don't require disclosure, and for several years the Federal Trade Commission suspended the requirement to disclose lasering in the United States. This position was reversed—disclosure is now required and compliance is assumed—but as always, guard yourself against unscrupulous practices by asking direct questions and getting the information in writing. If a lab report does not accompany the stone, you must be sure to ask explicitly, and verify it with an independent gemologist-appraiser.

Fracture Filling

Fractures—cracks or breaks—that would normally be visible and detract from the beauty of a diamond can often be filled with a nearly colorless, glasslike substance. After filling, these breaks virtually disappear and will no longer be seen, except under magnification. Filling is *not* a permanent treatment, and special precautions are required when cleaning and repairing jewelry containing a filled diamond. With proper care, such stones may remain beautiful for many years. Careless handling, however, can cause the filler to leave the stone or change color, resulting in a much less attractive diamond. Some filling materials are much more stable than others, but at present it is usually not possible to know what filler has been used in a given stone. Should the filler be accidentally removed, your jeweler can have the treatment repeated to restore the stone's original appearance. The GIA will not issue a grading report on a filled diamond, but some labs will (indicating the grade it *appears* to be *after* filling).

Filled diamonds cost much less than other diamonds, usually 40 to 60 percent less, depending on the number of filled cracks. They can be a very attractive and affordable alternative as long as you know what you are buying, understand the limitations, and pay the right price. Be sure to ask explicitly whether or not the stone has been fracture filled, and if the stone does not have a report from a respected lab (see appendix), get a statement *on the bill of sale* as to whether or not it is fracture filled.

How Does the Position of a Flaw Affect a Diamond's Grading and Value?

As a general rule, the position of any given inclusion will progressively downgrade and devalue a diamond as indicated below:

- *If seen only from the pavilion side,* or seen *clearly* only from the pavilion side, a flaw has the least adverse effect, since it is the least visible from the top.
- *If positioned near the girdle,* while perhaps more visible than described above, a flaw is still difficult to see, and hardly noticeable from the top. Such flaws can be easily covered with the prong of a setting.
- *Under any crown facet* (other than a star facet), a flaw is more easily visible, except when near the girdle.
- *Under a star facet,* a flaw will be much more easily visible.
- *Under the table* is the least desirable position, as it places the flaw where it is most noticeable, and may have the greatest effect on brilliance or fire, depending on the stone's size or color.

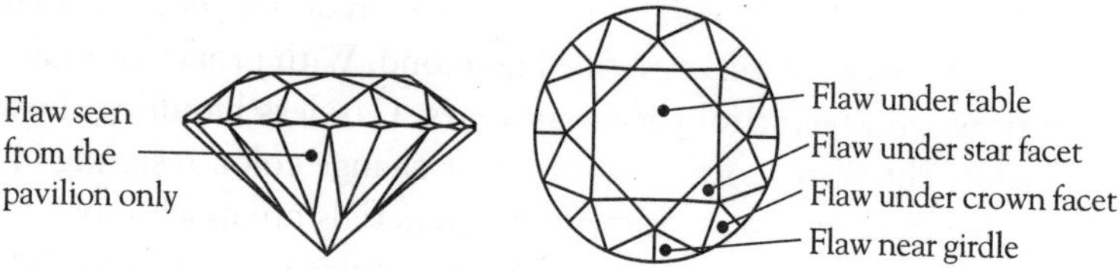

Sometimes a small black or white flaw may be in such a position that it is reflected within the stone. It may be seen as a reflection to the opposite side of the stone, or, more unfortunately, it may reflect itself as many as *eight times* around the bottom or near the culet of the stone. A diamond with such a flaw might otherwise be classified as a VS_1 or VS_2, but because of the eightfold reflection resulting from its unfortunate position, the flaw grade will be lowered.

Remember, a diamond does not have to be flawless to be a very fine stone and to have a high value. Personally, I prefer a stone that might be slightly imperfect but has fine color and brilliance over a flawless stone with less sparkle and a less fine color. Color and brilliance are considered the most important factors in terms of a stone's *desirability. And remember*: Even a diamond graded I_3 can be beautiful and brilliant.

Commonly Used Diamond Clarity Grading Systems

There are several recognized clarity grading systems in use worldwide, but the system used most widely in the United States and an increasing number of other countries was developed by the GIA (Gemological Institute of America). Other widely recognized clarity grading scales were introduced by these organizations:

- AGS (American Gem Society)
- Scan D.N. (Scandinavian Diamond Nomenclature)
- CIBJO (The World Jewellery Confederation). Participating member nations that use this system include Austria, Belgium, Canada, Denmark, Finland, France, Germany, Great Britain, Italy, Japan, Netherlands, Norway, Spain, Sweden, Switzerland, and the United States
- HRD (Hoge Raad voor Diamant, the Diamond High Council of Belgium)

The terms *clarity grade* and *flaw grade* are interchangeable, but today *clarity grade* is more common.

GIA	AGS	SCAN D.N.	CIBJO UNDER 0.47 CT	CIBJO 0.47 CT AND OVER	HRD
FL	0	FL	Loupe clean	Loupe clean	Loupe clean
IF (Internally Flawless)	1	IF			
VVS_1		VVS_1	VVS	VVS_1	VVS_1
VVS_2	2	VVS_2		VVS_2	VVS_2
VS_1	3	VS_1	VS	VS_1	VS_1
VS_2	4	VS_2		VS_2	VS_2
SI_1	5	SI_1	SI	SI_1	SI_1
SI_2	6	SI_2		SI_2	
I_1 (Imperfect)	7 8	1st Piqué	Piqué I	Piqué I	P_1
I_2		2nd Piqué	Piqué II	Piqué II	P_2
I_3	9 10	3rd Piqué	Piqué III	Piqué III	P_3

VV = Very, Very
V = Very
S = Slight or Small
I = Inclusion or Included or Imperfect (Imperfection)

For example, VVS may be translated to mean Very, Very Slightly (Included); or Very, Very Small (Inclusion); or Very, Very Slightly (Imperfect). Some jewelers prefer to classify the stone as "very, very small inclusion" rather than "very, very slightly imperfect" because the former description may sound more acceptable to the customer. There is, in fact, no difference.

CHAPTER EIGHT

Weight

What Is a Carat?

Diamonds are sold by the *carat* (ct), not to be confused with *karat* (kt), which in the United States refers to gold purity. Since 1913, most countries have agreed that a carat weighs 200 milligrams, or 1/5 gram.

Before 1913, the carat weight varied depending on the country of origin—usually weighing *more* than the modern carat. The Indian carat didn't weigh the same as the English carat; the French carat was different from the Indian and the English. This is important if you have, or are thinking of buying, a very old piece that still has the original bill of sale indicating carat weight. Since the old carat usually weighed *more* than the post-1913 *metric carat,* an old three-carat stone will often weigh more than three carats by modern standards. Today the term *carat* means the metric carat, the 200-milligram carat with five carats weighing one gram.

What are points? Jewelers often refer to the carat weight of diamonds in terms of *points*. This is particularly true of stones under one carat. There are 100 points to a carat, so if a jeweler says that a stone weighs 75 points, he means it weighs 75/100 of a carat, or 3/4 carat. A 25-point stone is 1/4 carat. A 10-point stone is 1/10 carat.

The carat is a unit of weight, not size. I wish to stress this point, since most people think that a one-carat stone is a particular size. Most people, therefore, would expect a one-carat diamond and a one-carat emerald, for example, to look the same size or to have the same apparent dimensions. This is not the case.

Comparing a one-carat diamond with a one-carat emerald and a one-carat ruby easily illustrates this point. First, emerald weighs less than diamond, and ruby weighs more than diamond. This means that a one-carat emerald will look larger than a one-carat diamond, while the ruby will look smaller than a diamond of the same weight. Emerald, with a mineral composition that is lighter, will yield greater mass per carat; ruby, with its heavier composition, will yield less mass per carat.

Let's look at the principle another way. If you compare a one-inch cube of pine wood, a one-inch cube of aluminum, and a one-inch cube of iron, you would easily choose the cube of iron as heaviest, even though it has the same *volume* as the other materials. The iron is like the ruby, while the wood is like the emerald and the aluminum like the diamond. Equal *volumes* of different materials can have very different weights, depending on their density, also called specific gravity.

Equal volumes of materials with the same density, however, should have approximately the same weight, so that in diamond, the carat weight has come to represent particular sizes. These sizes, as I've discussed, are based on diamonds cut to ideal proportions. Consequently, if properly cut, diamonds of the weights given in the chart on page 77 should be approximately the sizes illustrated. Remember, however, that *these sizes will not apply to other gems.*

How Does Carat Weight Affect Value in Diamonds?

Diamond prices are usually quoted *per carat*. Diamonds of the finest and rarest quality are sold for the highest price per carat, and diamonds of progressively less rare quality are sold for a progressively lower price per carat. For example, a rare-quality diamond might sell for $20,000 per carat. So, a stone in this quality weighing 1.12 carats would cost $22,400. On the other hand, a stone of exactly the same weight, in a less rare quality, might sell for only $10,000 per carat, or $11,200.

Also, as a rule, the price increases per carat as we go from smaller to larger stones, since the larger stones are rarer and more limited in supply. For example, stones of the same quality weighing ½ carat will sell for more per carat than stones weighing ⅓ carat; stones weighing ¾ carat will sell for more per carat than stones of the same quality weighing ½ carat. For example, the per-carat price of a particular quality ½-carat stone might be $5,000, while the per-carat price for a ⅓-carat stone of the same quality would be $3,000. The stones would cost $2,500 (½ x $5,000) and $1,000 (⅓ x $3,000) respectively.

Furthermore, stones of the same quality weighing exactly one carat will sell for *much* more than stones weighing 90 to 96 points. Thus, if you want a one-carat stone of a particular quality, but you can't afford it, you may find you can afford it in a 95-point stone—and a 95-point stone will give the impression of a full one-carat stone when set. You might be able to get your heart's desire after all.

As you will see, the price of a diamond does not increase proportionately; there are disproportionate jumps. And the larger and finer the stone (all else being equal in terms of overall quality), the more disproportionate the increase in cost per carat may be. A top-quality two-carat stone will not cost twice as much as a one-carat stone; it could easily be *three* times as much. A top-quality five-carat stone would not be five times the cost of a one-carat stone; it could easily be as much as ten times what a one-carat stone might cost.

What Is *Spread?*

The term *spread* may be used in response to the question "How large is this diamond?" But it can be misleading. Spread refers to the size the stone *appears* to be, based on its diameter. For example, if the diameter of the stone measured the same as you see in the diamond size charts (see pages 77 and 78), which represent the diameter of a perfectly proportioned stone, the jeweler might say it "spreads" one carat. But this does not mean it *weighs* one carat. It means it *looks* the same size as a perfectly cut one-carat stone. It may weigh less or more—usually less.

Diamonds are generally weighed before they are set, so the jeweler can give you the exact carat weight, since you are paying a certain price per carat. Remember, also, that the price per carat for a fine stone weighing 96 points is much less than for one weighing one carat or more. So it is unwise to accept any "approximate" weight, even though the difference seems so slight.

As you can see here, it is also important when buying a diamond to realize that since carat refers to weight, the manner in which a stone is cut can affect its apparent size. A one-carat stone that is cut shallow (see chapter 5) will appear larger in diameter than a stone that is cut thick (heavy). Conversely, a thick stone will appear smaller in diameter.

Furthermore, if the diamond has a thick girdle (see chapter 5), the stone will appear smaller in diameter. If this girdle is faceted, it tends to hide the ugly, frosted look of a thick girdle, but the fact remains that the girdle is thick, and the stone suffers because it will appear smaller in diameter than one would expect at a given carat weight. These stones are therefore somewhat cheaper per carat.

Sizes and Weights of Various Diamond Cuts

Weight (ct)	Emerald	Marquise	Pear	Brilliant
5				
4				
3				
2½				
2				
1½				
1¼				
1				
¾				
½				

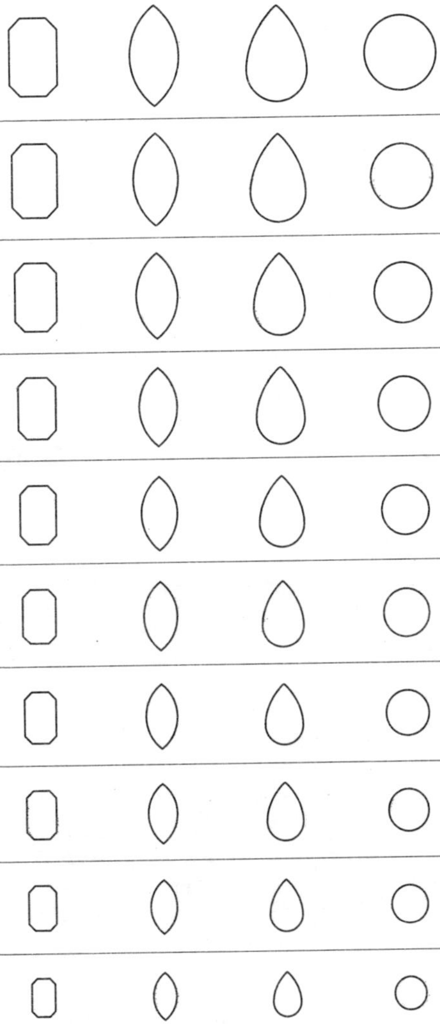

Diameters and Corresponding Weights of Round Brilliant-Cut Diamonds

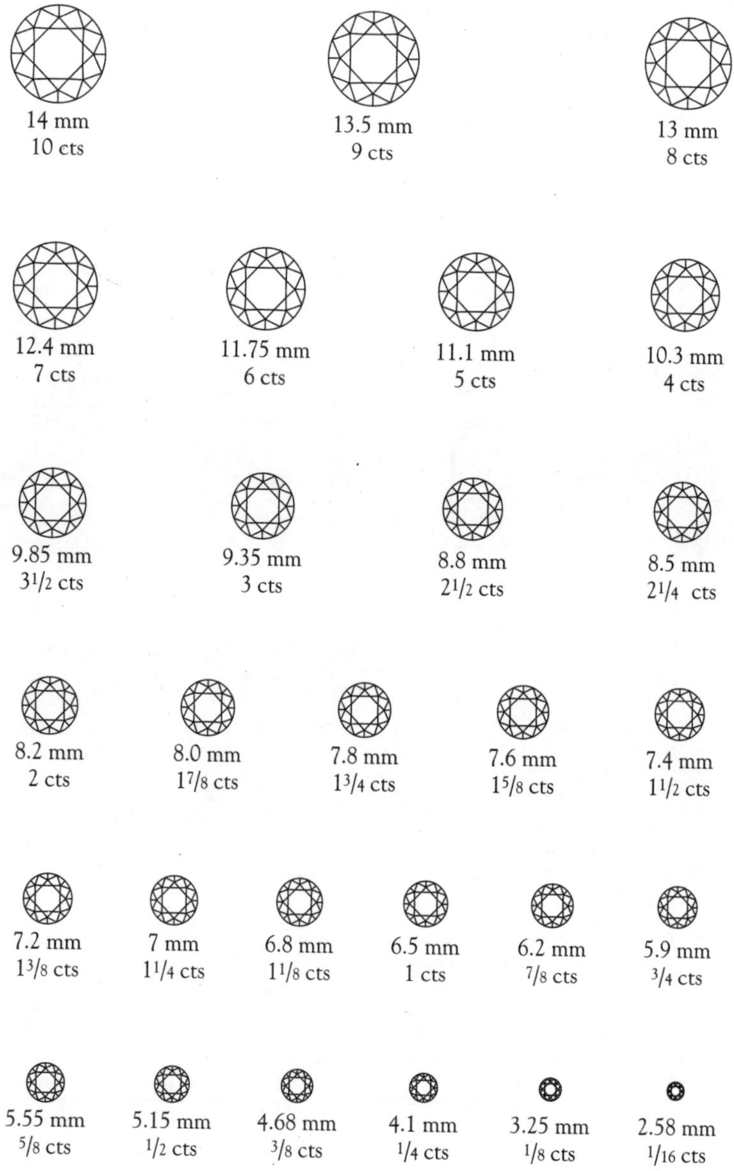

CHAPTER NINE

How to Read Diamond Grading Reports

Today, few fine diamonds over one carat are sold without a diamond grading report (or certificate, as they are also called) from a respected laboratory. Reports issued by the GIA Gem Trade Laboratory are the most widely used in the United States and in many countries around the world, but reports from other laboratories (see appendix) are also highly respected. Here we will discuss reports on diamonds in the D–Z range. Fancy-color diamond reports will be discussed separately in chapter 12.

A grading report does more than certify the stone's genuineness; it fully describes the stone and evaluates each of the critical factors affecting quality, beauty, and value. Grading reports can be very useful for a variety of reasons. The information they contain can provide verification of the "facts" as represented by the seller and enable one to make a safer decision when purchasing a diamond. Another important function of reports is to verify the identity of a specific diamond at some future time—if, for example, it has been out of one's possession for any reason. For insurance purposes, the information provided on the report will help ensure replacement of a lost or stolen diamond with one that is truly of "comparable quality."

Reports aren't necessary for every diamond, and many beautiful diamonds used in jewelry are sold without them. But when considering the purchase of a very fine diamond weighing one carat or more, I strongly recommend that the stone be accompanied by a report from one of the laboratories listed in the appendix, even if it means having a stone removed from its setting (no reputable lab will issue a full grading report on a mounted diamond) and then reset. If you are considering a stone that lacks a report, it is easy for your jeweler or an appraiser to obtain one.

The availability and widespread use of these reports can, when properly understood, enable even those without professional skills to make valid comparisons between several stones and more informed buying decisions. The key is found in *knowing how to read the reports properly.*

Don't Rely on the Report Alone

Reports can be an important tool to help you understand differences affecting rarity and price. But I must caution you not to let them interfere with what you *like* or really want. Remember, some diamonds are very beautiful even though they don't adhere to established standards. In the final analysis, use your own eyes and ask yourself how you *like* the stone.

I had a customer who was trying to decide between several stones. Her husband wanted to buy her the stone with the "best" report, but she preferred another stone which, according to what was on the reports, wasn't as "good." They decided against the "best" stone and bought the one that made her happiest. The important thing is that they knew exactly what they were buying and paid an appropriate price for that specific combination of quality factors. In other words, they made an *informed* choice. The reports gave them assurance as to the facts and greater confidence that they knew what they were really comparing.

Improper Use of Reports Can Lead to Costly Mistakes

As important as diamond grading reports can be, they can also be misused and lead to erroneous conclusions and costly mistakes. The key to being able to rely on a diamond report—and having confidence in your decision—lies in knowing how to read it properly.

When trying to decide between two diamonds accompanied by diamond grading reports, buyers all too often make a decision by comparing just two factors evaluated on the reports—*color* and *clarity*—and think they have made a sound decision. This is rarely the case. No one can make a sound decision based on color and clarity alone. In fact, when significant price differences exist between two stones of the same color and clarity, you will find that often the cheaper stone is *not* the same quality, nor the better value.

Color and clarity provide only part of the total picture and differences in price usually indicate differences in quality that you may not see or

Classic Diamond Shapes

Heart

Marquise

Round Brilliant

Pear

Oval

Emerald Cut

The Shape of Things to Come...

Classic Radiant

Gabrielle®
Rectangle

Crisscut®

Royal Asscher®

Gabrielle® Square

Quadrillion™

Lucida™

Tiana™

The Reiss Cushion—a traditional cutting style that evokes an heirloom feeling

...A Blend of Old and New

Biro 88™

Spirit Sun®

EightStar®
"Super" Ideal

Trilliant

Lily Cut®

Gabrielle® Heart

...And Distinctive Shapes to Accentuate

Briolette

Step-cut lozenge or kite shape creates unique elements.

Rondelles

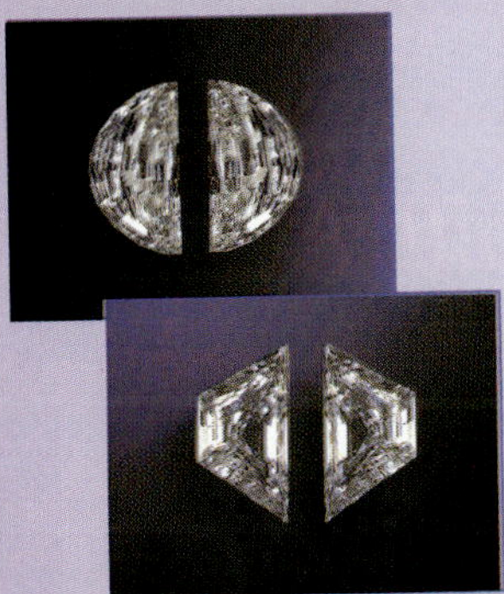

Step-cut half-moons and trapezoid shapes

Crisscut® baguette and tapered baguette

Fancy Natural-Color Diamonds...

Rare and Distinctive

Diamonds occur naturally in more colors and more shades of color than any other gemstone—virtually every color in the rainbow. *Above*: The Bulgari Blue.

...For Jewels That Stand Apart

Rudolf Friedmann's leaf brooch captures the color of fall with fancy cognac-color diamonds.

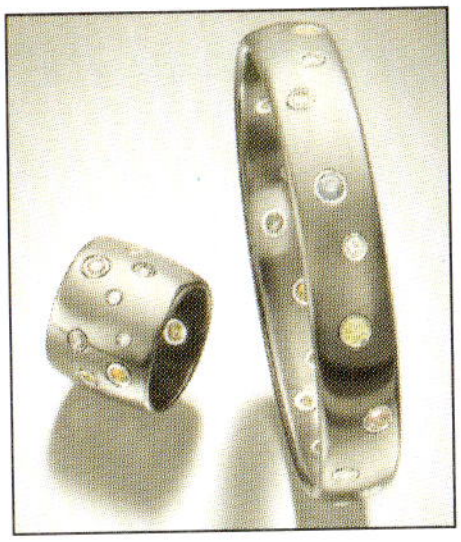

Etienne Perret's sophisticated ceramic bangle and ring with natural colorless and treated-color diamonds stand apart.

Manak's black and white diamond rings (*above*) reflect the latest mono-chromatic trend. Small diamonds and intricate platinum wirework with floral motifs by Janet Alix (*below*) combine for a soft, feminine feel.

Martin Gruber's award-winning necklace featuring a fancy deep orangy yellow diamond (*above*), and a lovely suite weaving white and natural pink and yellow diamonds into the Attia Collection by Eli Jewels (*left*)

Raymond Hak's contrasting brushed platinum and black and colorless pavé (*left*) create a bold and commanding look.

Diamonds Sparkle Any Time...

Graduated diamond "Riviera" necklaces by Kwiat (*above*) make a timeless choice, and their diamond "Flower Girl" bracelet (*right*) and entwined ring (*below*) are pure romance.

Classic elegance using Bellataire™ HPHT-processed diamonds

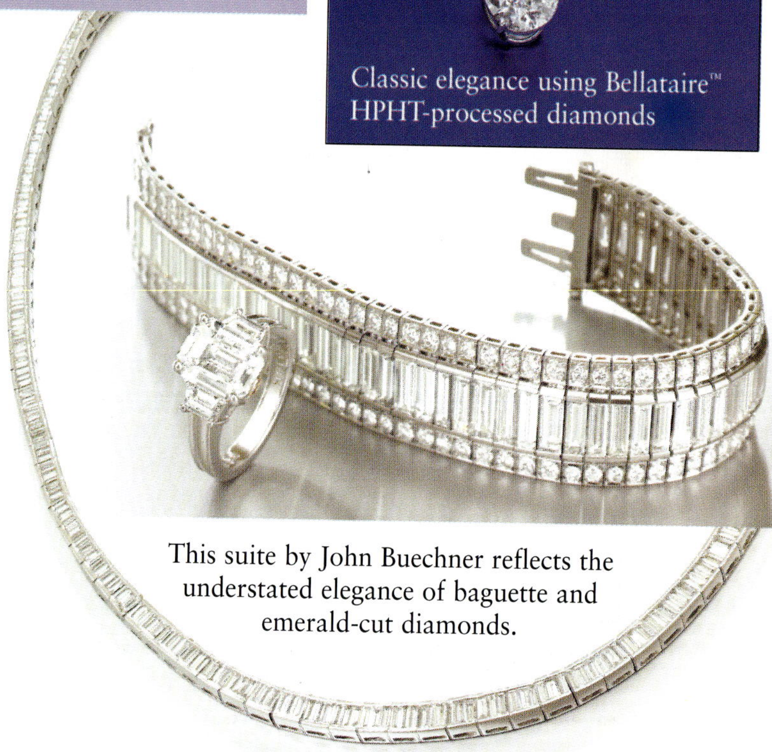

This suite by John Buechner reflects the understated elegance of baguette and emerald-cut diamonds.

...For Any Occasion

Jewelry using the new Gabrielle® round diamonds

Fancy shapes and fancy colors in earrings (*left*) create memorable jewels by Doron Isaak.

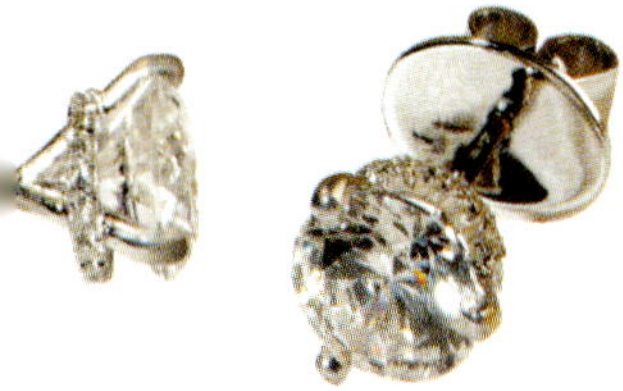

Micro-pavé work adds a subtle twist to these classic studs by Mark Silverstein.

Pink gold—a natural for white and pink diamond rings by Carl Blackburn.

Whimsical use of fancy-color and colorless diamonds, in bands by Christian Bauer

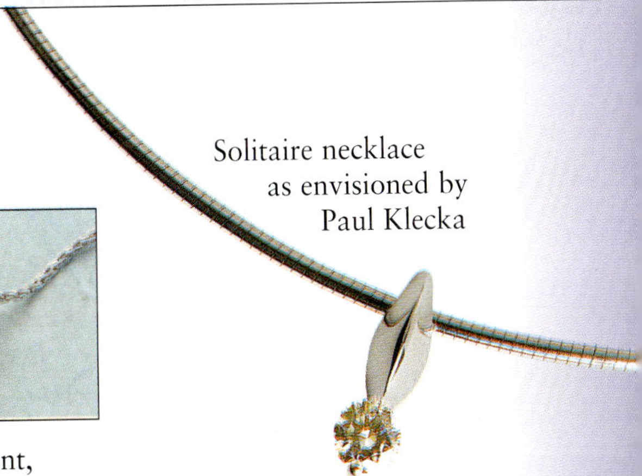

Solitaire necklace as envisioned by Paul Klecka

Pavé heart pendant, an affordable classic by James Breski

In Contemporary & Classic Designs

Inspired sundial by John David Cooney

Diamonds in vibrant *hair hues* inspire the elegant, glamorous Frédéric Fekkai by H. Stern jewelry collection.

Sethi Couture adds a touch of yesteryear with fancy-color diamonds, oxidized gold, and cascading flower earrings.

Yossi Harari uses oxidized gold, old cuts, and warm colors in a style evoking the Ottoman Empire.

Award-winning earrings by Joshua J are a sheer delight.

Carl Blackburn's cuff links combine grace and strength.

Baguettes alternating with rounds, in diamonds or combined with gemstones, create a popular new "classic" (*above*).

Scott Keating adds distinctive contemporary diamond "profile accents" in this ring from his Viewpoints Collection (*left*).

Three-stone Asscher-cut ring by J. Birnbach

Use of rose-cut, "foil-backed" diamonds against black-oxidized, low-karat gold combined with 24K gold makes a bold fashion statement by Yossi Harari.

Designer Doron Isaak contrasts the fancy intense yellow color of these radiant-cut diamonds with colorless round and baguette-cut diamonds for stronger impact.

Details such as engraving and milgraining along the diamond channels create modern heirlooms by Scott Kay.

Popular Ring Styles

Three-Stone Rings

Three-stone ring using color for contrast

Classic round three-stone ring

Three-stone ring with radiant-cut diamonds

Five Variations of the Classic "Solitaire"

Classic Tiffany-style six-prong ring

Paul Klecka's Floater® ring in platinum

Lazare Kaplan's solitaire with a "twist" (*right*) and classic yet bold two-tone ring (*left*)

Whitney Boin blends simplicity with strength

Christopher Designs' stunning use of fancy-color diamonds with colorless stones

Old Is New Again

Skilled artisans create intricate "heirloom" reproductions, by Varna (*left*) and Richard Kimball (*right*).

Micro-pavé Is All the Rage

Simple micro-pavé ring from J. Birnbach

Striking contrast in 18K white and yellow gold from Alishan's diamond collection

Creative Use of Side Stones

André Chervin uses tiny channel-set stones that lead the eye to the center.

Classic round with tapered baguettes

Interesting pavé work adds drama to the round center stone. From the Diana® Collection.

Kwiat's heart-shaped prongs add a clear message that his "princess" has his heart.

Wedding Bands for Today

Classic bands with a contemporary touch compliment designer Jean-François Albert's solitaire.

Five-stone bands with oval-cut, bar-set diamonds

Diamonds encircling the finger: baguette-cut diamonds in channel setting *(left)*; emerald-cut diamonds in bar-set band *(right)*

Bands and stacking rings

Artcarved creates a very feminine and romantic engagement ring and wedding band duo that recalls the feeling of bygone eras, but with a look of its own.

Elegant diamond bands in a variety of prong styles

For the right hand or left, with its clean lines combining channel and bezel setting, this "new" classic from Whitney Boin is timeless.

For the woman who loves variety, MJ Wilman provides the perfect solution.

Use of contrasting metal textures, black onyx, and diamonds for a bold new look for her…or for him.

Natural Diamonds in Treated Colors...

Offer a Rainbow of Affordable Hues

Natural diamonds that have been treated by the HPHT annealing process to obtain a "fancy" color

...and Synthetic Diamonds in New Colors, Too

Synthetic diamonds—red, yellow, orange, and blue

understand. With *round* diamonds, *all* the information you need is on the report, but you need to understand what all the information means before you can make valid comparisons.

Properly used, diamond grading reports can give you a more *complete* picture, enable you to make sounder comparisons, and determine who is offering good value. Reading reports may seem complicated at first, but if you take time to learn, and seek the help of a knowledgeable jeweler, you'll be amazed at how much more interesting—and unique—you'll find each diamond will become!

Before beginning, however, I must offer one important word of caution: *Don't make a purchase relying solely on any report without making sure the report matches the stone, and that the stone is still in the same condition described.* Always seek a professional gemologist, gemologist-appraiser, or gem-testing laboratory to confirm that the stone accompanying the report is, in fact, the stone described there, and that the stone is still in the same condition indicated on the report. I know of instances where a report has been accidentally sent with the wrong stone. And, in some cases, deliberate fraud is involved.

I want to stress that there are an increasing number of *counterfeit* GIA reports in use, accompanying diamonds sold in wholesale districts worldwide and on the Internet. GIA reports incorporate security features such as a hologram, security screen, microprint lines, and other components, with which a report can be readily identified as legitimate or counterfeit. You can verify the authenticity of a GIA diamond grading report, and the validity of the information provided at the time it was originally issued, by calling the GIA Laboratory in Carlsbad, California at (760) 603-4500.

Laser Inscription and Ion Beam Technology

Today, some laboratories are routinely providing a laser inscription of the number of the report along the girdle edge of diamonds on which they are issuing reports. This offers some means of ensuring that the stone and report do, in fact, match. If the diamond you are considering does not have a laser inscription, an independent gemologist can confirm that the stone and report match. Should you wish to have the report number inscribed on the girdle, a jeweler or gemologist can make arrangements with a lab for a nominal charge. European Gemological Laboratory and the Gemological Institute of America are among the companies providing laser inscription services. In addition to lasering, some labs offer a service that uses ion beam technology to mark a diamond in an innovative manner that is noninvasive. This new technology can also be used to apply a "brand" mark that will be visible only with a special viewer, thus making it more difficult to counterfeit branded diamonds. It will be more difficult to falsify or eradicate such marks as a result of the process itself, so this technology may ultimately replace laser inscriptions.

How to Read a Diamond Grading Report

Check the date issued. It is very important to check the date on the report. It's always possible that the stone has been damaged since the report was issued. This sometimes occurs with diamonds sold at auction. Since diamonds can become chipped or cracked with wear, one must always check them. For example, you might see a diamond accompanied by a report describing it as D–Flawless. If this stone were badly chipped *after the report was issued,* however, the clarity grade could easily drop to VVS, and in some cases, even lower. Needless to say, in such a case, value would be dramatically reduced.

Who issued the report? Check the name of the laboratory issuing the report. Is the report from a laboratory that is known and respected? If not, the information on the report may not be reliable. In the United States, respected laboratories that issue diamond reports include the Gemological Institute of America Laboratory (GIA), American Gemological Laboratories (AGL), American Gem Society (AGS), Professional Gem Sciences (PGS), and Gem Certification and Assurance Lab (GCAL). Respected European labs issuing diamond reports include the Belgian Diamond High Council (HRD), Gübelin Gem Lab (Swiss), and Swiss Gemmological Institute (SSEF). See the appendix for additional information on these and other laboratories.

Whichever report you are reading (see the end of this chapter for sample reports), all will provide similar information, including:

- *Identity of the stone.* This verifies that the stone is a diamond. Some diamond reports don't make a specific statement about identity because they are called *diamond* reports and are only issued for genuine diamonds. If the report is not called a "diamond grading report," then there must be a statement attesting that the stone described is a genuine diamond.

- *Weight.* The exact carat weight must be given.
- *Dimensions.* Any diamond, of any shape, should be measured and the dimensions recorded as a means of identification, especially for insurance/identification purposes. The dimensions given on a diamond report are very precise and provide information that is important for several reasons. First, the dimensions can help you determine that the diamond being examined is, in fact, the same diamond described in the report, since the likelihood of having two diamonds with exactly the same carat weight and millimeter dimensions is slim. Second, if the diamond has been damaged and recut since the report was issued, the millimeter dimensions may provide a clue that something has been altered, which might affect the carat weight as well. Any discrepancy between the dimensions that you or your jeweler get by measuring the stone and those provided on the report should be a red flag to check the stone very carefully.

  Finally, the dimensions on the report also tell you whether the stone is *round* or *out-of-round.* Out-of-round diamonds sell for less than those that are more perfectly round. Roundness is explained below in greater detail.
- *Proportioning, finish, girdle thickness, culet, color, and clarity.* These are covered individually on the following pages.

Round Brilliant-Cut Diamonds Are "Well-Rounded"

In round diamonds, the stone's *roundness* will affect value, so it is determined very carefully from measurements of the stone's diameter, gauged at several points around the circumference. For a round diamond,

Acceptable Tolerances for "Round" Diamonds

Weight	Diameter (in mm)	Acceptable Deviation (in mm)
1 ct	6.50	0.10
2 cts	8.20	0.12
3 cts	9.35	0.14
4 cts	10.30	0.16
5 cts	11.10	0.17
10 cts	14.00	0.21

To calculate an acceptable deviation on a particular stone, take the average between the high and low diameter dimensions given; multiply that number by 0.0154. For example, if the dimensions given are 8.20–8.31, the diameter averages 8.25. Multiply 8.25 by 0.0154 = 0.127. The acceptable deviation allowable for this stone will be 0.12–0.13. The actual deviation in this example is 0.11 (8.31 minus 8.20), well within the tolerance, so this diamond would be "round." Some flexibility is permitted on diamonds over two carats.

the report will usually give two diameters, measured in millimeters and noted to the hundredth: for example, 6.51 rather than 6.5; or 6.07 rather than 6.0, and so on. These indicate the highest and the lowest diameter. Diamonds are very rarely perfectly round, which is why most diamond reports will show two measurements. Recognizing the rarity of truly round diamonds, some deviation is permitted, and the stone will not be considered "out-of-round" unless it deviates by more than the established norm, which, in a one-carat stone, is approximately 0.10 millimeter. As the size of a diamond increases, the tolerances also increase.

Depending on the degree of out-of-roundness, price can be affected by 10 to 15 percent, or much more if the stone is noticeably out-of-round. The greater the deviation, the lower the price should be.

Dimensions for Fancy Shapes

While the dimensions for fancy shapes are not as important as they are for round diamonds, there are length-to-width ratios that are considered "normal" and deviations may result in price reductions of 15 percent or more. The following reflect acceptable ranges:

Pear	1.50:1 to 1.75:1
Marquise	1.75:1 to 2.25:1
Emerald	1.30:1 to 1.50:1
Oval	1.35:1 to 1.70:1

To better understand what this means, let's look at a pear-shaped diamond as an example. If its report showed the length to be 15 millimeters and the width to be 10 millimeters, the length-to-width ratio would be 15 to 10, or 1.50:1. This would be acceptable. If, however, the dimensions were 30 millimeters long by 10 wide, the ratio would be 30 to 10, or 3:1. This would be unacceptable; the ratio is too great, and the result is a stone that looks much too long for its width. A pear-shaped diamond with an unacceptable length-to-width ratio should sell for at least 10 percent less than another pear-shaped diamond. *Note*: A long pear shape is not necessarily bad, and some people prefer a longer shape, but it is important to understand that such stones should sell for less than those with "normal" lengths. Always keep in mind the length-to-width ratio of fancy cuts, and adjust the price for stones that are not in the "acceptable" range.

Evaluating the Cutting from the Report

As discussed earlier, good cutting is essential to revealing the beauty of a diamond. Regardless of the shape, it is the cutter's skill that will release the brilliance and fire in a specific stone. The cutting also has a dramatic impact on price: The difference in cost between a diamond with excellent cutting and one that is not well cut can easily be 40 percent, and in some cases, even more.

Since cutting is so important, diamond grading reports include information related to it, but few have a cut *grade* per se. Instead, most reports provide information that professionals can interpret and use—along with their trained eye—to evaluate the cutting and judge the overall appearance of the stone. Information pertaining to cut includes important details such as depth percentage, table percentage, girdle thickness, crown angles, and so on. These details will be discussed later in this chapter in order to help you interpret the information provided on reports that do *not* include a cut grade.

Today, in addition to the information mentioned above, an increasing number of laboratories, including GIA, now issue diamond grading reports that do include a cut grade. I will discuss the GIA cut grade below.

Understanding the GIA Cut Grade on Diamond Reports

Today, the GIA provides a cut grade on its Diamond Grading Reports and its Diamond Dossier® for all standard round brilliant-cut diamonds (those with fifty-eight facets) that fall within the GIA D-to-Z color scale, and Flawless-to-I_3 clarity scale. At this time, they do not provide cut grades on reports for diamonds with fancy shapes, or on reports for any fancy-color diamond.

The GIA cut grading system assigns one of five grades to describe the overall quality of the cutting:

GIA Cut Grading Scale
Excellent
Very Good
Good
Fair
Poor

In addition, the GIA report now includes a detailed diagram of the diamond, shaped to the *actual proportions of the particular stone on which the report has been issued.* The diagram shows total depth percentage, table percentage, crown and pavilion angles, length of important facets, girdle thickness, and culet size.

With the new reports, the nonprofessional doesn't have to interpret anything to figure out whether or not the diamond is well cut. But this does *not* eliminate the importance of looking at diamonds to compare them side by side whenever possible, for the reasons we explained in chapter 5. With the new GIA system, two stones having identical cut *grades* can have very different personalities!

The GIA system incorporates a wide range of table-percentage and depth-percentage *combinations*—wider than what has previously been accepted within the gemological community—for each grade. Following years of research and the application of new technology in measuring light movement in diamonds, GIA's findings revealed that previously established standards were not always reliable indicators of the quality of cutting or its effect on the beauty of a diamond. Thus, the GIA system was designed to incorporate the new findings, which also allow for individual taste differences. Among diamonds with an "Excellent" rating, for example, some will have more brilliance, while others may have more fire; some may have more contrast in the patterns seen when you peer into the stone, others less contrast, and so on.

To sum up, having a cut grade on a diamond grading report may remove your anxiety about being able to judge whether or not a diamond is well cut, and provide greater reassurance with regard to its value, but with new parameters being used today, it becomes even *more* important to look at diamonds firsthand to ensure they exhibit the personality that you like best.

Understanding "Depth Percentage" and "Table Percentage"

Most European laboratories do *not* include a cut grade, and most reports prior to the year 2006 do not include a cut grade. In the absence of a cut grade, you will need to understand how to evaluate the cutting and proportioning for yourself. The following information is provided to help you understand how to do that. Again, this applies only to standard round brilliant-cut diamonds (having fifty-eight facets).

In round diamonds, the proportioning has a significant impact on the light performance and, thus, on the overall beauty of the stone (unfortunately there are no universally accepted parameters for fancy shapes, and you will need to rely on your own eye to a much greater degree). The key to understanding the proportioning is found in the "depth percentage" and the "table percentage." But remember that research has recently shown that there are other cutting details in addition to a stone's proportioning—such as the length of certain facets, crown angles, and pavilion angles—that affect the beauty of any diamond. *In light of recent research findings, avoid relying rigidly on the numbers shown below, and learn to rely on your own eye and personal preference.*

To determine whether or not a round stone's proportioning is good, look at the section of the report that describes *depth percentage* and *table percentage*. The depth percentage represents the depth of the stone—the distance from the table to the culet—as a percentage of the width of the stone. The table percentage represents the width of the table as a percentage of the width of the entire stone. These numbers are good indicators of how well a round stone has been cut in terms of its proportioning, but there can be exceptions. Your eye may be able to see differences in sparkle and brilliance, but you may not be able to discern the subtleties of proportioning. The percentages on the report should fall within certain ranges in order for the stone to be judged acceptable, excellent, or poor.

I will not discuss how one calculates these percentages, but it is important for you to know what the ranges are, as outlined in the "Depth Percentage Guidelines" below. Some reports also provide information about the *crown angle* and *pavilion angle*. The crown angle is more critical. It tells you the angle at which the crown portion has been cut. This angle will affect the depth and table percentage. Normally, if the crown angle is between 34 and 36 degrees, the table and depth will be excellent; between 32 and 34, good; between 30 and 32 degrees, fair; and less than 30 degrees, poor. If the exact crown angle is not given, it is probably considered acceptable. If not, there is normally a statement indicating that the crown angle exceeds 36 degrees, or is less than 30 degrees. But once again, use your own eye to determine whether or not you like what you see. I've seen diamonds that are very beautiful despite having angles that are not within the norm.

Depth Percentage

A round diamond cut with a depth percentage between 58 and 64 percent is normally a lovely, lively stone. You should note, however, that girdle thickness will affect depth percentage. A high depth percentage could result from a thick or very thick girdle, so when checking the depth percentage on the diamond report, check the "girdle" information as well.

Stones with a depth percentage over 64 percent or under 57 percent will normally be too deep or too shallow to exhibit maximum beauty and should sell for less. If the depth percentage is too high, the stone will also look smaller than its weight indicates. If the depth percentage is exceptionally high, brilliance can be significantly reduced and a darkish center may also be produced. If the depth percentage is too *low,* brilliance will also be significantly affected. I've seen diamonds that were so shallow—stones with such low depth percentages—that they had no brilliance and liveliness at all. When dirty, such stones look no better than a piece of glass. I avoid stones with depth percentages over 64 percent or under 57 percent. If you are attracted to such stones, remember that they should sell for much less per carat.

*Depth Percentage Guidelines Used Generally**

Depth Percentage	Effect on Price
Excellent†—approximately 58 to 60%	20 to 30% more
Very Good†—60+ to 62%	10 to 20% more
Good†—62 to 64%	———
Fair†—64 to 66%	15 to 25% less
Poor†—over 66% or less than 57%	20 to 40% less

*For *round* diamonds, combined with the right table percentage and fine overall cutting.

†Do not confuse these terms with the cut *grade* seen on GIA reports.

Table Percentage

Round stones cut with tables ranging from 53 to 64 percent usually result in beautiful, lively stones. Diamonds with smaller tables usually exhibit more *fire* than those with larger tables, but stones with larger tables may have more *brilliance.* As you will see, table width affects the stone's personality, but deciding which personality is more desirable is a matter of personal taste.

*Table Percentage Guidelines Used Generally**

Table Percentage	Effect on Price
Excellent†—from 53 to 58%	20 to 30% more
Very Good†—up to 60% (up to 62% in stones under ½ carat)	10 to 20% more
Good†—up to 64%	——
Fair†—over 64 to 70%	15 to 30% less
Poor†—over 70%	30 to 40% less

*For *round* diamonds, combined with the right depth percentage and fine overall cutting.

†Do not confuse these terms with the cut *grade* seen on GIA reports.

Finish

Under *finish* on the diamond report you will find an evaluation of the stone's *polish* and *symmetry.* Polish serves as an indicator of the care taken by the cutter. The quality of the stone's polish is a factor that cannot be ignored in evaluating the overall quality of a diamond, as well as its cost and value. As with a pair of fine leather shoes, the better the polish, the brighter the surface luster!

Polish can be described on the report as *excellent, very good, good, fair,* or *poor.* The price per carat should be less on stones with "fair" or "poor" polish. Cost per carat is usually more for stones that have "very good" or "excellent" polish.

Symmetry describes several factors, including: (1) how the facet edges align with one another; (2) whether or not the facets from one side of the diamond match corresponding facets on the opposite side; and (3) whether or not facets in the top portion of the diamond are properly aligned with corresponding ones in the bottom portion. When the symmetry is described as "fair"—or worse—something is usually out of line.

When evaluating symmetry, the most important area to check is the alignment of the crown (top) to the pavilion (bottom). If it is not good, it will make a visual difference in the beauty of the stone, and correspondingly in its price. To check for proper alignment here, simply look at the stone from the side to see whether or not the facets just above the girdle align with the facets just beneath the girdle.

When the top and bottom facets don't line up, it indicates sloppy cutting, and, more important, diminishes the overall beauty of the diamond. This will reduce price more than other symmetry faults.

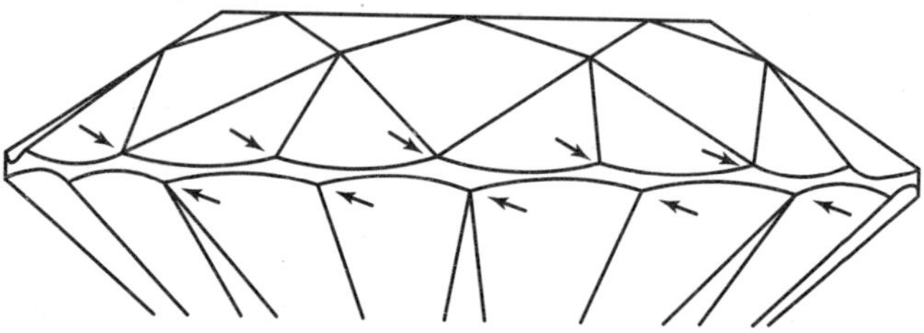

Misalignment of crown and pavilion

How Does the Girdle Affect Value?

The girdle is another important item described on diamond grading reports. The report will indicate whether or not the girdle is polished or faceted, and how thick it is. (On GIA reports dated prior to 2006, this information is provided on the left side of the report; on new reports, it is provided in the diagram in the lower center of the report.) Girdle thickness is very important for two reasons: (1) it affects *value* and (2) it affects the stone's *durability.*

Girdle thickness ranges from extremely thin to extremely thick. Diamonds with girdles that are excessively thin or thick normally sell for less than other diamonds. An extremely thin girdle increases the risk of chipping. Remember that despite their legendary hardness, diamonds are brittle, so a very thin edge poses a greater risk.

If a diamond has an extremely thick girdle, its cost should also be reduced somewhat because the stone will look smaller than another diamond of the same weight with a more normal girdle thickness. This is because extra weight is being consumed by the thickness of the girdle itself. (See chapter 8.)

There are some cases in which a very thick girdle is acceptable. Shapes that have one or more points, such as the pear shape, heart, or marquise, can have thick to very thick girdles in the area of the points and still be in the acceptable range. Here the extra thickness in the girdle helps protect the points themselves from chipping.

Generally, a diamond with an extremely thin girdle should sell for less than one with an extremely thick girdle because of the stone's increased vulnerability to chipping. However, if the girdle is much too thick (as in some older diamonds), the price can also be significantly less because the stone can look significantly smaller than other stones of comparable weight. The GIA factors girdle thickness into its overall cut grade since it can affect durability.

The Culet

The culet looks like a point at the bottom of the stone, but it is normally another facet—a tiny, flat, polished surface. This facet should be *small or very small.* A small or very small culet won't be noticeable from the top. Some diamonds today are actually pointed. This means that there really is no culet, that the stone has been cut straight down to a point instead. The larger the culet, the more visible it will be from the top. The more visible, the lower the cost of the stone. Stones described as having a large or "open" culet, as in old-European or old-mine cut diamonds (see chapter 5), are less desirable because the appearance of the culet causes a reduction in sparkle or brilliance at the very center of the stone. For the same reasons, a chipped or broken culet will seriously detract from the stone's beauty and significantly reduce the cost.

Color and Clarity Grades

The color and clarity grades found on a diamond report are the items with which most people are familiar, and I have already discussed them in detail in chapters 6 and 7. They are important factors in terms of determining the value of a diamond, but as the preceding discussion has shown, they do not tell the whole story.

The placement, number, type, and color of internal and external flaws will be indicated on a diamond report (note "Key to Symbols" on a GIA report), and may include a plotting—a diagram showing all the details. Be sure you carefully note *all* the details in addition to the cumulative grade. Remember, the *placement* of imperfections can affect value (see chapter 7). You should pay special attention to the section that says "Key to Symbols." This is where lasering will be indicated if the diamond is lasered. This means that the clarity grade indicated is *after* lasering. Its cost should be 15 to 20 percent less than another diamond with the "same" clarity grade. With regard to *fracture filling*, a reliable diamond grading report cannot be issued on a fracture-filled diamond, so most laboratories will not grade diamonds that have been clarity enhanced by this method. Most will return the stone *ungraded*, with a notation that it is fracture filled. Some labs will provide a "qualified" clarity grade, indicating it is fracture filled and that the grading cannot be precise.

A Word about Fluorescence

Fluorescence, if present, will also be indicated on a diamond grading report (see chapter 6 for additional important information about fluorescence). It will be graded *faint, weak, moderate, strong,* or *very strong.* Some reports indicate the color of the fluorescence (blue, yellow, white, and so on). If the fluorescence is moderate to very strong and the color is not indicated, you should ask the jeweler to tell you what color the stone fluoresces. A stone with strong yellow fluorescence should sell for less since it will appear more tinted when worn outdoors in daylight or a few inches away from a fluorescent light. The presence of blue fluorescence will not detract and in some cases may be considered a bonus, since it may make the stone appear whiter than it really is when seen in daylight or within a few inches of fluorescent lighting. However, if the report shows a *very strong* blue fluorescence, be sure to view the stone in daylight or fluorescent light to see whether or not there is an oily or murky appearance to the diamond. If so, it should sell for less; if not, then value should not be affected.

Pay Attention to "Comments"

On the GIA diamond grading report, and on most other reports issued by major laboratories, there is a section in which additional comments are provided. Any notes here are important, and you should be sure you understand what they mean. Here you will find comments on characteristics such as the presence of "graining" (see page 64). Graining may not affect the appearance or value of a stone at all, but sometimes graining can reduce brilliance, so you should look more closely at the stone to make sure it doesn't affect its beauty. Here you will also find special notations regarding "crown" or "pavilion" angles, indicating that the angle at which the upper or lower portion of the stone has been cut may be less than or greater than the norm. Here again, you must look carefully at the stone to be sure its beauty has not been diminished by faulty cutting. And last but not least, this is where you will find any notation regarding certain treatments, such as clarity enhancement or the new high-pressure/high-temperature (HPHT) process used to enhance diamond color; if the laboratory issues a report on a diamond that has been treated in some manner, the presence of some type of enhancement will be noted under "Comments."

A Final Word about Reports

Diamond grading reports provide a very useful tool to aid in comparing diamonds and evaluating quality and value. But the key to their usefulness is proper understanding of how to read them.

Today we are seeing new diamond reports accompanying diamonds and diamond jewelry that are *not* as thorough as the full "diamond *grading* reports" issued by major laboratories. While they provide a briefer and less detailed description or identification of the diamond and do not usually include a clarity plotting, they do serve a useful purpose and help retailers provide greater assurance to customers regarding the quality of the stones they are selling, at a more reasonable cost than doing a full report. For smaller diamonds or diamonds that are already set in jewelry, these documents are more practical. Among this new genre you will see the GIA's *Diamond Dossier®* that is issued for diamonds weighing 0.18 to 0.99 carats, and the European Gemological Laboratory's *Gem Passport*, which they will issue with mounted diamonds (which may be necessary when it is not possible or practical to remove stones from a setting).

For fine-quality diamonds weighing one carat or more, I highly recommend a full diamond grading report from a respected gem testing laboratory (see appendix), even if it means removing the stone from the setting.

Take time to learn and understand what *all* the information on the report really means, as well as differences in the type and quality of information provided. When you do, you will really understand what you are buying, and make a wiser choice.

The following pages provide sample diamond grading reports from respected laboratories.

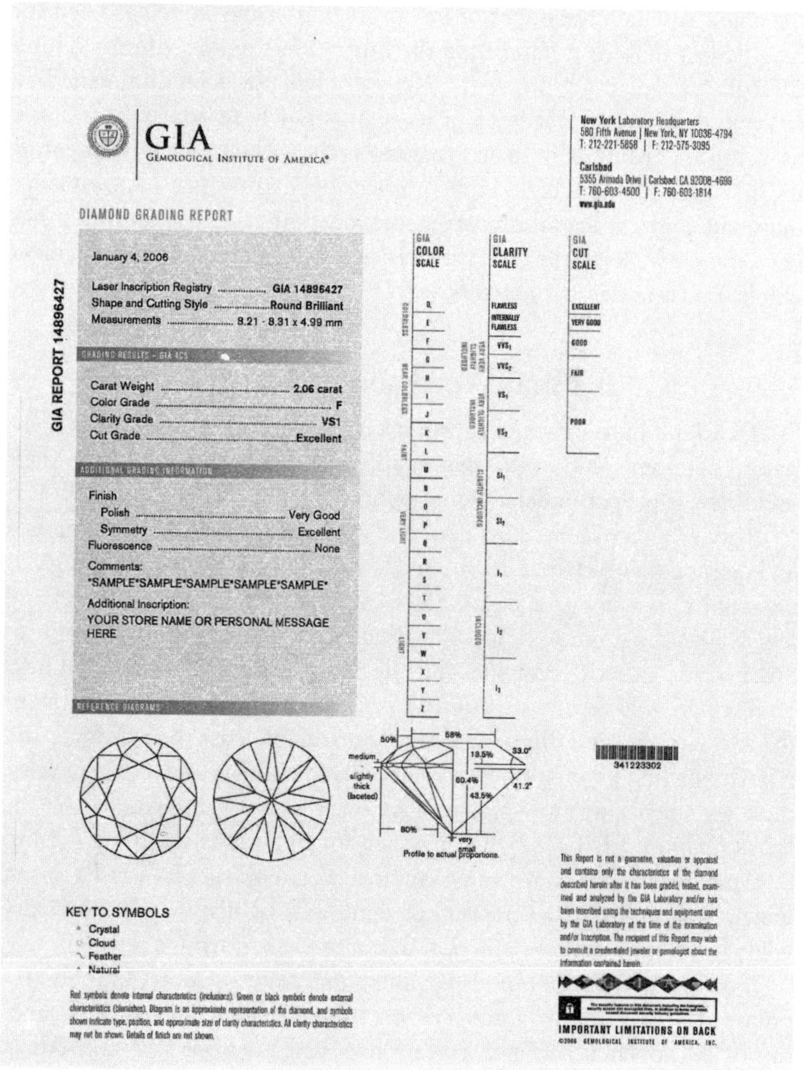

GIA
GEMOLOGICAL INSTITUTE OF AMERICA®

New York Laboratory Headquarters
580 Fifth Avenue | New York, NY 10036-4794
T: 212-221-5858 | F: 212-575-3095

Carlsbad
5355 Armada Drive | Carlsbad, CA 92008-4699
T: 760-603-4500 | F: 760-603-1814
www.gia.edu

GIA REPORT 14896427

DIAMOND GRADING REPORT

January 4, 2006

Laser Inscription Registry .... GIA 14896427
Shape and Cutting Style .... Round Brilliant
Measurements .... 8.21 - 8.31 x 4.99 mm

GRADING RESULTS - GIA ACS

Carat Weight .... 2.06 carat
Color Grade .... F
Clarity Grade VS1
Cut Grade .... Excellent

ADDITIONAL GRADING INFORMATION

Finish
Polish .... Very Good
Symmetry .... Excellent
Fluorescence .... None
Comments:
*SAMPLE*SAMPLE*SAMPLE*SAMPLE*SAMPLE*
Additional Inscription:
YOUR STORE NAME OR PERSONAL MESSAGE HERE

REFERENCE DIAGRAMS

GIA COLOR SCALE: D E F G H I J K L M N O P Q R S T U V W X Y Z (COLORLESS, NEAR COLORLESS, FAINT, VERY LIGHT, LIGHT)

GIA CLARITY SCALE: FLAWLESS, INTERNALLY FLAWLESS, VVS1, VVS2, VS1, VS2, SI1, SI2, I1, I2, I3 (VERY VERY SLIGHTLY INCLUDED, VERY SLIGHTLY INCLUDED, SLIGHTLY INCLUDED, INCLUDED)

GIA CUT SCALE: EXCELLENT, VERY GOOD, GOOD, FAIR, POOR

50% 58% 19.5% 33.0° medium slightly thick (faceted) 60.4% 41.2° 43.5% 80% very small
Profile to actual proportions.

341223302

KEY TO SYMBOLS
- Crystal
- Cloud
- Feather
- Natural

Red symbols denote internal characteristics (inclusions). Green or black symbols denote external characteristics (blemishes). Diagram is an approximate representation of the diamond, and symbols shown indicate type, position, and approximate size of clarity characteristics. All clarity characteristics may not be shown. Details of finish are not shown.

This Report is not a guarantee, valuation or appraisal and contains only the characteristics of the diamond described herein after it has been graded, tested, examined and analyzed by the GIA Laboratory and/or has been inscribed using the techniques and equipment used by the GIA Laboratory at the time of the examination and/or inscription. The recipient of this Report may wish to consult a credentialed jeweler or gemologist about the information contained herein.

IMPORTANT LIMITATIONS ON BACK
©2006 GEMOLOGICAL INSTITUTE OF AMERICA, INC.

The new GIA Diamond Grading Report showing a cut *grade* and "profile" for the stone. Note under the "Comments" section that GIA will also add a personal inscription.

SOURCE: © GEMOLOGICAL INSTITUTE OF AMERICA. REPRINTED BY PERMISSION.

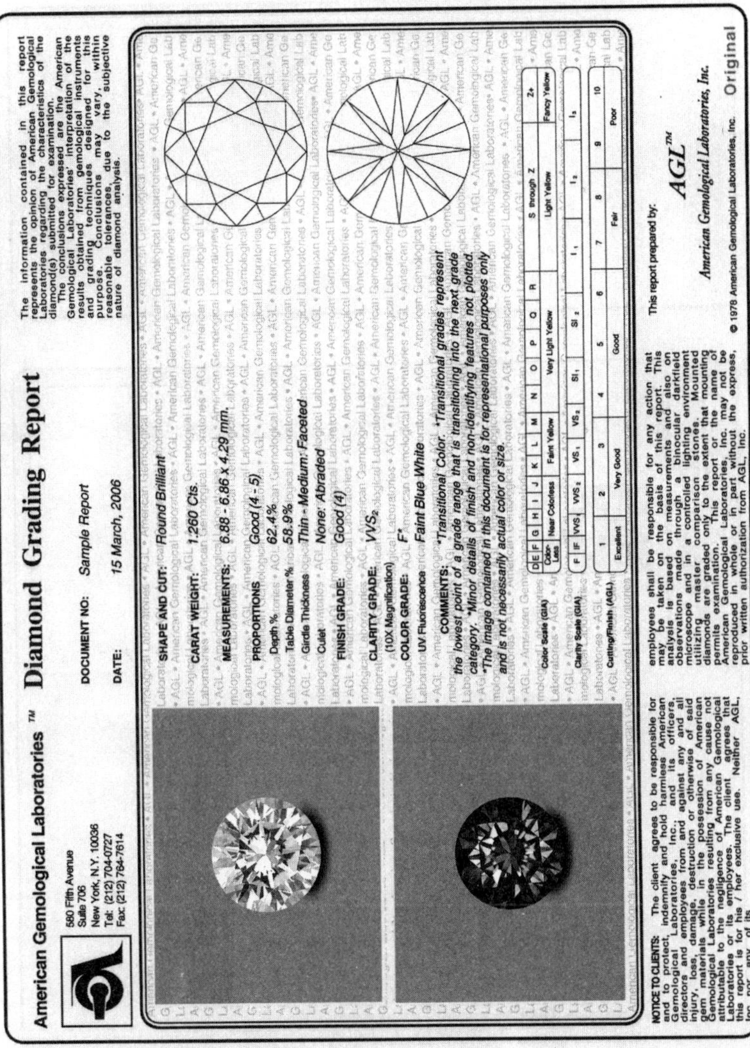

American Gemological Laboratories ™ **Diamond Grading Report**

580 Fifth Avenue
Suite 706
New York, N.Y. 10036
Tel: (212) 704-0727
Fax: (212) 764-7614

DOCUMENT NO: *Sample Report*

DATE: *15 March, 2006*

The information contained in this report represents the opinion of American Gemological Laboratories regarding the characteristics of the diamond(s) submitted for examination.

The conclusions expressed are the American Gemological Laboratories' interpretation of the results obtained from gemological instruments and grading techniques designed for this purpose. Conclusions may vary, within reasonable tolerances, due to the subjective nature of diamond analysis.

SHAPE AND CUT: *Round Brilliant*
CARAT WEIGHT: *1.260 Cts.*
MEASUREMENTS: *6.88 - 6.86 x 4.29 mm.*
PROPORTIONS *Good (4 - 5)*
Depth % *62.4%*
Table Diameter % *58.9%*
Girdle Thickness *Thin - Medium: Faceted*
Culet *None: Abraded*
FINISH GRADE: *Good (4)*
CLARITY GRADE: (10X Magnification) *VVS₂*
COLOR GRADE: *F**
UV Fluorescence *Faint Blue White*
COMMENTS: **Transitional Color. *Transitional grades represent the lowest point of a grade range that is transitioning into the next grade category. *Minor details of finish and non-identifying features not plotted. *The image contained in this document is for representational purposes only and is not necessarily actual color or size.*

Color Scale (GIA)	D	E	F	G	H	I	J	K	L	M	N	O	P	Q	R	S through Z	Z+
	Color-Less			Near Colorless				Faint Yellow			Very Light Yellow					Light Yellow	Fancy Yellow

Clarity Scale (GIA)	F	IF	VVS₁	VVS₂	VS₁	VS₂	SI₁	SI₂	I₁	I₂	I₃

Cutting/Finish (AGL)	1	2	3	4	5	6	7	8	9	10
	Excellent	Very Good		Good			Fair		Poor	

NOTICE TO CLIENTS: The client agrees to be responsible for and to protect, indemnify and hold harmless American Gemological Laboratories, Inc., and its officers, directors and employees from and against any and all injury, loss, damage, destruction or otherwise of said gem materials while in the possession of American Gemological Laboratories resulting from any cause not attributable to the negligence of American Gemological Laboratories or its employees. The client agrees that this report is for his / her exclusive use. Neither AGL, Inc. nor any of its employees shall be responsible for any action that may be taken on the basis of this report. This analysis is based on measurements and also on observations made through a binocular darkfield microscope and in a controlled lighting environment utilizing master comparison stones. Mounted diamonds are graded only to the extent that mounting permits examination. This report or the name of American Gemological Laboratories, Inc. may not be reproduced in whole or in part without the express, prior written authorization from AGL, Inc.

This report prepared by:

AGL™

American Gemological Laboratories, Inc.

© 1978 American Gemological Laboratories, Inc. Original

AGL reports describe the cut and finish and provide a numerical grade.

SOURCE: AMERICAN GEMOLOGICAL LABORATORIES

Cut Scale

AGS	0	1	2	3	4	5	6	7	8	9	10
	AGS Ideal	AGS Excellent	AGS Very Good	AGS Good		AGS Fair			AGS Poor		

Color Scale

AGS	0	0.5	1.0	1.5	2.0	2.5	3.0	3.5	4.0	4.5	5.0	5.5	6.0	6.5	7.0	7.5	8.0	8.5	9.0	9.5	10.0	To		Fancy Yellow
GIA	D	E	F	G	H	I	J	K	L	M	N	O	P	Q	R	S	T	U	V	W	X	Y	Z	Fancy Yellow
	COLORLESS			NEAR COLORLESS				FAINT YELLOW			VERY LIGHT YELLOW					LIGHT YELLOW								

Clarity Scale

AGS	0	1	2	3	4	5	6	7	8	9	10
GIA	FLAWLESS / IF	VVS1	VVS2	VS1	VS2	SI1	SI2	I1		I2	I3

Key to Symbols

Bruise	Crystal	Laser Drill Hole
Cavity	Extra Facet	Natural
Chip	Feather	Needle
Cleavage	Indented Natural	Pinpoint
Cloud	Knot	Twinning Wisp

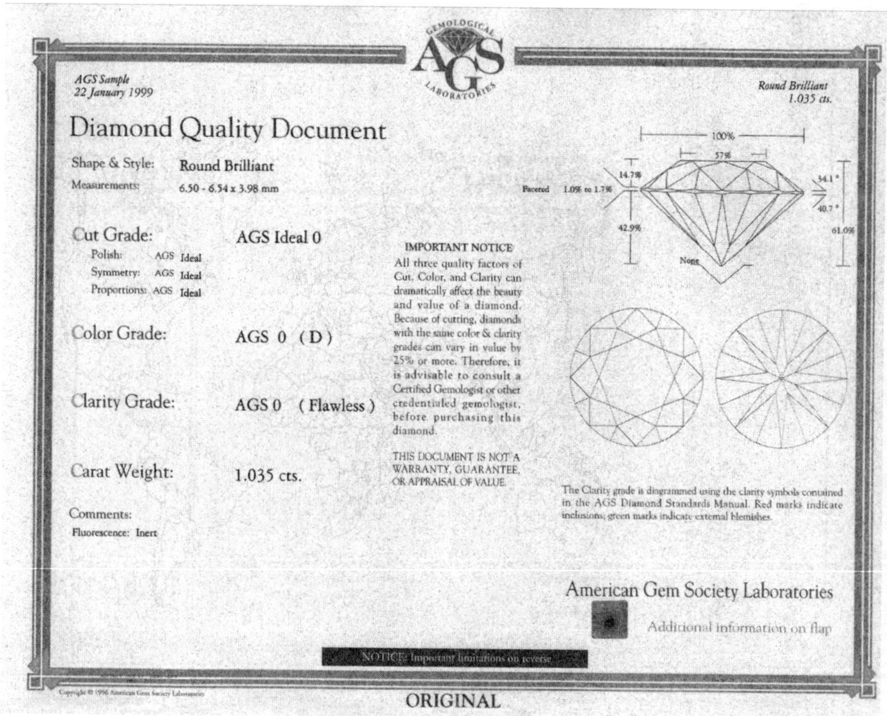

GEMOLOGICAL AGS LABORATORIES

AGS Sample
22 January 1999

Round Brilliant
1.035 cts.

Diamond Quality Document

Shape & Style: Round Brilliant
Measurements: 6.50 - 6.54 x 3.98 mm

Cut Grade: AGS Ideal 0
Polish: AGS Ideal
Symmetry: AGS Ideal
Proportions: AGS Ideal

Color Grade: AGS 0 (D)

Clarity Grade: AGS 0 (Flawless)

Carat Weight: 1.035 cts.

Comments:
Fluorescence: Inert

IMPORTANT NOTICE
All three quality factors of Cut, Color, and Clarity can dramatically affect the beauty and value of a diamond. Because of cutting, diamonds with the same color & clarity grades can vary in value by 25% or more. Therefore, it is advisable to consult a Certified Gemologist or other credentialed gemologist, before purchasing this diamond.

THIS DOCUMENT IS NOT A WARRANTY, GUARANTEE, OR APPRAISAL OF VALUE.

The Clarity grade is diagrammed using the clarity symbols contained in the AGS Diamond Standards Manual. Red marks indicate inclusions; green marks indicate external blemishes.

American Gem Society Laboratories
Additional information on flap

NOTICE: Important limitations on reverse

ORIGINAL

AGS reports provide a cut grade. Note the scale they use to indicate the quality of cutting.

SOURCE: AMERICAN GEM SOCIETY LABORATORIES

BELTEST

EN 45001
ISO/IEC GUIDE 25
ISO 9002

The HRD Certificates Department is BELTEST accredited for the quality examination of polished diamonds under ref. N° 047.

This certificate is established in conformity with the "International Rules for Grading Polished Diamonds", approved by the World Federation of Diamond Bourses and the International Diamond Manufacturers Association at the May 1978 Congress (rev. ed. 1995), and may not be reproduced by any means whatsoever unless complete.

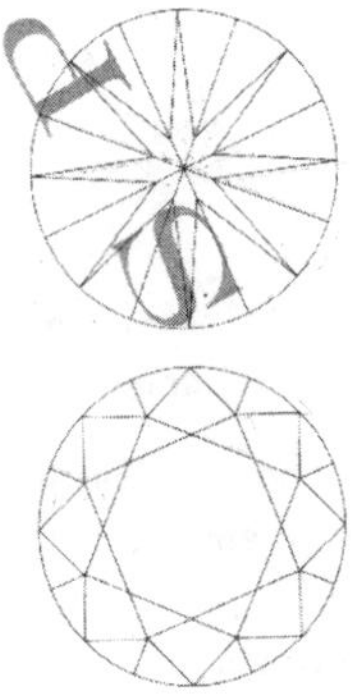

identification marks :
negligible external characteristics

Red symbols refer to internal and green symbols to external characteristics. The symbols do not usually reflect the actual size of the characteristics. The characteristics have been indicated in order to clarify the description and/or for further identification.

HRD

certificate no. 000000000

The stone in accordance with the above mentioned number has been identified as a natural gem diamond and has the following description :

shape	brilliant
weight	1.02 ct
clarity grade	loupe-clean
fluorescence	nil
colour grade	exceptional white (E)
measurements	6.58-6.64mm x 3.89mm
proportions	very good
girdle	thin 2.5%
culet	pointed
table width	65%
cr. height	12.5%
pav. depth	44%
finish grade	very good
comments	

antwerpen, 11/03/1996

gemmologists

The characteristics of the above mentioned diamond have been established by scientific measurements and observations, carried out in the laboratory of the Diamond High Council.

clarity grade (magnification 10 ×)

clarity grade	
loupe-clean	X
vvs 1	
vvs 2	
vs 1	
vs 2	
si 1	
si 2	
p 1	
p 2	
p 3	

colour grade

colour grade	
exceptional white +	
exceptional white	X
rare white +	
rare white	
white	
slightly tinted white	
tinted white	
tinted colour	

proportions

proportions	
very good	X
good	
unusual	

finish grade

finish grade	
very good	X
good	
medium	
poor	

HRD describes the quality of the cut and finish.

SOURCE: HOGE RAAD VOOR DIAMANT (THE DIAMOND HIGH COUNCIL OF BELGIUM)

LON 0091285

The Gem Testing Laboratory of Great Britain

LONDON DIAMOND REPORT

Carat weight: 2.30

Colour grade: F RARE WHITE +

Clarity grade: VVS 2

Shape and cutting style: ROUND BRILLIANT

Measurements: 9.06 - 9.13 x 5.16 mm

Proportions: Height: 56.7%

Table: 68 %

Polish: VERY GOOD

Symmetry: GOOD

Girdle: VERY THIN TO THIN

UV-fluorescence: FAINT

Comments:

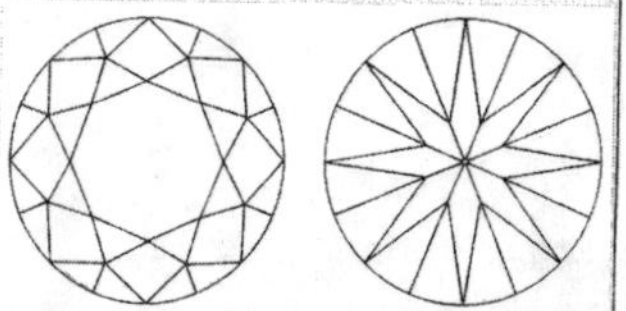

This Report does not make any statement with respect to the monetary value of the diamond.
Only the original report with signature and embossed stamp is a valid identification document.

The Gem Testing Laboratory of Great Britain is the official CIBJO recognised Laboratory for Great Britain.

The Gem Testing Laboratory of Great Britain

GAGTL, 27 Greville Street,
London, ECIN 8SU, Great Britain

Telephone: +44 171 405 3351
Fax: +44 171 831 9479

Signed SAMPLE

Date 22nd May 2001

No cut grade is provided although essential information pertaining to cutting is given.

Note: The Gem Testing Laboratory of Great Britain formally ceased grading diamonds and closed its laboratory in September 2008, but documents prior to this date are still in circulation and are seen in the marketplace.

SOURCE: THE GEM TESTING LABORATORY OF GREAT BRITAIN

PROFESSIONAL GEM SCIENCES
An Independent Laboratory for the Study and Grading of Diamonds and Gemstones

5 S. Wabash Avenue, Suite 1905
Chicago, IL 60603
Phone (312) 920-1541
Fax (312) 920-1547

550 S. Hill Street, Suite 1595
Los Angeles, CA 90013
Phone (213) 622-2387
Fax (213) 622-3138

Toll Free (800) 235-3287

www.progem.com

CERTIFICATE OF QUALITY

IDENTIFICATION

Species	Natural Diamond	Report Number	XdSAMPLE
Variety	Diamond	Date	May 08, 2001
Shape & Cut	Round Brilliant Cut		
Carat Weight	0.75 ct.	*Precision Weight*	0.7565 ct.
Clarity Grade*	VS1	*Graining*	Nil
Color Grade**	F	*Fluorescence*	Very Faint

Clarity Representation
Internal Characteristics are shown in red. External Characteristics are shown in green. Extra facets are shown in black. Symbols indicate the position of identifying characteristics, not necessarily their size. Hairline feathers in the girdle, minor bearding, and minor details of polish and finish are not shown.

KEY TO SYMBOLS

Feather *Crystal*
Cloud *Natural*

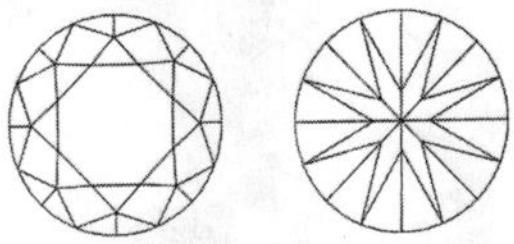

CUT INFORMATION

Dimensions	5.78 - 5.87 x 3.62 mm.	Total Depth	62.1%
Table Width	56%		
Crown Angle	35.5°	Crown Height	16.0%*
Pavilion Angle	40.5°	Pavilion Depth	43.0%*
Girdle Thickness	Thin to Slightly Thick, Frosty, Smooth	Average	3.1%*
		*TOTAL	62.1%
Culet Size	Small, Polished (1.0%)		

FINISH

Polish Very Good to Excellent
Symmetry Good to Very Good

COMMENTS
Ideal Cut. Additional pinpoints not shown.

* Clarity grade determined at 10x magnification with a corrected loupe.
** Color grade determined by comparison to approximately 1 carat size, master comparison diamonds.
*** Color Analysis determined by comparison to Munsell color order standards as presented in the book *The World of Color*.

Note: Please read the important limitations to this report printed on the reverse side.

Security Control Number
SAMPLE

QUALITY CONTROL By:
Thomas E. Tashey, Jr., G.G., F.G.A.

This report provides a cut grade in the "Comments" section. Here the cut is graded "ideal."

SOURCE: PROFESSIONAL GEM SCIENCES

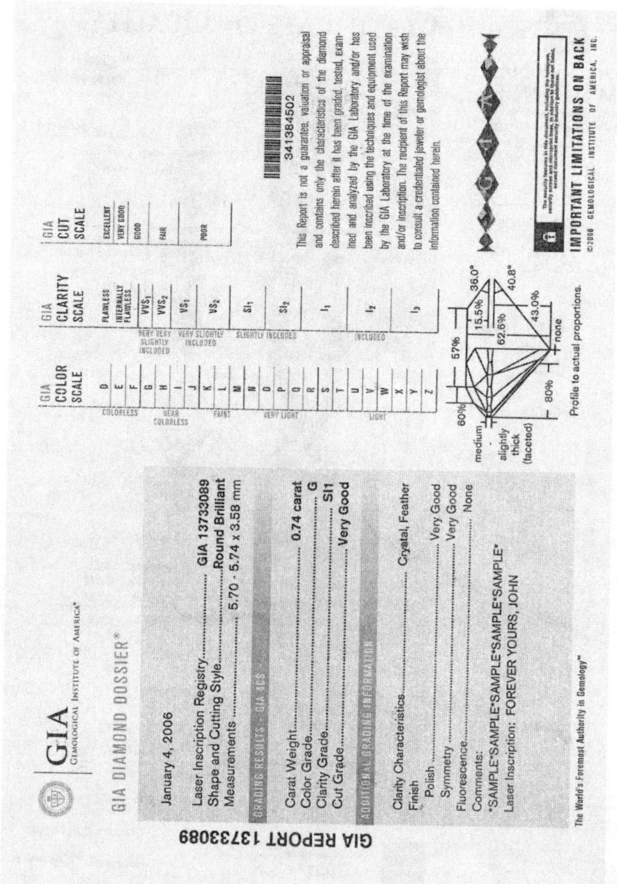

GIA REPORT 13733089

GIA | Gemological Institute of America®

GIA DIAMOND DOSSIER®

January 4, 2006

Laser Inscription Registry.................... GIA 13733089
Shape and Cutting Style.................... Round Brilliant
Measurements .... 5.70 - 5.74 x 3.58 mm

GRADING RESULTS - GIA 4CS

Carat Weight.................... 0.74 carat
Color Grade.................... G
Clarity Grade.................... SI1
Cut Grade.................... Very Good

ADDITIONAL GRADING INFORMATION

Clarity Characteristics.................... Crystal, Feather
Finish
Polish .... Very Good
Symmetry .... Very Good
Fluorescence.................... None
Comments:
*SAMPLE*SAMPLE*SAMPLE*SAMPLE*SAMPLE*
Laser Inscription: FOREVER YOURS, JOHN

The World's Foremost Authority in Gemology™

341384502

This Report is not a guarantee, valuation or appraisal and contains only the characteristics of the diamond described herein after it has been graded, tested, examined and analyzed by the GIA Laboratory and/or has been inscribed using the techniques and equipment used by the GIA Laboratory at the time of the examination and/or inscription. The recipient of this Report may wish to consult a credentialed jeweler or gemologist about the information contained herein.

IMPORTANT LIMITATIONS ON BACK

©2006 GEMOLOGICAL INSTITUTE OF AMERICA, INC.

The new GIA Diamond Dossier® (issued for diamonds weighing 0.18 carat–0.99 carat) showing a cut *grade* and profile. Note that the Dossier does *not* provide a diagram showing the type and placement of inclusions; this is only provided on the full Diamond Grading Report.

SOURCE: © GEMOLOGICAL INSTITUTE OF AMERICA. REPRINTED BY PERMISSION.

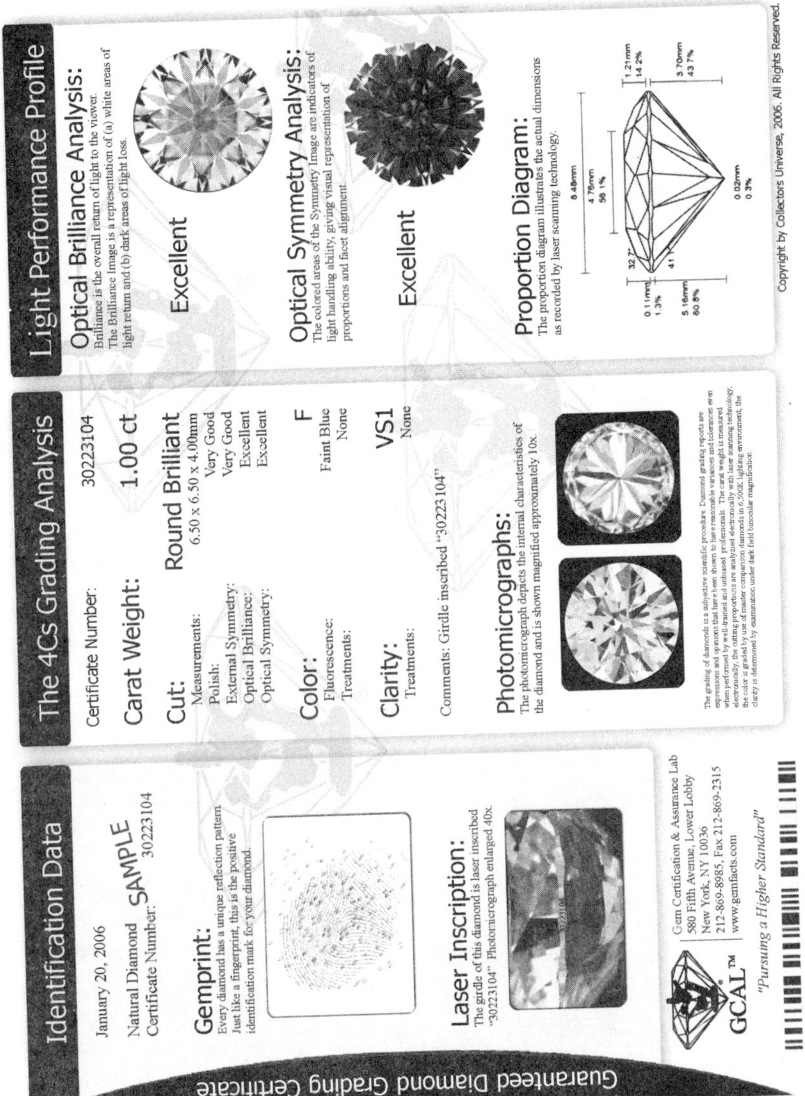

GCAL's Five Star Guaranteed Grading Certificate provides direct assessment of optical light performance as well as a Gemprint image that is filed in GCAL's international database, which is available to law enforcement agencies in the search and recovery of lost or stolen diamonds.

SOURCE: GEM CERTIFICATION AND ASSURANCE LAB. REPRINTED BY PERMISSION.

CHAPTER TEN

False Claims & Costly Bargains

How to Spot Fraud and Avoid Misrepresentation

As you have seen, many factors affect quality and value in diamonds. When the average person is looking at a stone already set, it is very difficult, if not impossible, to *see* differences that can dramatically affect cost. For this reason, I recommend buying any important diamond *unmounted,* and mounting it only after all the facts have been verified. But you don't have to be a gemologist or fear buying jewelry. Anyone who follows a few simple steps can buy with confidence.

Four Key Steps to Avoiding Fraud or Misrepresentation

- *The first step is to buy from someone both accessible and knowledgeable.* Sellers should have the skill to know for sure what they themselves are buying and selling. This is not to say that there aren't bargains to be found in flea markets, estate sales, and so on, but you run a higher risk when purchasing in such places because of possible misinformation, intentional or otherwise. You must weigh the risk versus the potential reward. In addition, before making a final purchasing decision, ask yourself whether or not you will be able to find the seller again if what you bought turns out to be misrepresented. This is equally true when you are traveling and are considering a jewelry purchase abroad.

  Keep in mind that unless the jeweler also does business in the country where you live, it may be cost prohibitive to try to rectify any misrepresentation if it occurs.

- *Second, ask the right questions.* Don't be afraid to ask direct, even pointed questions. The key to getting complete information about what you are buying is asking good questions so you can be sure you are aware of important factors affecting quality and value. (To help you ask the right questions, I provide a complete list in chapter 18.)
- *Third, get the facts in writing.* Be sure the seller is willing to put *in writing* the answers to the questions you ask and any representations made about the gem or jewelry you are considering. If not, I recommend against purchasing from this seller unless there is an unconditional return policy that allows merchandise to be returned within a reasonable period of time for a full refund (not a store credit). In this case, follow the next step to be safe.
- Finally, *verify the facts with a gemologist-appraiser.* It's especially important to verify whatever has been put in writing with a professional gemologist-appraiser (see chapter 21). Some unscrupulous dealers are willing to put anything in writing to make the sale, knowing that written assurances or claims about the stone are often sufficient to satisfy buyers' doubts. So this last step may be the most important to ensure that you have made a wise decision.

In general, you need not worry about fraud or misrepresentation, whether deliberate or unintentional, if you simply follow these four easy steps. They may require a little more time and nominal additional expense, but the end result will be greater knowledge—and assurance—about your jewelry choice and your jeweler, and they may save you from a costly mistake.

Types of Misrepresentation

Beware of Bargains!

Erroneous Identification

Colorless natural stones such as colorless sapphire, quartz, and zircon are sometimes represented as diamonds, especially when mounted in ancient or antique pieces of jewelry and when they occur in antique cuts. One of the most convincing examples I ever saw was a colorless sapphire cut into an octahedral shape simulating a diamond crystal and set in an antique mounting. While it didn't have the right "look" on the surface for a genuine diamond crystal, the seller really believed the piece contained a natural diamond crystal.

Small colorless zircons have often been used as accent stones in jewelry containing colored gemstones because, with their high brilliance, they look so much like diamonds. My father once gave me a beautiful amethyst ring surrounded by colorless zircons that people always complimented (and I'm sure they thought the zircons were diamonds). Unfortunately, it was stolen several years ago—I'm sure by someone who also thought they were diamonds!

Never assume that small brilliant, colorless accent stones are diamonds. Be sure to ask explicitly whether or not they are diamonds, and get the answer in writing.

Diamonds Represented to Be Better Than They Are

Beware of bargains. Most are not. When a price seems too good to be true, it usually is, unless the seller doesn't know the piece's true value (which reflects badly on the seller's expertise).

A large, well-established jewelry store in Philadelphia that had built a large clientele over many years was found guilty of misrepresenting the quality of diamonds it was selling. Sales staff consistently represented their diamonds to be several color grades and/or flaw grades better than they actually were. As a result, their prices seemed much more attractive than those of other jewelers. For many years customers thought they were getting a much better buy from this firm than from others in the area, which may not have been the case; since customers didn't know the true quality of the stones they were buying, they couldn't make a fair comparison with what other jewelers were offering. Other jewelers in the area were, in fact, giving better value on stones comparable to what was actually being sold by this "bargain" firm.

Such firms can be found in every city. Many are even willing to put everything in writing, often including a full "appraisal." Such dishonest practices often go undetected because most people assume that when a seller is willing to "put it in writing," he or she is properly representing the item. Most buyers never bother to have the facts verified.

Are Wholesale Prices Really Wholesale?

It is natural to be lured by the promise of getting a diamond at a wholesale price: a price significantly below what most retailers charge. I've already discussed some of the pitfalls, but many fall into the trap of believing that even if they don't get exactly what they are told, they will still get it at a price below what they might have paid at a local jewelry store. Yet, this is frequently not the case.

I recently went undercover for one of the TV networks and made a purchase from a diamond dealer touting "wholesale" prices. In addition to misrepresentation of quality, the price I paid for the diamond was *double* the stone's *retail* value. I purchased a stone described by the seller as having a color grade of J–K and a clarity grade of SI_2. He gave me an appraisal with all the representations stated clearly in writing. The diamond was actually X-color, and the clarity was no better than I_2. It was also fracture filled, despite the fact that he had shown me fracture-filled diamonds, explaining what they were—and supposedly gaining my confidence by so doing—and I had told him explicitly that I did not want a fracture-filled diamond! I paid $3,200 for the stone; the *retail* value was $1,400 to $1,500. I could have purchased this stone from any retail jeweler for less. The moral: Don't assume you get a good buy just because you are in a "wholesale" jewelry district.

Scams Involving "Appraisals" Prior to Sale

Beware of jewelers who are not willing to put the facts in writing but who offer to let you take the stone, before the sale, to an appraiser in the neighborhood. This may be a scam. It is often seen in wholesale districts like New York's famous 47th Street.

The first step in this scam is to build you up with all the reasons why you are going to get an exceptional buy because the seller "bought it right" (whatever that means), or wants to "pass the savings on to you," or isn't greedy ("I don't care who I sell to at wholesale; after all, a sale is a sale"), and so on. When you find something you are seriously interested in buying, the seller then explains, for a variety of seemingly valid reasons, why he or she will not put any information pertaining to the quality of the stone in writing on the bill of sale. The salesperson offers to permit you to go with one of the firm's "bonded guards" to a local appraiser so that you can verify the facts and learn for yourself what a bargain you are getting. Many people are immediately hooked, and conclude erroneously that since they can get an appraisal if they choose, everything must be in order. So they don't. And they become the victims of intentional misrepresentation.

Those who do wish to get an appraisal usually face another problem. They don't know any appraiser—or certainly not any in the neighborhood. Many visitors to 47th Street, for example, are from out of town and don't know anyone local. Unscrupulous sellers often count on this because it gives them the opportunity to recommend several "reliable" appraisers. Or, rather than be so obvious, they suggest you "choose" your own (some even make a fuss about not wanting to know whom you choose). Many purchasers make a big mistake here because they don't realize that *all appraisers are not the same, nor are all appraisers equally competent or reliable* (see chapter 21). Unfortunately, the "reliable appraiser" in this situation often means that the seller can rely on the appraiser to tell the prospective buyers what the seller wants them to hear.

One must always be careful of recommendations from the seller. While legitimate jewelers usually know better than anyone else who the best gemologist-appraisers are in their communities, and their recommendations should be respected, you must still be sure to check the credentials yourself to avoid such scams. Unfortunately, especially in the jewelry districts of major cities, far too many appraisers are not qualified, and some are in collusion with unscrupulous jewelers.

One of my clients had an experience that provides an excellent example of how this type of scam can work. She went to a 47th Street firm in New York. She was offered a five-plus carat diamond ring at a price that was one-fourth the price most retailers had been quoting for what appeared to be comparable quality. She thought the ring looked very beautiful and became very excited about being able to get such a bargain. But when she asked the seller if he would back up his description of the quality of the diamond in writing, he said it was against his store policy, but he would be happy for her to take the ring to a neighborhood appraiser before she purchased it.

This made her cautious, especially since she didn't know any local appraiser. Luckily, I was in New York at the time and was able to use a colleague's lab to examine the ring carefully (it was awkward for the seller to refuse). Not surprisingly, the quality was not as represented. The flaw grade had been misrepresented by *four* grades, and the color had been enhanced *seven grades* by "painting" (painted diamonds have a coating that doesn't come off with normal cleaning and may take months or years to wear off). We had to clean the stone chemically to determine that it was painted and to reveal its true color!

In this particular case, given the true value of the diamond, the price being asked for the ring was certainly not the "steal" it appeared to be. It wasn't a bad price, but other retailers were offering comparable stones at comparable prices or less.

Such practices are overtly dishonest, of course, but all too often they leave honest jewelers in a bad light as a result. In such cases, the dishonest jeweler will appear to be offering the best price, while the honest jeweler—who may actually be offering the best value—falsely appears to be charging "too much."

In general, you need to guard against fraud or misrepresentation in one of the following four areas:

- Weight misrepresentation
- Color alteration and misgrading
- Flaw concealment and misgrading
- Certification—alteration and counterfeit certificates

Weight

Giving "total weight" of all stones where more than one is involved, rather than the exact weight of the main stone, is another form of misrepresentation. This is in strict violation of Federal Trade Commission rulings. When the weight is given, particularly on any display card, descriptive tag, or other type of advertising for a particular piece of jewelry, the weight of the main stone or stones should be clearly indicated as well as the total weight of all the stones.

Thus, if you purchase a "three-carat diamond" ring with one large center stone and two small side stones (as found in many engagement rings), the center stone's weight should be clearly stated; for example, "The weight of the center stone is 2.80 carats, with side stones that weigh 0.10 carats each, for a total weight of 3.00 carats." There is a tremendous price difference between a single stone weighing three carats and numerous stones having a total weight of three carats. A single three-carat stone of good quality could sell for $50,000, while three carats consisting of numerous stones (even with some weighing as much as a carat or more) of the same quality could sell anywhere from $5,000 to $20,000, depending on how many there are and the weight of each.

When inquiring about the weight of a diamond, don't ask the wrong question. Usually the jeweler will be asked how *large* the stone is, rather than how much it *weighs*. In any case, the answer should provide the exact carat weight. Beware when the response includes the word spread: "This stone *spreads* one carat." *A stone that spreads one carat does not weigh one carat;* it simply *looks* like a one-carat stone in its width (see chapter 8).

Color

Failure to Disclose Permanent Treatments

Diamonds can be treated in many ways to improve their color. Some are temporary and others are permanent. Regardless of permanence, any treatment should be disclosed so that you know you are paying an appropriate price.

***High-pressure/high-temperature annealing* (HPHT).** This is a new treatment being used to enhance diamonds. The process can transform very tinted, off-white diamonds (as low as Q–Z colors) into colorless and near-colorless stones—even D, E, F! It can also be used to create or improve fancy colors. Fancy colors include greenish yellow, yellowish green, and even very rare shades of pink and blue. The change is permanent, but detection requires sophisticated equipment that can be found only in major gem-testing laboratories.

In the case of colorless diamonds, this particular treatment process is effective only on very rare diamond types (Type IIa and Type Ia/b). Where consumers are concerned, this is fortunate because a competent gemologist can determine whether or not a diamond is one of these rare types. If a diamond is not one of these types, then it could not have been treated in this manner; if it is, only then must it be submitted to a major laboratory such as the GIA to determine whether or not the color has been enhanced by HPHT annealing. The GIA and other labs will issue a diamond grading report on diamonds treated in this manner, indicating the treatment under the "comments" section of the report.

It has been estimated that fewer than 2 percent of all diamonds are Type IIa; Type Ia/b is even rarer. They represent a larger percentage of jewelry-quality diamonds, however, and some are unusually large and clean. Therefore, if a diamond is transformed from a strongly tinted yellow or brown color into a "colorless" stone, the cost difference could be very great. It is more important than ever to have laboratory documentation on any fine diamond purchased today.

A word of caution: Diamonds treated by HPHT annealing entered the marketplace before the gemological community was aware of the use of this technology on diamonds and before they understood how to distinguish them from natural diamonds. *We recommend that any colorless or near-colorless diamond that has a diamond report issued between January 1996 and June 2000 be examined by a gemologist to determine whether or not it is Type IIa or Ia/b, and if so, that it be resubmitted to a major gem-testing lab (see appendix) for verification.*

Fancy-color diamonds produced by the HPHT annealing process, especially pink and blue diamonds, are more difficult to detect and involve not only Type IIa and Ia/b diamonds but other diamond types as well, so merely having a gemologist confirm whether or not the stone is Type IIa and Ia/b will not necessarily be useful. We highly recommend that fancy-color blue and pink diamonds purchased recently be accompanied by a lab report issued by a major lab, and that if a report already accompanies the stone, that it be resubmitted if the report predates December 2000.

Radiation treatment. Exposing off-color diamonds such as yellowish or brownish tinted stones (and also badly flawed stones in which the flaws would be less noticeable against a colored background) to certain types of radiation can result in the production of fancy-colored stones. This treatment produces rich yellows, greens, and blues, and greatly enhances salability because these colors are very desirable. In and of itself, radiation is not fraud; in fact, it may make a "fancy" color diamond affordable to someone otherwise unable to afford one. But again, just be sure that the stone is properly represented and you know what you are buying, and that you are getting it at the right price—which should be much lower than that of a natural fancy-color stone.

Temporary Color Enhancement to Improve Colorless Diamonds

Touching the culet with ink. Touching the culet, or side, of a slightly yellow stone with a coating of purple ink, such as found in an indelible pencil, neutralizes the yellow, producing a whiter-looking stone. This can be easily detected by washing the stone in alcohol or water. If you have any questions about the color, tactfully request that the stone be washed (in front of you) for better examination. A reputable jeweler should have no objection to this request.

Improving the color by using a sputtering technique. This technique (also called "painting" the diamond) involves sputtering a very thin coating of a special substance over the stone or part of the stone, usually the back, where it will be harder to detect when mounted. The girdle area can also be "painted" with the substance and create the same effect. The substance, like indelible pencil, also neutralizes the yellow and thereby improves the color by as much as seven color grades, but unlike indelible ink, *the substance will not wash off.* It can be removed in two ways: by rubbing the stone briskly and firmly with a cleanser, or by boiling the stone carefully in sulfuric acid. If the stone is already mounted and is coated on the back, using cleanser is not feasible. The sulfuric acid method is the only way. *But please note:* Using sulfuric acid can be extremely dangerous and must be done only by an experienced person. I cannot overstate the hazards of conducting this test.

This technique is not frequently used, but stones treated in this manner do appear often enough to be worth mentioning.

Coating the diamond with chemicals and baking it in a small lab-type oven. This technique also tends to neutralize some of the yellow, thereby producing a better color grade. This coating will be removed eventually by repeated hot ultrasonic cleanings, which will gradually erode the coating. A more rapid removal can be accomplished by the more dangerous method of boiling in sulfuric acid.

Treated stones must be represented as "treated stones" and should be priced accordingly. Unfortunately, too often, in their passage through many hands, the fact that they have been treated ("radiated" or "bombarded") is overlooked or forgotten—intentionally or accidentally. Whether the color is natural or treated can often be determined by spectroscopic examination, which can be provided by a gem-testing laboratory (see appendix). Not all gemologists, however, are competent with spectroscopic procedures, and some fancy-color diamonds require examination with very sophisticated equipment not available to most labs. If your gemologist lacks the skill or equipment, stones can be submitted to a laboratory such as the GIA Laboratory for verification. Most *natural* fancy-color diamonds sold by jewelers in the United States are accompanied by a GIA report.

"Fancy Color" Diamonds Colored by Surface Coatings

With demand increasing and prices rising for rare and valuable fancy-color diamonds, we are now finding artificially colored diamonds entering the marketplace in which their color is the result of a surface coating. As with colorless diamonds, the color resulting from surface coatings is not permanent; the color can change back to its original color.

Depending on the color desired, various coatings can be used. While the color can be improved—or totally changed—by applying the coating to the entire diamond or to an area of the girdle, it is usually applied to the bottom (pavilion), which makes it more difficult to detect. While there is nothing wrong with buying a "coated" diamond as long as you know the color change is not permanent and results from a surface coating and have paid a fair price for it, this is rarely the case; most people buying them don't know what they are buying and are overpaying for what they are getting.

Since fancy-color diamonds are usually accompanied by a laboratory report from a respected gem-testing lab, be suspicious of any fancy-color diamond without a report and take it to a gemologist to confirm what you have. In larger stones it is easy for a gemologist to detect the coating using a simple carbide scriber, but in small sizes used for pavé work, this is not the case.

The biggest problem in the fancy-color diamond market today is the huge number of fancy-color diamond pavé jewelry pieces being sold with surface-coated stones. They are usually sold as something they are not, at inflated prices. This is especially true of pieces containing pink, blue, and intense yellow diamonds. I recommend that anyone buying any fancy-color diamond pavé piece submit it to a laboratory to confirm whether or not the color is natural, and if not, to determine how it was treated. If the color comes from HPHT treatment, irradiation techniques, or some combination thereof, the color will be permanent, and those stones can still be expensive. However, this is not the case with surface-coated stones.

Erroneous Color Grading

Mistakes in grading of color may be unintentional (resulting from insufficient training or experience, or simply from carelessness), or they may be deliberate. You're safer considering the purchase of a stone that has had such important data as color described in a diamond grading report (or certificate) issued by one of several different laboratories offering this service. Many jewelry firms now offer diamonds accompanied by grading reports; those issued by the GIA are the most widely used in the United States. Diamonds accompanied by reports usually sell for slightly more per carat, but they provide an element of security for the average consumer as well as credible documentation if you wish to sell the stone at some future time. If the stone you are considering is accompanied by such a report, be sure to verify that the information on the certificate is accurate by taking the stone to a competent gemologist or lab.

Clarity Enhancement and Flaw Concealment

Clarity Enhancement

Be especially alert to the possibility that clarity may be enhanced. The two most frequently used techniques are lasering inclusions and filling fractures. In both cases, dark inclusions or cracks that might normally be visible—in some cases, very visible—are concealed or become much less noticeable (these techniques are discussed in chapter 7). Be sure to ask whether or not the stone has been lasered or filled. As long as you know, and pay the right price, a clarity-enhanced diamond may be an attractive choice.

Flaw Concealment

Where possible, flaws are concealed by their settings. A good stone setter will try to set a stone in such a manner that the setting will help to conceal any visible imperfections. For this reason, flaws near or at the girdle will downgrade a stone less than those in the center of a stone; since most settings cover all or part of the girdle, they are simply less visible here. Indeed, a setting can make a flaw "invisible."

There is nothing fraudulent in such uses of settings as long as the stone is properly represented. The only danger is that not only the customer but also the jeweler may not have seen the imperfection concealed by the setting.

Can concealment affect value? In most diamonds other than grade FL or grade IF, the presence of a minor flaw concealed under a prong will not affect the price significantly. However, given the difference in price between diamonds graded FL or IF and VVS_1, a minor blemish or inclusion hidden by the setting that might result in a VVS_1 stone being graded FL could have a significant effect on value, especially if the stone has exceptionally fine color. For this reason, FL or IF stones should be viewed *unmounted.*

Certification of Diamonds

Today, most fine diamonds weighing one carat or more are carefully evaluated by a respected laboratory, such as the GIA or the American Gemological Laboratories (AGL), before being set and are issued a diamond grading report. That report both certifies the diamond as genuine and describes it, providing such important information as color grade, flaw grade, weight, cutting and proportioning, and so on. If you are considering the purchase of a very fine diamond weighing one carat or more and it is *not* accompanied by such a report, we would strongly recommend that you or the seller have the stone evaluated by the GIA or another respected laboratory before purchase. You should do so even if it means having a stone that is already set removed from the setting and reset. Given the significant difference in cost that can result from a grading error in the rarer grades, we believe this procedure is worth the inconvenience and expense.

Unfortunately, the confidence of the public in stones accompanied by certificates has given rise to the practice of altering and counterfeiting them. While you can be relatively sure that "certificated" stones sold by reputable, established jewelry firms are what they claim to be, some suppliers and dealers seize opportunities to prey on the unsuspecting. This is one compelling reason to seek a gemologist-appraiser with respected credentials to examine the diamond and accompanying documentation (see chapter 21).

Altering Certificates

Sometimes information is changed on an otherwise valid certificate; for example, the flaw or color grade may be altered. If you have any question regarding the information on the certificate, a phone call to the lab, giving them the certificate number and date, will enable you to verify the information on the certificate.

Counterfeit GIA Certificates and Certification from Nonexistent Laboratories

Certificates from nonexistent labs are an increasingly common problem, as is the use of counterfeit reports purportedly issued by GIA when they are not. A major New York diamond dealer was recently arrested for selling diamonds on the Internet with counterfeit GIA diamond grading reports. Stones accompanied by fancy "certificates" from impressive-sounding labs that don't exist are also appearing more and more frequently. If the certificate is not from one of the recognized labs (see appendix), it should be carefully checked. Have reputable jewelers in the area heard of this lab? Has the Better Business Bureau had any complaints? If the lab seems legitimate, call to verify the information on the certificate, and if all seems in order, you can probably rest comfortably. Otherwise, you may need to have the facts verified by another gemologist or recognized lab.

Some jewelers may not allow verification of an existing certificate by a little-known lab simply because they've been victims themselves or it isn't worth the inconvenience to them. In this case, you might ask the jeweler to get the stone certificated by one of the recognized labs. Many jewelers today are happy to provide this service. If not, then you must decide how badly you want the stone, how much you feel you can trust the jeweler, and what degree of monetary risk you can afford.

Switching the Stone Described on a Report

In some cases the report is bona fide but the stone has been switched. To protect both the consumer and the lab, some labs are taking advantage of ingenious techniques to ensure against switching. For example, a service called Gemprint uses laser technology to display a diamond's unique pattern of reflection and then records it photographically. The result is an electronic "fingerprint" of the diamond, which can be used for identification purposes (see chapter 17). In addition, the GIA and other labs can now actually inscribe its report number, which is visible only under magnification, directly onto the diamond along the girdle. By so doing, one can very easily be sure a specific stone matches a specific certificate simply by matching the numbers. There is an additional fee for this service.

In the absence of such a mark, one clue to a switched stone might be provided by comparing the carat weight and dimensions given on the report. If the measurements and weight match exactly, the probability is slim that the stone has been switched, provided the report hasn't been altered. But it's always a good idea to contact the lab to confirm the details of the report, and then double-check all the information. If the measurements don't match, the type and placement of inclusions or blemishes might enable you to determine if the stone in question is the one described on the report but has been altered; the dimensions might differ if, for example, the stone was nicked or chipped and subsequently recut or repolished. In such a case, ask the jeweler to place the stone under the microscope to enable you to see what should be in the stone.

Unfortunately, if the stone has been mounted, it may be difficult to get precise measurements to compare. In this case, if there is any cause for suspicion, you may be taking a risk to buy the stone unless the seller allows you to have the stone removed from the setting and to have both the report and the stone verified by a qualified gemologist-appraiser. This arrangement requires an understanding in writing that the stone can be returned within a certain time limit if the customer learns it is not as represented.

Always make sure in this situation, for both your protection and the jeweler's, that the jeweler writes down on the bill of sale or memo *all* of the stone's dimensions as best as can be determined: diameter or length and width, depth, and weight. This is to help ensure that you aren't accused of switching the stone after leaving the premises in the event you must return it.

Avoid "Bargains"—and Avoid Costly Mistakes

Take time to do your homework first, to learn what to look for and what questions to ask. Keep my recommended four-step procedure in mind, then shop carefully and compare stones being offered by several fine jewelers in your community. This will give you a chance to get a clearer sense of what something should legitimately sell for, decide whether or not something sounds "too good to be true," and, most important, make sounder decisions about which jeweler is asking a *fair* price.

And remember: No one gives away a valuable gem. There are very few "steals," and even fewer people are qualified to truly know a "steal" when they see one.

Is It a Diamond or a Diamond Imposter?

How can you tell if a stone is really a diamond? As I have said many times, unless you are an expert—or consult one—you cannot be sure about the identification of a stone. Nevertheless, there are a few simple tests you can perform that will show up most diamond imposters quite quickly. Here are a few things to look for.

Is newsprint readable or observable through the stone? If the stone is a round, modern-cut stone and is loose or mounted in such a way as to allow you to place it table-down over some small newsprint, check whether you can see or read any portion of the lettering. If so, it is not a diamond. Refraction of light within a genuine diamond will prevent you from being able to see any of the letters in the newsprint.

Is the stone glued into the setting? Diamonds are seldom glued in. Rhinestones often are.

Is the back open or closed? If the stone is a properly set diamond, the back of the setting will usually be open, allowing you to readily see a portion of the pavilion. Some *antique* pieces containing rose-cut or single-cut diamonds may have closed backs, and some of today's finest custom designers may use a closed-back technique. Otherwise, if a piece has a closed back it is probably rhinestone, the back being closed to conceal silver foil applied to the back of the stone to create greater brilliance.

Recently a young woman called and asked if I would examine an antique diamond ring she'd inherited from her great-grandmother. She mentioned that as she was cleaning it, one of its two diamonds had fallen out of the setting, and inside the setting she saw what she described as pieces of "mirror." She added, "Isn't that strange?" Of course my suspicions were immediately aroused, and upon examination of the piece, they were completely confirmed.

When I saw the ring, I could immediately understand why she felt it was a valuable heirloom. It was beautiful, with a classic design. It held two "diamonds" appearing to be approximately one carat each. The ring mounting was finely worked platinum filigree. But the design of the mounting, which had been common in her great-grandmother's day, made viewing the stones from the side of the ring almost impossible. The top of the stone and the beautiful platinum work were visible, but little more. Furthermore, the back was not completely enclosed; a small round hole would easily have led to the assumption that the stones were the real thing, since the setting wasn't completely closed, as were most imitations at that time. The "set" diamond appeared to be a well-proportioned old-mine cut with very good color. The loose stone, however, with some of the "shiny stuff" still clinging to it, lacked brilliance and fire.

This was one of the finest examples of fraud I had seen in a long time. The "stones" were well cut and proportioned; the mounting was beautifully worked in a precious metal; the stones were held by very small prongs, which was typical of good design at that time. But inside the mounting, backing the stones, was silver foil. They were not genuine diamonds but foil-backed glass.

The use of silver foil is an effective method to "create" a diamond. It acts as a mirror to reflect light and makes the stone appear so brilliant and lively that it can pass as a diamond. The foiling seen today consists of making the back facets into true mirrors and then giving the backs of these mirrors a protective coating of gilt paint. These are then set in jewelry so that their backs are hidden.

It's a sad story, but not an altogether uncommon one. I don't know how many more rings as cleverly done exist today, but approximately 5 percent of the antique jewelry we see is set with fake gems. Fine glass imitations (often referred to as "paste") have been with us since the Venetians of the Renaissance period perfected the art of glassmaking. Fraud, unfortunately, has been with us since time immemorial. Don't allow yourself to be deluded into believing that something you possess is "genuine" simply because it is "antique" or has "been in the family" for a long time.

How many facets are visible on the top? In cheaper glass imitations, only nine top facets are usually visible, as opposed to thirty-three visible top facets in a diamond or "good" simulation. Single-cut or Swiss-cut diamonds (see chapter 5) will also show only nine facets on top, but they will be set in open-back mountings, whereas cheap glass imitations are usually set in closed-back mountings.

Does the girdle of the stone appear to be "frosted"? The girdles of most diamonds are unpolished, with a ground-glasslike appearance that suggests frostiness. Some diamond imitations also have a frosted appearance, but of all of these, a diamond has the whitest frostiness—like clean, dry, ground glass. On the other hand, some diamonds do have polished or faceted girdles, and thus no frostiness will be present. You can develop an eye for this by asking a reliable jeweler to point out the differences between a polished girdle, an unpolished girdle, and a faceted girdle.

Is the cut symmetrical? Since diamond is so valuable and symmetry so important to its overall appearance and desirability, the symmetry of the faceting on a diamond will be very carefully executed, whereas in diamond simulations the symmetry of the facets may be sloppy. For example, the eight kite-shaped facets (sometimes called bezel facets) will often be missing one or more points on the side, or on the top or bottom, showing a small straight edge rather than a point. This sloppy faceting can be an important indication that the stone in question is not a diamond, since it indicates that the cutter did not take proper care. It should be noted that some poorer-grade or old-cut diamonds may also show sloppiness.

Are the crown and the pavilion of the stone properly aligned? While occasionally a diamond may show partial misalignment, imitations are frequently and often badly misaligned.

Are the facet edges or faces scratched, chipped, or worn? Diamond imitations include some stones that are very soft and/or brittle, such as zircon, gadolinium gallium garnet (GGG; an artificial simulation), Fabulite (an artificial diamond simulation also known as Wellington Diamond), and glass. Because of their lack of hardness and, in the case of zircon, possible brittleness, these imitations will show wear easily, and one can often detect scratches or chips on the facet edges or faces. The edges are somewhat more vulnerable, and scratches or chips may be more easily seen there, so check the edges first. Then check the flat faces for scratches. Check both the areas that would be most exposed and the areas around the prongs, where a setter might have accidentally scratched the stone while setting it.

Zircon, a stone found in nature that is often confused with cubic zirconia (CZ), an artificial imitation, is relatively hard but very brittle, so it will almost always show chipping at the edges of the facets if the stone has been worn in jewelry for a year or more. Glass and Fabulite will also show scratches after minimal exposure to handling and wear. Fabulite further differs from diamond in its fire; it will show even more fire than diamond, but with a strong bluish cast.

In addition, with a very good eye or the aid of a magnifier, you can examine the lines or edges where the facets come together in these imitation materials. In diamond, these facet edges are very sharp because of the stone's spectacular hardness. In most simulations, however, since the stone is so much softer, the final polishing technique rounds off those edges, and that sharpness is absent.

Some diamond look-alikes, however, are more durable and resistant to noticeable wear. These include colorless synthetic spinel, colorless synthetic sapphire, colorless quartz, yttrium aluminum garnet (YAG; artificial), and CZ. While these may scratch or chip over time with regular wear and daily abuse, scratches or chips are not as numerous and will be less noticeable.

An Important Word about Cubic Zirconia

Cubic zirconia is the best diamond simulation made to date, and even some jewelers have mistaken these stones for diamonds. Shortly after its appearance, several well-known jewelers in Washington, D.C., found themselves stuck with CZ instead of the one-carat diamonds they thought they'd purchased. The crooks were very clever. A well-dressed couple would arrive at the diamond counter and ask to see various one-carat round brilliant-cut loose diamonds. Because of their fine appearance and educated manner, the jewelers relaxed their guard. The couple would then leave, not making a purchase decision just then, but promising to return. When the jewelers went to replace their merchandise, something didn't seem quite right. Upon close examination, the jewelers discovered that the "nice couple" had pocketed the genuine diamonds and substituted CZ.

Cubic zirconia is almost as brilliant as diamond, has even greater fire (which masks its lesser brilliance), and is relatively hard, giving it good durability and wearability. It is also being produced today in fancy colors—red, green, and yellow—and can provide a nice diamond alternative as a means to offset or dress up colored stones in jewelry if diamonds are unaffordable.

But make sure you *know* what you are buying. For example, if you are shown a lovely amethyst or sapphire ring dressed up with "diamonds," make sure to ask whether the colorless stones are diamonds. And if you are having your own piece of jewelry custom made, you might want to consider using CZ. You can ask your jeweler to order them for you. CZ makes attractive jewelry that can be worn every day without worry.

How Can You Tell If You Have a CZ?

Some of the tests already discussed may help you detect a CZ. The following, however, may eliminate any remaining doubt.

If it is a loose stone, have it weighed. If you are familiar with diamond sizes (see pages 77 and 78) or have a spread gauge (which can be purchased for under $10), you can estimate the diamond carat weight by its spread. A loose stone can be weighed on a scale, which most jewelers have handy, and you can determine how much it should weigh if it is truly a diamond. If the weight is much greater than the diamond weight should be, based on its spread, then it is not a diamond. A CZ is approximately 75 percent heavier than a diamond of the same spread. For example, a CZ that looks like a 1-carat diamond size-wise will weigh 1¾ carats; a CZ that looks like a ¼-carat diamond in terms of size will weigh approximately 40/100 carat.

Look at the girdle. If the girdle is frosted, a subdued whiteness resembling slightly wet or oiled frosted glass will indicate CZ. Unfortunately, looking at girdles to differentiate between the appearance of frosted CZ and frosted diamond girdles requires considerable experience.

Test the stone with a carbide scriber. CZ can be scratched with a fine-point carbide scriber, also available at most jewelry supply houses for under $15. If the scriber is forcibly pushed perpendicularly to any of the facets (the table being the easiest) and then drawn across this flat surface, you will scratch it. You cannot scratch a diamond except with another diamond. But be sensible and considerate. Don't heedlessly scratch merchandise that doesn't belong to you—particularly if the jeweler or seller doesn't represent the stone as a diamond.

Examine the stone, loose or mounted, for fluorescence. Both CZ and diamond fluoresce, but the colors and intensities will be different.

Use an electronic diamond tester. There are pocket-size diamond testers for under $175 that will tell you whether or not you have a diamond. If you follow the instructions, they are easy to use and fairly reliable. Most won't tell you what you have if it's *not* diamond; they will only confirm whether or not it *is* diamond.

If after these tests you have some questions, take the stone to a qualified gemologist with lab facilities for positive identification.

Synthetic Moissanite—A Sparkling Newcomer

A new diamond imitation is being sold today under the name *moissanite,* although it should be called *synthetic moissanite,* since what is being sold in jewelry stores is not natural but created in laboratories. It is silicon carbide, named after Dr. Henri Moissan, the French scientist who discovered it. Advertisements describe it as one of nature's rarest gems, but it does not occur in nature as a gemstone, only as a microscopic inclusion.

It made news upon its introduction because it fooled most electronic diamond testers (those measuring thermal conductivity), indicating "diamond" when tested! Many concluded from this that it was indistinguishable from diamond, but this is far from the case. It has several distinctive characteristics that immediately separate it from diamond. Nevertheless, synthetic moissanite is being misrepresented as diamond in new and antique jewelry, and there have been several cases in which jewelers have switched stones substituting synthetic moissanite for the original diamond. Gemologists can quickly and easily separate diamond from synthetic moissanite with simple tests, in most cases using only a 10x loupe. There is also new diamond testing equipment that can instantly distinguish between the two.

Synthetic moissanite is lighter than diamond, so weighing it is a quick way to distinguish it from diamond if the stone is unmounted. While moissanite is not as hard as diamond, it is harder than CZ and even harder than ruby and sapphire, which means it is a very durable material that can take a very high polish. It has even greater brilliance and much more dispersion (fire) than either diamond or CZ. One disadvantage in comparison with CZ is that it is much more expensive, costing approximately a tenth of what a comparable diamond costs.

Synthetic moissanite has a distinctive appearance and may make an attractive choice for those who want something new and different. As a diamond imitation, given its high cost and the fact that CZ actually looks more like diamond, only time will tell whether or not it will replace CZ as the diamond imitation of the twenty-first century.

Comparison of Diamonds and Diamond Look-Alikes

Name of Stone	Hardness (Mohs' Scale 1–10) 1 = Softest, 10 = Hardest	Read-through*	Degree of Dispersion (Fire, Flashes of Color Observed)	Wearability
Diamond	10 (Hardest natural substance in existence)	None, if properly cut	High; lots of fire and liveliness	Excellent
Cubic zirconia (CZ)	8.5 (Hard)	Slight	Very high; lots of life	Very good
Gadolinium gallium garnet (GGG; produced very briefly)	6.5 (Somewhat soft)	Moderate	High; almost identical to diamond	Fair—scratches easily; wears badly; sunlight causes brownish discoloration
Glass	5–6.5 (Soft)	Very strong	Variable—low to good depending on quality of glass and cut	Poor; susceptible to scratches, chipping, and excessive wear
Strontium titanate (also known as Fabulite or Wellington Diamond)	5–6 (Soft)	None, if properly cut	Extremely high; too high (much more than diamond); shows lots of blue flashes	Poor—scratches and wears badly
Synthetic moissanite	9.25 (Very hard)	None	Extremely high; much too high for diamond; higher than CZ	Excellent
Synthetic rutile (shows yellowish color)	6.5 (Soft)	None	Extremely high; lots of life—but strong yellowish flashes	Poor; scratches easily and shows excessive wear
Synthetic sapphire	9 (Very hard)	Very strong	Very low; little life or display of color flashes	Very good
Synthetic spinel	8 (Hard)	Very strong	Low; little life	Very good
Yttrium aluminum garnet (YAG; used extensively)	8.5 (Hard)	Strong	Very low; almost no visible display of fire	Good
Zircon	7.5 (Moderately hard)	Moderate	Good; lively	Fair—hard but brittle, so chips easily and shows wear equivalent to much softer stones

*This technique—the ability and ease with which one can read print while looking through the stone—is reliable only when looking at round brilliant-cut stones (although it is *sometimes* useful for ovals and some fancy cuts).

CHAPTER ELEVEN

Comparing Colorless Diamond Prices

All too often, people look for easy answers to complex problems. Many would like to have a simple list of diamond grades and corresponding prices, by size. Unfortunately, market conditions are constantly changing, and, more important, significant differences in price often result from subtle differences in quality not readily discernible to any but the professional. Therefore, it is not possible to provide a simple answer to this complex question.

But that does not mean I cannot provide you with some general guidelines that will help you understand the *relative* effects of each of the four primary factors used to determine the value of diamonds. The following charts are not intended as hard price lists of what you should be paying in a jewelry store; instead, they should be used as a guideline—a foundation on which you can place more current information that reflects the variations in a constantly fluctuating market. Keep in mind that these prices are for unmounted stones. Fine settings and custom-designed one-of-a-kind pieces can add substantially to the price.

Extreme differences between the prices given on the following pages and a price you might be quoted for a diamond should be examined carefully; if the price is *much lower,* be sure to seek a gemologist or gemologist-appraiser to check the quality and verify that the stone is as represented. If the price is *much higher,* do some comparison shopping in your community to be sure the seller is offering good value.

Note that the prices given here are for diamonds with good proportioning; stones with excellent proportioning will sell for more, while stones with poor proportioning can sell for much less. Diamonds having fancy shapes—shapes other than round—normally sell for anywhere from 5 to 15 percent less than round cuts. However, if a particular shape is in great demand, the price can be higher than for round stones.

Finally, before relying too heavily on the prices listed in this chapter, be sure you read the information on diamond grading reports. This knowledge will give you additional input on adjusting diamond prices according to the more subtle factors that affect quality and value. Finally, if you are contemplating the purchase of a particular stone, be sure to have the facts verified by a qualified gemologist-appraiser.

*Retail Price Guide for Round Brilliant-Cut Diamonds**

Notice both the tremendous price fluctuation among stones of the same size due to differences in the flaw grades and color grades and the disproportionate jumps in cost *per carat*, depending on size.

lightface indicates PRICE PER CARAT / **boldface indicates PRICE PER STONE** in U.S. dollars

3/4 Carat	COLOR GRADE							
FLAW (CLARITY) GRADE	D	E	F	G	H	I	J	K
IF†	15,400	11,200	10,400	9,200	8,200	6,740	6,075	5,625
	11,550	**8,400**	**7,800**	**6,900**	**6,150**	**5,055**	**4,550**	**4,220**
VVS_1	11,850	10,000	9,000	8,000	7,400	6,600	5,625	5,400
	8,890	**7,500**	**6,750**	**6,000**	**5,550**	**4,950**	**4,220**	**4,050**
VVS_2	9,600	9,000	8,200	7,400	6,800	6,525	5,400	4,725
	7,200	**6,750**	**6,150**	**5,550**	**5,100**	**4,890**	**4,050**	**3,540**
VS_1	8,300	8,000	7,600	7,000	6,500	6,070	5,175	4,500
	6,225	**6,000**	**5,700**	**5,250**	**4,875**	**4,550**	**3,880**	**3,375**
VS_2	7,600	7,000	6,875	6,750	6,300	5,850	4,725	4,275
	5,700	**5,250**	**5,150**	**5,060**	**4,725**	**4,390**	**3,540**	**3,200**
SI_1	6,400	6,200	6,075	5,850	5,400	5,175	4,500	4,050
	4,800	**4,650**	**4,550**	**4,390**	**4,050**	**3,880**	**3,375**	**3,040**
SI_2	6,300	6,075	5,500	5,175	4,950	4,610	4,275	3,825
	4,725	**4,550**	**4,125**	**3,880**	**3,710**	**3,460**	**3,200**	**2,870**
I_1	4,275	4,050	3,825	3,600	3,480	3,375	3,150	2,750
	3,200	**3,040**	**2,870**	**2,700**	**2,610**	**2,530**	**2,360**	**2,060**

* Prices compiled from *The Guide*, Gemworld International, Inc., and adjusted to retail.

† There is a minimal price difference between FL and IF stones in the rarest colors. Stones will cost approximately 5–8 percent more in D–F colors; 1–2 percent more in G–J colors; there is no cost difference in stones of less rare colors (below J).

Light (.90–.99) Carat	COLOR GRADE							
FLAW (CLARITY) GRADE	D	E	F	G	H	I	J	K
IF†	19,190	17,220	15,840	12,600	11,200	8,200	7,000	6,300
	17,270	**15,500**	**14,260**	**11,340**	**10,080**	**7,380**	**6,300**	**5,670**
VVS_1	16,200	15,900	14,400	11,600	10,000	8,000	6,800	6,075
	14,580	**14,310**	**12,960**	**10,440**	**9,000**	**7,200**	**6,120**	**5,470**
VVS_2	14,800	13,300	12,480	9,900	9,000	7,600	6,600	5,850
	13,320	**11,970**	**11,230**	**8,910**	**8,100**	**6,840**	**5,940**	**5,265**
VS_1	10,400	9,800	9,700	9,000	8,000	6,800	6,400	5,625
	9,360	**8,820**	**8,730**	**8,100**	**7,200**	**6,120**	**5,760**	**5,060**
VS_2	10,160	9,450	9,000	8,000	7,500	6,400	5,800	5,400
	9,140	**8,500**	**8,100**	**7,200**	**6,750**	**5,760**	**5,220**	**4,860**
SI_1	8,800	7,720	7,500	7,400	6,700	6,000	5,600	4,950
	7,920	**6,950**	**6,750**	**6,660**	**6,030**	**5,400**	**5,040**	**4,460**
SI_2	7,000	6,790	6,760	6,400	5,800	5,700	5,400	4,500
	6,300	**6,110**	**6,080**	**5,760**	**5,220**	**5,130**	**4,860**	**4,050**
I_1	5,400	5,175	4,950	4,725	4,500	4,275	4,050	3,600
	4,860	**4,660**	**4,460**	**4,250**	**4,050**	**3,850**	**3,650**	**3,240**

1 Carat	COLOR GRADE							
FLAW (CLARITY) GRADE	D	E	F	G	H	I	J	K
IF†	36,860	25,270	22,040	16,240	13,960	11,800	10,300	8,400
	36,860	**25,270**	**22,040**	**16,240**	**13,960**	**11,800**	**10,300**	**8,400**
VVS_1	26,790	22,230	19,760	15,600	13,000	11,060	9,700	8,000
	26,790	**22,230**	**19,760**	**15,600**	**13,000**	**11,060**	**9,700**	**8,000**
VVS_2	23,560	19,350	18,900	14,840	12,160	10,000	9,340	7,700
	23,560	**19,350**	**18,900**	**14,840**	**12,160**	**10,000**	**9,340**	**7,700**
VS_1	17,800	15,500	14,400	12,800	10,600	9,280	8,400	7,300
	17,800	**15,500**	**14,400**	**12,800**	**10,600**	**9,280**	**8,400**	**7,300**
VS_2	13,700	12,500	11,840	10,900	9,600	8,400	7,200	6,600
	13,700	**12,500**	**11,840**	**10,900**	**9,600**	**8,400**	**7,200**	**6,600**
SI_1	10,940	9,900	9,600	9,300	8,450	7,880	6,760	6,200
	10,940	**9,900**	**9,600**	**9,300**	**8,450**	**7,880**	**6,760**	**6,200**
SI_2	9,300	8,900	8,000	7,800	7,500	7,050	6,500	6,190
	9,300	**8,900**	**8,000**	**7,800**	**7,500**	**7,050**	**6,500**	**6,190**
I_1	7,000	6,750	6,525	6,300	5,625	5,175	4,950	4,725
	7,000	**6,750**	**6,525**	**6,300**	**5,625**	**5,175**	**4,950**	**4,725**

* Prices compiled from *The Guide*, Gemworld International, Inc., and adjusted to retail.

† There is a minimal price difference between FL and IF stones in the rarest colors. Stones will cost approximately 5–8 percent more in D–F colors; 1–2 percent more in G–J colors; there is no cost difference in stones of less rare colors (below J).

2 Carat	COLOR GRADE							
FLAW (CLARITY) GRADE	**D**	**E**	**F**	**G**	**H**	**I**	**J**	**K**
IF†	57,600	46,800	45,360	30,210	23,370	20,520	17,800	13,600
	115,200	**93,600**	**90,720**	**60,420**	**46,740**	**41,040**	**35,600**	**27,200**
VVS$_1$	49,500	44,460	41,990	29,260	21,660	19,700	16,200	13,200
	99,000	**88,920**	**83,980**	**58,520**	**43,320**	**39,400**	**32,400**	**26,400**
VVS$_2$	47,310	39,710	35,530	26,410	19,570	19,000	15,800	12,800
	94,620	**79,420**	**71,060**	**52,820**	**39,140**	**38,000**	**31,600**	**25,600**
VS$_1$	38,760	33,060	29,260	22,990	19,000	17,200	14,400	11,800
	77,520	**66,120**	**58,520**	**45,980**	**38,000**	**34,400**	**28,800**	**23,600**
VS$_2$	26,220	25,650	24,510	21,850	18,200	15,400	14,000	11,000
	52,440	**51,300**	**49,020**	**43,700**	**36,400**	**30,800**	**28,000**	**22,000**
SI$_1$	20,710	19,610	18,810	18,200	16,500	14,400	11,800	10,000
	41,420	**39,220**	**37,620**	**36,400**	**33,000**	**28,800**	**23,600**	**20,000**
SI$_2$	17,280	17,000	15,680	14,600	14,200	13,400	11,000	9,400
	34,560	**34,000**	**31,360**	**29,200**	**28,400**	**26,800**	**22,000**	**18,800**
I$_1$	10,400	10,200	10,000	9,600	8,600	8,400	7,800	7,000
	20,800	**20,400**	**20,000**	**19,200**	**17,200**	**16,800**	**15,600**	**14,000**

3 Carat	COLOR GRADE							
FLAW (CLARITY) GRADE	**D**	**E**	**F**	**G**	**H**	**I**	**J**	**K**
IF†	125,100	90,360	69,480	52,020	43,890	30,590	24,700	19,380
	375,300	**271,080**	**208,440**	**156,060**	**131,670**	**91,770**	**74,100**	**58,140**
VVS$_1$	97,920	83,340	68,850	48,960	41,610	29,830	23,940	18,810
	293,760	**250,020**	**206,550**	**146,880**	**124,830**	**89,490**	**71,820**	**56,430**
VVS$_2$	84,420	63,000	58,500	47,520	35,910	28,690	23,180	18,050
	253,260	**189,000**	**175,500**	**142,560**	**107,730**	**86,070**	**69,540**	**54,150**
VS$_1$	63,360	52,650	48,420	41,610	34,010	25,270	21,030	17,400
	190,080	**157,950**	**145,260**	**124,830**	**102,030**	**75,810**	**63,100**	**52,200**
VS$_2$	48,600	45,720	40,470	35,110	26,980	21,470	19,000	15,200
	145,800	**137,160**	**121,410**	**105,340**	**80,940**	**64,410**	**57,000**	**45,600**
SI$_1$	32,680	30,210	25,270	22,990	19,570	18,600	16,200	14,000
	98,040	**90,630**	**75,810**	**68,970**	**58,710**	**55,800**	**48,600**	**42,000**
SI$_2$	20,200	19,600	19,000	17,800	16,800	16,600	14,400	12,400
	60,600	**58,800**	**57,000**	**53,400**	**50,400**	**49,800**	**43,200**	**37,200**
I$_1$	13,400	12,200	11,800	11,200	10,600	9,800	8,600	8,200
	40,200	**36,600**	**35,400**	**33,600**	**31,800**	**29,400**	**25,800**	**24,600**

* Prices compiled from *The Guide*, Gemworld International, Inc., and adjusted to retail.

† There is a minimal price difference between FL and IF stones in the rarest colors. Stones will cost approximately 5–8 percent more in D–F colors; 1–2 percent more in G–J colors; there is no cost difference in stones of less rare colors (below J).

*Retail Price Guide for Old-European Cut Diamonds**

Prices are per carat in U.S. dollars.

Color	½ Carat	1 Carat	2–3 Carat
Color D–F			
VVS–VS	6,400	12,000	19,950–28,500
SI	4,725	9,200	13,000–17,000
I_1	3,500	4,950	7,000–9,000
Color G–H			
VVS–VS	5,850	9,700	17,000–26,980
SI	4,450	7,600	12,000–15,000
I_1	3,000	5,175	6,400–7,000
Color I–J			
VVS–VS	4,500	7,700	13,400–15,800
SI	3,480	6,525	9,800–11,800
I_1	2,500	4,500	6,300–6,600
Color K–M			
VVS–VS	3,600	5,625	8,000–10,400
SI	3,250	4,500	6,300–7,600
I_1	2,125	3,250	4,050–5,175

*Prices compiled from *The Guide*, Gemworld International, Inc., and adjusted to retail.

*Retail Price Guide for Rose-Cut Diamonds**

Prices are per carat in U.S. dollars.

Size	Carat	Color	Per Carat
3 mm	0.15	H–J	1,000–1,190
		K–M	750–940
4 mm	0.20	H–J	1,625–1,875
		K–M	1,250–1,500
5 mm	0.45	H–J	2,125–2,375
		K–M	1,625–1,875
6 mm	0.75	H–J	3,750–4,500
		K–M	2,500–3,750

*Prices courtesy of Michael Goldstein of Michael Goldstein Ltd.

*Retail Price Guide for Briolette-Cut Diamonds**

Prices are for bright goods, VS to SI clarity, and are per carat in U.S. dollars.

Weight	Brown	Cognac	K–M	H–I
½ carat	325–500	625–1,000	1,250–1,875	2,200–2,875
¾ carat	625–825	875–1,250	1,875–2,375	2,750–3,100
1 carat	825–1,250	1,200–1,625	2,750–3,450	3,300–3,800

*Prices compiled from *The Guide*, Gemworld International, Inc., and adjusted to retail.

CHAPTER TWELVE

Fancy-Color Diamonds

Natural-Color Diamonds— A Rainbow of Choices

Of all the gems on earth, nothing surpasses the palette of natural-color diamonds for beauty, distinctiveness, and desirability. Known as *fancy-color diamonds,* they occur in virtually every color and shade of color. Ruby-red, baby-pink, grass-green, and sapphire-blue diamonds rank among the rarest and most precious of all gems.

Fancy-color diamonds possess a distinctive look not found in any other colored gem. Whatever the actual "body" color seen in a fancy-color diamond, it is augmented by the presence of numerous pinpoint flashes of other colors that are the result of diamond's high dispersion—diamond's ability to break up each ray of reflected light into an array of spectral colors. For example, a "yellow" diamond may be yellow, but you may also see pinpoint reflections of green, blue, orange, and so on. The body color of the diamond, combined with its high dispersion, creates a fiery scintillation not found in any other gemstone. The latest rage is "brown" diamonds, from pale beige to rich cognac. The most affordable of the fancy colors—and more affordable than colorless and near-colorless diamonds—they were once considered too common to use in fine jewelry, but today they are being showcased by leading fashion and jewelry designers alike. Today, no fashion-conscious woman wants to be without one! Ranging from just a few hundred dollars per carat to under $10,000 per carat in larger sizes and deeper shades, these make a statement at a fraction of the price of colorless diamonds.

On the other end of the spectrum, diamonds in the rarest colors are breaking world records. It started in 1987 with the sale of the famous .95-carat red "Hancock" diamond that fetched $880,000—almost a million dollars per carat—for a stone under a carat in size! Today we're starting to see equally impressive figures, and stellar prices are now the norm. In 2009 a fancy *vivid*-blue cushion-cut diamond weighing 7.03 carats commanded $1,350,000 *per carat* as the hammer came down at almost $9.5 million, and in mid-2010, a 7.64-carat intense-blue cushion-cut diamond set a new per-carat record for intense-blue diamonds, at $1,050,000 per carat! One of the highlights of the past few years was the sale of one of the world's most famous diamonds—the 35+–carat Wittelsbach Blue—once part of the Austrian and Bavarian Crown jewels. It was sold at auction to Lawrence Graff for over £16 million (over $26 million). It is now known as the Wittelsbach-Graff Diamond, and at that price, he can name it whatever he likes!

What Causes the Color Seen in Fancy-Color Diamonds?

When we talk about fancy-color diamonds, we must remember that the color seen can be *natural* or the result of *treatment* used to transform off-color diamonds into lovely "fancy" colors.

Natural color in diamonds usually results from the presence of trace elements, although in some cases it can result from natural exposure to radiation, or from damage to the crystal lattice structure. Natural-color yellow diamonds get their color from the presence of nitrogen, for example, and blue diamonds, from boron or hydrogen. In diamonds where color is due to particular trace elements, the presence or absence of those trace elements can be ascertained through sophisticated testing procedures, providing an important key to determining whether color is natural or artificial.

The situation is different with green diamonds. The color seen in natural-color green diamonds does not result from the presence of trace elements; green diamonds owe their color to exposure to radiation as they were forming in the earth eons ago. This creates an unusual dilemma for gem-testing laboratories because there are also treated green diamonds that have been created by humans using modern radiation techniques. Since radiation is the cause of color in both cases, it poses some identification challenges for laboratories. In some cases a natural-color green diamond will contain certain unique identifying characteristics that distinguish it from the treated stone, and in some cases a treated green diamond will exhibit characteristics that identify it as treated, but many green diamonds lack conclusive evidence for positive identification. In such cases, a laboratory report will indicate that a positive determination cannot be made with gemological data currently available. This leaves the door open to the possibility that a positive determination might be made at some future time as new data comes to light from continued research and technological advances, but there are no guarantees. In any event, if you are considering a natural green diamond you must understand that it may be more difficult to find one with laboratory documentation confirming that the color is natural.

Fortunately, gem-testing laboratories are usually able to positively confirm origin of color in fancy-color diamonds, and cases where they cannot are the exception rather than the rule. For this reason, and since origin of color has such a significant impact on rarity and cost, I never recommend the purchase of a natural-color diamond without laboratory verification (see appendix) nor would I ever purchase one personally without such documentation.

Judging Fancy-Color Diamonds

Fancy-color diamonds have always attracted connoisseurs and collectors, but today they are capturing the attention of a much wider audience. Demand—and pricing—are setting new records. If a fancy-color diamond is what you seek, take time to learn as much as you can about the specific colors you like and what is available; some colors occur in a wider range of sizes than others, and some are much rarer. And most of all, before buying, no matter how rare the color, no matter how collectible or desirable to others, make sure you *like* it!

It is also important to take time to understand the four Cs as they relate to fancy-color diamonds—especially the subtle nuances of color and their impact on value—and to develop an eye for the important differences that affect not only the beauty and desirability of a particular stone, but its cost. And finally, since most natural-color diamonds are accompanied by a diamond report, be sure to take time to understand what the information provided on the report is really telling you.

Color—The Most Important Factor

While the four Cs apply to fancy-color diamonds as well as to colorless diamonds, the emphasis is clearly on "color." In general, the rarer the color, the less impact clarity and cutting have on its value; the less rare the color, the more important clarity and cutting become. Many reports on fancy-color diamonds do not even include a clarity grade or information regarding cutting and proportioning except for the stone's shape.

When judging a fancy-color diamond, color is so paramount that it is important to understand how color is graded. You must carefully evaluate each of the following:

- Purity of color
- Depth of color (tone and saturation)
- Color distribution throughout the stone

Whether or not the color is *natural*—the origin of color—is also critically important, as I've already discussed, in the overall evaluation of color and its impact on price.

To properly evaluate the color of a fancy-color diamond, the stone must be viewed from the *face-up* position—looking at it with the table up, as you would see it when mounted in a piece of jewelry—which is very different from evaluating colorless diamonds (see chapter 6). From the face-up position, you must now evaluate each of the following characteristics.

Purity of color. This refers to the hue and the purity of the hue. Let's take yellow as an example. The color of a fancy yellow diamond might be described as "yellow," "orangish yellow," "brownish yellow," "brown yellow," and so on. Understanding the differences in the wording is very important. The final word in the color description is the *hue;* the word or words preceding it are the *modifiers* of the hue. Having no modifier means the color is a pure hue, which, depending on the color, can be very rare. Some color combinations are rarer and costlier than others. For example, let's consider two diamonds where one is "orangy yellow" and the other is "brownish yellow." In both cases, the hue is "yellow" but since orange is rarer than brown, the orangy-yellow stone would be more valuable than the brownish-yellow stone.

Now let's look again at the description of the "brownish yellow" stone. Here the primary color is yellow, with a lesser degree of brown modifying the color. However, if the words were *reversed*—that is, yellowish *brown* rather than brownish *yellow*—the words would tell us the diamond is *brown* with some lesser amount of yellow modifying the color. Again, since brown is a much less rare color, a yellowish-brown diamond would have less value than a brownish yellow.

When considering a fancy-color diamond it is important to take time to understand the terminology used to describe the particular hue that interests you, what shades are available, and how they compare in terms of rarity and value.

Depth of color. This refers to the *saturation* of color combined with the *tone*. Saturation refers to the denseness of the color. A pure yellow or pink diamond, for example, has minimal color saturation, while a brown or blue diamond has heavy color saturation. Most fancy-color diamonds occur in less saturated colors such as yellow. With the exception of brown diamonds, heavily saturated colors can be very rare and costly; ruby red and sapphire blue are among the rarest and costliest of all gems.

Tone has to do with how light or dark the color is; that is, how much *white* or *black* is present (sometimes brown or gray will affect tone). If there is too much white, it will be too pale or even colorless; if there is too much black, brown, or gray, the stone will be overly dark. Fancy "black" diamonds are popular today. These are typically opaque (that is, not transparent) and heavily included and usually sell for much less than other fancy colors. It is important to note that today black diamonds are being used increasingly in designer lines, but most of the stones used are being treated to obtain the black color. There are also "white" diamonds that should not be confused with "colorless" stones. Fancy white diamonds are very rare, but they are usually milky or cloudy, which reduces their popularity and value.

Most diamond reports for fancy-color diamonds classify the depth of color using terminology similar to the following:

- *Faint*
- *Very Light*
- *Light*
  (Among "yellow" and "brown" diamonds, these first three categories are not truly "fancy colors" but at the lowest end of the D–Z scale for colorless stones.)
- *Fancy Light*
- *Fancy (Yellow, Orange, Brown, Blue, or whatever the color)*
- *Fancy Intense*
- *Fancy Deep*
- *Fancy Dark*
- *Fancy Vivid*

The classification pertaining to the depth of color is extremely important. One tonal difference can dramatically affect value. But it is important to understand that the *number of classifications* is *not the same for every color.* Generally speaking, less saturated colors (such as pure yellow or pure pink) have fewer classifications, and more heavily saturated colors (such as blue) will have more classifications. If you are interested in a yellow diamond, for example, and decide you want a color that is *richer* than "Fancy Yellow," the next classification following "Fancy Yellow" is usually "Intense," followed by "Dark"; it is rare to find a "Deep Yellow" classification (which would fall between "Intense" and "Dark"). "Dark Yellow" indicates the stone has more black but less saturation of yellow. So while "dark" yellow is a darker color, it has less *yellow* saturation, and therefore would be less valuable than "Intense Yellow," and "Vivid Yellow" would be the most valuable.

If you are looking at a diamond described as "Fancy *Brownish* Yellow"—which has a higher color saturation—you will find more tonal classifications, and it is not unusual to find a "Fancy Deep" classification that would have more color depth than "Fancy" but less than "Intense." It would also be more expensive than "Fancy Brownish Yellow" but less expensive than "Fancy Intense." In blue diamonds, you can also find a "Dark" and a "Deep" classification. And so on. What this really means is that *to accurately evaluate rarity and value, and to be sure you have found the depth of color that best suits your needs, you must be sure to find out what the specific tonal classifications are for the particular color you are considering.*

Evenness of color. A laboratory report will indicate whether or not the color is evenly dispersed under "Distribution." Ideally, the distribution of the color should be "even," but this is not always the case. Sometimes color occurs in zones, alternating with colorless zones, and the report will indicate "uneven" color distribution. Such stones may *appear* to have even color distribution when viewed from the top, and may be lovely and desirable, but they should cost less than one that has "even" distribution.

Is the Color Natural?

In addition to the rainbow of colors in which diamond occurs naturally, diamonds can also be transformed into beautiful, desirable colors by several techniques, as mentioned earlier. Radiation techniques have been used for many years to change tinted, off-white diamonds into various shades of yellow, green, and blue-green. In most cases (green diamonds are often an exception), these can be easily distinguished from the natural by any competent gemologist. But new techniques are creating new challenges, and determining whether or not color is natural may require very sophisticated, high-tech procedures only available at a major gem-testing laboratory.

HPHT process creates "fancy-color" diamonds. Earlier I mentioned a new technique known as *high-pressure/high-temperature annealing* (HPHT) that can be used to transform very off-white and brownish diamonds into colorless and near-colorless diamonds (see page 48). HPHT techniques can also transform tinted, off-white, and brownish diamonds into a variety of "fancy" colors, from yellowish green and greenish yellow to exquisite shades of pink and blue. While the yellowish-green and greenish-yellow stones often have a distinctive look that sets them apart from most natural diamonds of comparable color, this is not the case with the pink and blue stones, which exhibit a color and other characteristics that make it very difficult to distinguish them from the natural. A round, 10.09-carat natural brown diamond was transformed by HPHT techniques into an exquisite *intense* pink diamond with VS clarity! Currently the world's largest, it was named the *Provo Rose*.

Since natural fancy-color diamonds can be costlier than many colorless diamonds—with fancy-color blue and pink diamonds *much* costlier because of their rarity—I recommend that you obtain a laboratory report for any fancy-color diamond represented to have natural color. Most major labs will grade diamonds treated in this manner, indicating the treatment in a special comment on the report (see sample fancy diamond reports at the end of this chapter).

There is nothing wrong with buying a diamond that has obtained its color through some form of treatment. Increasingly, fine jewelry designers are using color-treated diamonds to create very distinctive jewelry at attractive prices. But it is important to know whether the color is natural or the result of some treatment process so that you know you have paid an appropriate price.

An extra word of caution regarding pink and blue diamonds: Anyone considering the purchase of a diamond represented to be *natural blue* or *natural pink* must be sure it is accompanied by a *current* report—*a report issued by a major laboratory after December 2000*. If the date on the report is earlier than December 2000, request that the stone be resubmitted to a major lab for verification, or make the sale contingent on getting this documentation (see appendix). Most laboratories were unaware of the use of HPHT techniques to create blue and pink colors until the year 2000, and diagnostic data with which to detect the treatment was not available until later that year. Since prior testing techniques would not have revealed the treatment, earlier reports may not be accurate.

Surface coatings. As discussed earlier, with demand increasing and prices rising for rare and valuable fancy-color diamonds, we are now finding artificially colored diamonds entering the marketplace in which the color seen is the result of a surface coating. The color resulting from surface coatings is not permanent; the color can change back to its original color (see chapter 10).

Clarity

Many fancy-color diamond reports do not include a clarity grade, especially if the color is exceptional or very rare. When a clarity grade is provided, the grading is based on the same criteria used for colorless diamonds (see chapter 7). It is important to understand that in fancy-color diamonds, flawlessness is even rarer than in colorless diamonds. Fancy-color diamonds are often graded "slightly imperfect" (SI), and "imperfect" (I) grades are also common. In fancy-color stones, SI and I grades do not carry the stigma associated with these grades in colorless diamonds, especially if the stone has a rare or unusually rich, saturated color. This is not to say that there are no "flawless" fancy-color diamonds, or stones in the rarer clarity grades, but if the color is rare, and the stone also has a rarer clarity grade, the cost will be disproportionately *much* higher.

As with colorless diamonds, enhancement techniques are also being used to improve the appearance by filling fractures and lasering black inclusions so they will no longer be visible. Be sure to take the precautions recommended in chapter 7.

Cutting and Proportioning

As already mentioned, most reports on fancy-color diamonds lack information pertaining to cutting and proportioning. As with clarity, the deeper and/or rarer the color, the less important the cutting. However, I should mention here that certain shapes are more common among fancy-color diamonds because, in addition to its proportioning, the shape itself and the cutting style (that is, step cut versus brilliant cut) can affect the intensity or evenness of the color.

Shape Can Affect Intensity and Evenness of Color

If you are interested in a fancy-color diamond, you must allow some flexibility where shape is concerned. Certain shapes are rare and difficult, if not impossible, to find in fancy colors, while other shapes are much more readily available in almost any color. The emerald cut is one that is especially difficult to find, and even round stones may be difficult to find in a particular color. The radiant cut, however, is frequently found.

Today's modern radiant and princess cuts have become especially popular for fancy-color diamonds, because the shape, proportioning, and facet arrangement *intensify the color*. On the other hand, it is extremely rare to find a fancy-color diamond in an emerald cut, because the color won't look as intense. In fact, when emerald-cut diamonds with fancy colors are found in old jewelry, many diamond cutters immediately recut them into one of the new cuts, such as the radiant or princess, to intensify the color so they can obtain a report with a rarer color grade. I searched for an emerald-cut diamond with an "Intense Yellow" color for a client and it took many months to find just three stones, because "Intense Yellow" emerald-cut diamonds, recut and resubmitted to a laboratory, often receive a "*Vivid*" grade, the rarest and costliest of yellow diamonds.

The result is that emerald-cut diamonds in fancy colors are becoming ever more difficult to find. One of the most beautiful diamonds I ever saw was a square emerald-cut diamond, with a report that graded the color "Vivid Yellow." Imagine an emerald cut with a "Vivid" grade, and the intensity of color! The stone's personality was truly regal, and I would certainly never want to see this stone recut because I appreciate its rarity—not just because its color is "Vivid" but because it is a "Vivid" emerald cut.

Some shapes are not desirable in a fancy-color diamond because they may cause the color to appear uneven. This is often the case when a fancy-color diamond is cut into a pear shape or marquise shape. This is because these shapes usually exhibit a *bow tie* effect across the center of the stone—an effect created by light leakage—which usually causes the color to appear lighter across the area of the bow tie. Sometimes the difference is slight; sometimes it is pronounced. Such stones should sell for less; the more visible the color difference, the more impact on cost.

Now that you have a better understanding of how fancy-color diamonds are judged, you're ready to start searching for that special stone. It may seem somewhat complicated at first, but if you focus on the factors discussed here, it won't be long before you discover what is important to you and what you really like; it will quickly become a fascinating and exciting journey filled with wonder and joy.

To help you become more familiar with fancy-color diamond reports and the types of documentation that you might encounter, the following pages provide sample reports from some of the world's most respected laboratories.

GIA
GEM TRADE LABORATORY

New York Headquarters
580 Fifth Avenue | New York, NY 10036-4794
T: 212-221-5858 | F: 212-575-3095

Carlsbad
5355 Armada Drive | Carlsbad, CA 92008-4699
T: 760-603-4500 | F: 760-603-1814

112565702

COLORED DIAMOND
GRADING REPORT

GIA REPORT 10958099

January 03, 2000

Laser Inscription Registry .... GIA 10958099

Shape and Cutting Style .... CUT-CORNERED RECTANGULAR MODIFIED BRILLIANT

Measurements .... 6.59 x 5.99 x 3.75 mm

Weight .... 1.18 carat

Proportions

Depth .... 62.6 %

Table .... 63 %

Girdle .... MEDIUM TO SLIGHTLY THICK

Culet .... VERY SMALL

Finish

Polish .... VERY GOOD

Symmetry .... VERY GOOD

Clarity Grade VS1

Color

Origin .... NATURAL

Grade .... FANCY YELLOW

Distribution .... EVEN

Fluorescence .... NONE

Comments:
Sample Sample Sample Sample Sample Sample

Additional Inscription .... FOREVER YOURS, JOHN

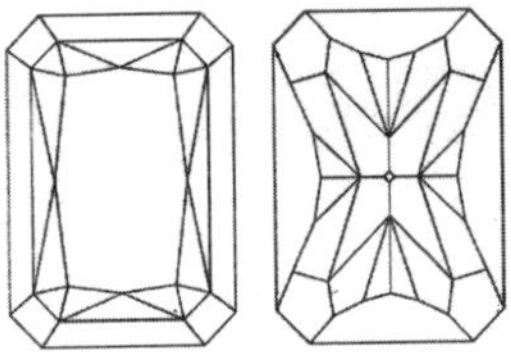

KEY TO SYMBOLS
Crystal
Feather
Natural

GIA CLARITY SCALE

FLAWLESS
INTERNALLY FLAWLESS
VVS_1, VVS_2 — VERY VERY SLIGHTLY INCLUDED
VS_1, VS_2 — VERY SLIGHTLY INCLUDED
SI_1, SI_2 — SLIGHTLY INCLUDED
I_1, I_2, I_3 — INCLUDED

GIA COLORED DIAMOND SCALE

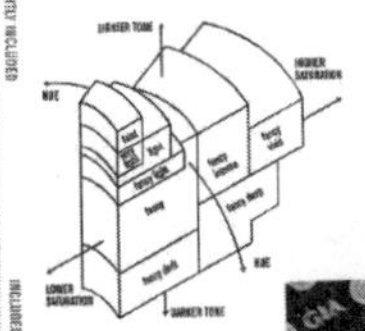

This Report is not a guarantee, valuation or appraisal. This Report contains only the characteristics of the diamond described herein after it has been graded, tested, examined and analyzed by GIA Gem Trade Laboratory under 10X magnification, and/or has been inscribed, using the techniques and equipment available to GIA Gem Trade Laboratory at the time of the examination and/or at the time of being inscribed, including fully corrected triplet loupe and binocular microscope, master color comparison diamonds, standardized viewing environment and light source, electronic carat balance, high intensity short wave fluorescence imaging system, optical measuring device, micro laser inscribing device, ProportionScope®, ultraviolet lamps, millimeter gauge, additional visual color comparators, spectroscope, Illuminator Polariscope®, immersion liquids, ultraviolet-visible and infrared spectrometers, X-ray fluorescence spectrometer, gamma-ray spectroscopy systems, beta radiation scintillation detector, radiation survey meter, X-ray luminescence equipment, and ancillary instruments as necessary. Red symbols denote internal characteristics (inclusions). Green or black symbols denote external characteristics (blemishes). Diagram is an approximate representation of the diamond, and symbols shown indicate type, position, and approximate size of clarity characteristics. All clarity characteristics may not be shown. Details of finish are not shown. The recipient of this Report may wish to consult a credentialed Jeweler or Gemologist about the importance and interrelationship of cut, color, clarity and carat weight.

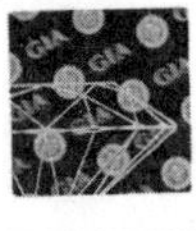

IMPORTANT DOCUMENT, STORE SAFELY

NOTICE: IMPORTANT LIMITATIONS ON BACK

Here you will find information indicating origin of color ("natural"), depth of color ("fancy"), and distribution ("even"), along with other essential information describing the overall quality. Note the information under "Comments." GIA will also issue reports pertaining to color only.

SOURCE: GIA GEM TRADE LABORATORY, © GEMOLOGICAL INSTITUTE OF AMERICA

SCHWEIZERISCHES GEMMOLOGISCHES INSTITUT
INSTITUT SUISSE DE GEMMOLOGIE
SWISS GEMMOLOGICAL INSTITUTE

SSEF

Gemstone Report
Expertise de pierre précieuse No. 35888
Edelstein-Expertise

Weight / Poids / Gewicht	2.046 ct
Cut / Taille / Schliff	octagonal, step cut
Measurements / Dimensions / Masse	7.71 x 7.54 x 4.91 mm
Colour / Couleur / Farbe	purplish red (fancy intense colour)
IDENTIFICATION / IDENTIFIKATION	D I A M O N D of natural coloration
Comments / Commentaires / Bemerkungen	The analysed properties confirm the authenticity of its coloration.

SAMPLE

Important note

The conclusions on this Gemstone Report reflect our findings at the time it is issued. A gemstone could be modified and / or enhanced at any time. Therefore, the SSEF may reconfirm at any time that a stone is in line with the Gemstone Report.

See other comments on reverse side.

Note importante

Les conclusions de cette expertise reflètent nos résultats au moment de son émission. A tout moment, une pierre précieuse, peut être modifiée et / ou son aspect amélioré. Par conséquent, le SSEF peut a tout moment contrôler la conformité entre la pierre et le certificat.

Voir autres commentaires au dos.

Wichtige Anmerkung

Die Befunde in dieser Edelstein - Expertise beschreiben den Zustand zum Zeitpunkt ihrer Erstellung. Ein Edelstein kann jederzeit verändert und / oder behandelt werden. Deshalb kann die SSEF die Übereinstimmung des Steins mit dem Zertifikat jederzeit nachprüfen.

Beachten Sie die Bemerkungen auf der Rückseite.

magnification 2.0x

SCHWEIZERISCHES GEMMOLOGISCHES INSTITUT
INSTITUT SUISSE DE GEMMOLOGIE
SWISS GEMMOLOGICAL INSTITUTE

SSEF

Basel, 17 July 2000 ss

Dr. L. Kiefert, FGA

Prof. Dr. H.A. Hänni, FGA

Falknerstrasse 9 CH-4001 Basel Tel. + 41 (0)61 262 06 40 Fax + 41 (0)61 262 06 41

This report provides essential information related to the color—depth ("Fancy Intense") and origin ("natural")—but there is no information about clarity or cutting. The lab provides more detailed reports, but the owner of this stone requested information pertaining to its color only.

SOURCE: SCHWEIZERISCHES GEMMOLOGISCHES INSTITUT (SWISS GEMMOLOGICAL INSTITUTE)

GÜBELIN
GEM LAB

DIAMANT-BERICHT · RAPPORT DE DIAMANT
DIAMOND REPORT

No.	**SPECIMEN**
Datum · Date	16 May 2001
Gewicht · Poids · Weight	**2.34 ct**
Schliff · Taille · Cut	pear-shape, brilliant cut
Abmessungen · Dimensions · Measurements	10.52 x 7.96 x 4.50 mm
Proportionen · Proportions · Proportions	
- Höhe · Hauteur · Depth	56.5 %
- Tafel · Table · Table	66 %
Rundiste · Rondiste · Girdle	medium to very thick
Kalette · Calette · Culet	none
Politur · Poli · Polish	**good**
Symmetrie · Symétrie · Symmetry	**good**

Innere Merkmale rot eingezeichnet, äussere Merkmale grün. Siehe Legende der Symbole. Caractéristiques internes marquées en rouge, caractéristiques externes en vert. Voir légende. Internal characteristics shown in red, external characteristics in green. See key to symbols.

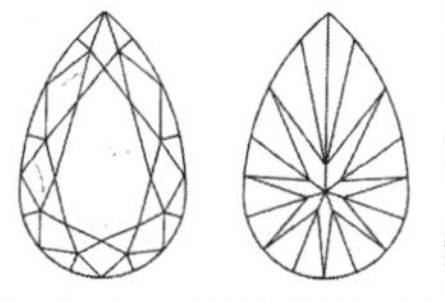

Reinheitsgrad · Degré de pureté · Clarity grade	VS 2
Farbgrad · Degré de couleur · Colour grade	**Fancy vivid yellow**
Fluoreszenz · Fluorescence · Fluorescence	medium yellow
Bemerkungen · Commentaires · Comments	Natural colour.

GEMMOLOGISCHES LABOR · LABORATOIRE GEMMOLOGIQUE · GEMMOLOGICAL LABORATORY
Maihofstrasse 102 · CH-6000 Lucerne 9 · Switzerland · Tel. (41) 41 - 429 17 17 · Fax (41) 41 - 429 17 34
www.gubelinlab.com · e-mail: gubelinlab@compuserve.com

Christopher P. Smith, G.G. C. Dunaigre, A.G., DUG

Wichtige Anmerkungen und Einschränkungen auf der Rückseite · Remarques au verso · Important notes and limitations on the reverse.

Here you will find information pertaining to the color, along with overall quality grading. Gübelin will also issue reports on color only.

SOURCE: GÜBELIN GEM LAB (SWISS)

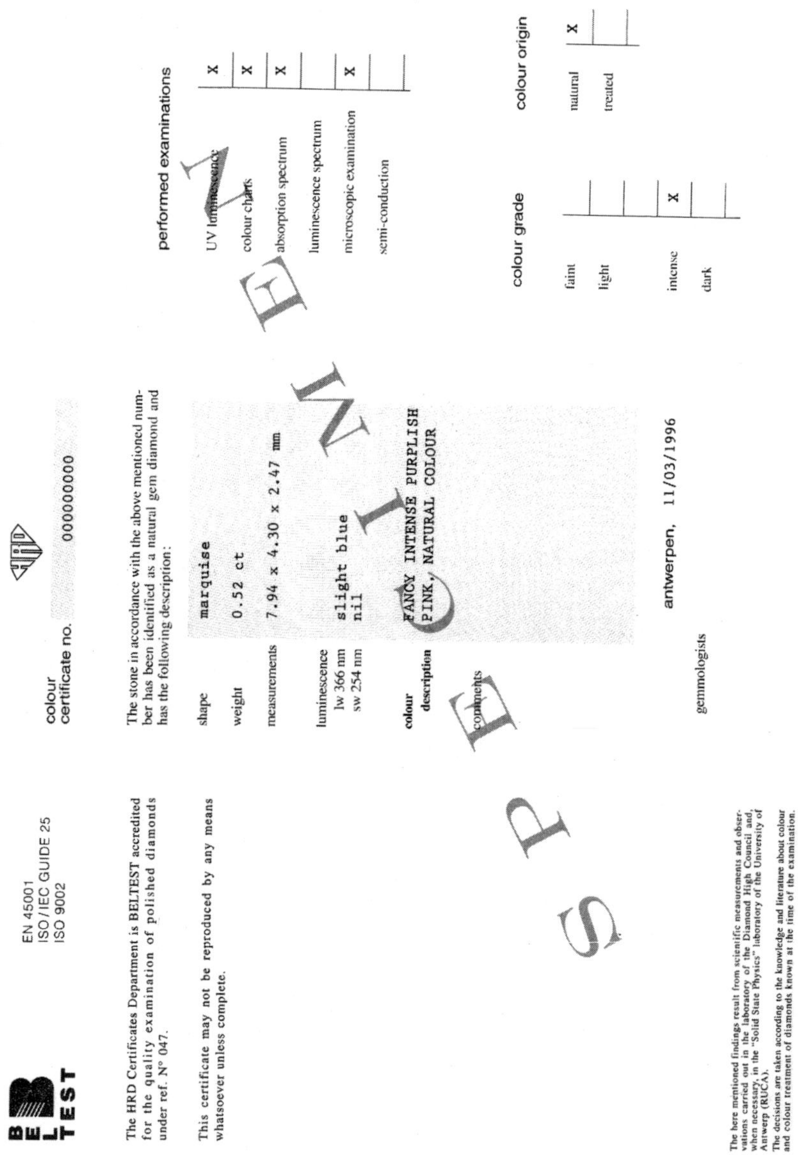
EN 45001
ISO/IEC GUIDE 25
ISO 9002

BELTEST

The HRD Certificates Department is BELTEST accredited for the quality examination of polished diamonds under ref. N° 047.

This certificate may not be reproduced by any means whatsoever unless complete.

colour certificate no. 000000000

The stone in accordance with the above mentioned number has been identified as a natural gem diamond and has the following description:

shape	marquise
weight	0.52 ct
measurements	7.94 x 4.30 x 2.47 mm
luminescence lw 366 nm	slight blue
sw 254 nm	nil
colour description	FANCY INTENSE PURPLISH PINK, NATURAL COLOUR
comments	

antwerpen, 11/03/1996

gemmologists

performed examinations

UV luminescence	X
colour charts	X
absorption spectrum	X
luminescence spectrum	
microscopic examination	X
semi-conduction	

colour grade

faint	
light	
intense	X
dark	

colour origin

natural	X
treated	

The here mentioned findings result from scientific measurements and observations carried out in the laboratory of the Diamond High Council and, when necessary, in the "Solid State Physics" laboratory of the University of Antwerp (RUCA).
The decisions are taken according to the knowledge and literature about colour and colour treatment of diamonds known at the time of the examination.

This report was issued to confirm color only—purity, depth, and origin—without information on clarity or cutting. Overall quality reports are also available.

SOURCE: HOGE RAAD VOOR DIAMANT (THE DIAMOND HIGH COUNCIL OF BELGIUM)

1242555

The Gem Testing Laboratory of Great Britain

SAMPLE

GEM TESTING REPORT

Examined a loose, yellow, oval, faceted stone, measuring approximately 16.30 x 12.15 x 7.85 mm. and weighing 10.20 ct.

Found to be a **NATURAL DIAMOND** of **NATURAL COLOUR.**

COLOUR GRADE : FANCY INTENSE YELLOW

The Gem Testing Laboratory of Great Britain is the official CIBJO recognised Laboratory for Great Britain

Only the original report with signatures and embossed stamp is a valid identification document.
This report is issued subject to the conditions printed overleaf.

The Gem Testing Laboratory of Great Britain

GAGTL, 27 Greville Street,
London, ECIN 8SU, Great Britain

Telephone: +44 171 405 3351
Fax: +44 171 831 9479

SAMPLE

Signed________________ Signed________________

Sarah Mahoney FGA DGA Stephen J. Kennedy FGA DGA

Date 21st May 2001

This report provides information about color only, but some reports include clarity and cutting.

Note: The Gem Testing Laboratory of Great Britain formally ceased grading diamonds and closed its laboratory in September 2008, but documents prior to this date are still in circulation and are seen in the marketplace.

SOURCE: THE GEM TESTING LABORATORY OF GREAT BRITAIN

CHAPTER THIRTEEN

Comparing Fancy Natural-Color and Treated-Color Diamond Prices

The following price charts are intended as a guide to help you understand the pricing of the many fancy-color diamond choices now available. In particular, they show how each of the four Cs affects the value of natural fancy-color diamonds, how their prices compare to color-treated diamonds, and a sampling of what rare fancy-color diamonds are bringing today at auction. Since some fancy-color diamonds are so rare, the auction arena often provides the best indication of current value.

*Retail Price Guide for Fancy Natural-Color Diamonds**

Prices are per carat in U.S. dollars.

C1–C4 TOP LIGHT BROWN				
Wt.	**FL–VVS**	**VS**	**SI**	**I_1**
Melee†	NA	1,250–2,500	1,060–1,750	875–1,250
¼ ct	NA	1,500–2,750	1,250–2,500	1,250–1,875
½ ct	NA	1,750–5,400	1,375–4,050	1,250–3,750
¾ ct	NA	1,875–7,500	1,500–4,950	1,375–3,825
1 ct	NA	3,250–9,000	3,125–7,000	1,750–5,175
2 ct	NA	4,050–8,000	3,825–7,600	1,875–6,180
3 ct	NA	6,075–9,600	4,500–10,000	3,750–7,200
4 ct	NA	7,000–12,000	6,750–11,000	5,400–8,000
5 ct	NA	10,000–15,000	9,600–14,000	6,750–10,000

* Retail prices are based on *The Guide*, Gemworld International, Inc., and adjusted to retail.
† Melee refers to small diamonds weighing less than ⅕ carat (usually between 0.001 to 0.19 carat).

C5–C7 FANCY LIGHT BROWN TO FANCY BROWN				
Wt.	FL–VVS	VS	SI	I_1
Melee†	NA	1,375–2,625	1,125–1,875	1,000–1,500
¼ ct	NA	1,625–3,000	1,375–3,000	1,250–2,000
½ ct	NA	1,875–6,400	1,500–4,500	1,310–3,710
¾ ct	NA	3,000–6,600	1,625–5,400	1,500–3,940
1 ct	NA	3,750–7,000	3,375–7,500	1,875–5,625
2 ct	NA	4,500–10,000	3,940–8,000	2,750–6,750
3 ct	NA	6,750–12,000	5,625–10,400	3,710–9,000
4 ct	NA	7,200–13,000	6,400–12,000	5,625–10,000
5 ct	NA	11,000–16,000	10,000–15,000	6,400–11,000

FANCY LIGHT YELLOW				
Wt.	FL–VVS	VS	SI	I_1
Melee†	810–1,500	680–1,430	625–1,310	500–1,060
¼ ct	1,625–3,500	1,250–3,000	1,125–2,500	1,000–1,625
½ ct	4,500–5,400	3,750–4,500	3,250–4,050	2,000–2,250
¾ ct	5,175–5,625	4,500–5,175	3,600–4,275	3,000–3,750
1 ct	7,200–7,600	5,625–7,000	4,500–5,625	3,750–4,500
2 ct	9,000–11,000	7,000–8,000	6,600–7,600	6,000–6,600
3 ct	10,000–11,000	8,000–10,000	7,200–8,000	6,400–7,000
4 ct	10,000–11,600	9,000–11,000	8,400–9,400	7,600–8,000
5 ct	13,000–15,000	12,000–14,000	11,000–13,000	9,000–10,000

FANCY YELLOW				
Wt.	FL–VVS	VS	SI	I_1
Melee†	1,625–3,125	1,500–2,750	825–2,500	625–2,125
¼ ct	3,250–5,625	3,375–4,725	2,125–4,950	1,375–3,750
½ ct	6,750–8,000	5,625–7,200	4,725–5,625	4,050–4,500
¾ ct	6,600–9,000	6,750–8,000	5,400–6,400	4,725–5,625
1 ct	9,000–13,000	7,000–11,000	6,750–11,000	6,400–7,600
2 ct	16,000–19,000	14,000–17,000	11,000–14,000	10,000–11,600
3 ct	17,000–19,950	14,400–18,600	13,800–16,600	11,000–12,400
4 ct	18,000–21,090	16,400–20,520	14,600–17,200	11,800–13,200
5 ct	19,000–25,080	18,000–23,750	16,000–18,000	12,600–14,400

* Retail prices are based on *The Guide*, Gemworld International, Inc., and adjusted to retail.

† Melee refers to small diamonds weighing less than ⅕ carat (usually between 0.001 to 0.19 carat).

FANCY INTENSE YELLOW				
Wt.	**FL–VVS**	**VS**	**SI**	**I_1**
Melee†	NA	NA	NA	NA
¼ ct	NA	NA	NA	NA
½ ct	6,800–8,400	6,700–7,600	6,000–7,000	4,500–6,075
¾ ct	11,000–12,600	9,600–12,000	8,600–9,800	6,700–7,800
1 ct	13,600–17,400	13,000–16,600	10,000–15,000	7,600–9,000
2 ct	20,330–23,560	20,000–22,800	16,000–20,000	11,000–13,600
3 ct	21,850–25,650	22,800–26,600	18,000–20,900	12,000–14,000
4 ct	25,080–33,250	26,600–30,400	19,400–21,850	13,000–15,400
5 ct	28,310–34,200	26,790–32,110	21,470–25,650	14,000–16,200

FANCY LIGHT PINK				
Wt.	**FL–VVS**	**VS**	**SI**	**I_1**
Melee†	3,625–4,050	2,750–3,600	2,500–3,500	2,250–3,375
¼ ct	7,200–9,600	6,600–8,600	6,000–8,000	5,850–7,200
½ ct	15,600–20,000	13,200–19,000	12,000–14,400	5,400–9,600
¾ ct	34,200–38,000	26,600–34,200	19,950–27,550	14,400–19,000
1 ct	39,900–47,500	36,100–45,600	34,200–40,850	25,080–29,450
2 ct	108,000–135,000	90,000–117,000	63,000–86,400	45,600–54,000
3 ct	118,800–161,500	126,000–153,000	97,200–132,600	64,800–75,600
4 ct	187,000–221,000	153,000–212,500	129,600–144,500	108,000–118,800
5 ct	238,000–255,000	204,000–224,400	161,500–204,000	129,600–163,200

FANCY PINK				
Wt.	**FL–VVS**	**VS**	**SI**	**I_1**
Melee†	NA	NA	NA	NA
¼ ct	31,350–60,300	24,700–49,500	22,800–45,600	11,000–20,900
½ ct	69,300–99,000	59,400–89,100	41,800–87,300	20,900–31,350
¾ ct	81,000–108,900	70,200–117,000	54,000–90,000	31,350–41,800
1 ct	135,000–170,000	108,000–136,000	90,000–135,000	48,600–68,400
2 ct	212,500–288,750	153,000–212,500	117,000–161,500	59,400–81,000
3 ct	280,500–453,750	233,750–363,000	168,300–238,000	136,000–187,000
4 ct	313,500–453,750	313,500–396,000	229,500–264,000	153,000–204,000
5 ct	437,250–600,000	363,000–520,000	272,250–520,000	264,000–387,750

* Retail prices are based on *The Guide*, Gemworld International, Inc., and adjusted to retail.
† Melee refers to small diamonds weighing less than ⅕ carat (usually between 0.001 to 0.19 carat).

FANCY BLUE				
Wt.	FL–VVS	VS	SI	I_1
Melee†	NA	NA	NA	NA
¼ ct	NA	NA	NA	NA
½ ct	117,000–126,000	76,500–117,000	58,500–81,000	41,800–49,500
¾ ct	135,000–144,500	99,000–136,000	79,200–99,000	59,400–69,300
1 ct	221,000–255,000	187,000–221,000	153,000–187,000	135,000–168,300
2 ct	313,500–396,000	272,250–363,000	229,500–321,750	99,000–136,000
3 ct	453,750–640,000	387,750–600,000	363,000–495,000	233,750–313,500
4 ct	520,000–680,000	495,000–640,000	404,250–528,000	272,250–363,000
5 ct	680,000–960,000	640,000–880,000	528,000–704,000	363,000–453,750

* Retail prices are based on *The Guide*, Gemworld International, Inc., and adjusted to retail.
† Melee refers to small diamonds weighing less than ⅕ carat (usually between 0.001 to 0.19 carat).

*Retail Price Guide for Fancy-Color Permanently Enhanced/Treated Diamonds**

Prices are per carat in U.S. dollars.

FANCY INTENSE IMPERIAL RED, INTENSE PINK								
Weight	VVS_1	VVS_2	VS_1	VS_2	SI_1	SI_2	I_1	I_2
0.01–0.09	3,300	3,170	3,030	2,890	2,750	2,620	2,200	1,790
0.10–0.19	4,950	4,750	4,540	4,340	4,130	3,920	3,300	2,690
0.20–0.29	6,770	6,490	6,210	5,920	5,640	5,360	4,510	3,670
0.30–0.39	7,920	7,590	7,260	6,930	6,600	6,270	5,280	4,290
0.40–0.49	8,250	7,910	7,570	7,220	6,880	6,540	5,500	4,470
0.50–0.59	9,900	9,490	9,080	8,670	8,250	7,840	6,600	5,370
0.60–0.69	10,560	10,120	9,680	9,240	8,800	8,360	7,040	5,720
0.70–0.79	11,220	10,760	10,290	9,820	9,350	8,890	7,480	6,080
0.80–0.89	11,880	11,390	10,890	10,400	9,900	9,410	7,920	6,440
0.90–0.99	12,540	12,020	11,500	10,980	10,450	9,930	8,360	6,800
1.00–1.24	17,820	17,080	16,340	15,600	14,850	14,110	9,900	8,050
1.25–1.49	19,800	18,980	18,150	17,330	16,500	15,680	11,000	8,940

* Retail prices are based on information provided by Lucent Diamonds.

*Retail Price Guide for HPHT-Treated Fancy-Color Diamonds**

Prices are per carat in U.S. dollars.

FANCY YELLOW, FANCY ORANGY YELLOW, FANCY GREENISH YELLOW									
Weight	VVS_1	VVS_2	VS_1	VS_2	SI_1	SI_2	I_1	I_2	I_3
0.01–0.07	1,390	1,320	1,280	1,210	1,100	990	770	730	510
0.08–0.17	1,650	1,590	1,520	1,460	1,320	1,130	800	660	530
0.18–0.29	1,890	1,830	1,750	1,680	1,520	1,310	930	760	610
0.30–0.37	2,460	2,380	2,270	2,170	1,980	1,790	1,200	800	700
0.38–0.49	2,970	2,840	2,730	2,610	2,380	2,150	1,430	950	840
0.50–0.69	4,400	4,230	4,040	3,870	3,530	3,170	2,120	1,420	1,060
0.70–0.89	5,280	5,070	4,850	4,640	4,230	3,800	2,550	1,710	1,280
0.90–0.99	5,790	5,570	5,330	5,120	4,640	4,180	2,790	1,880	1,400
1.00–1.24	6,960	6,680	6,390	6,120	5,570	5,020	3,340	2,240	1,680
1.25–1.49	7,500	7,200	6,890	6,580	6,000	5,390	3,600	2,400	1,810
1.50–1.99	8,610	8,280	7,920	7,570	6,890	6,210	4,140	2,780	2,070
2.00–2.99	9,900	9,500	9,100	8,720	7,920	7,130	4,750	3,180	2,380
3.00–3.99	11,870	11,400	10,930	10,460	9,500	8,560	5,720	3,810	2,870

FANCY INTENSE YELLOW, FANCY INTENSE ORANGY YELLOW, FANCY INTENSE GREENISH YELLOW, FANCY INTENSE YELLOWISH GREEN									
Weight	VVS_1	VVS_2	VS_1	VS_2	SI_1	SI_2	I_1	I_2	I_3
0.01–0.07	1,850	1,790	1,720	1,630	1,480	1,350	1,040	970	690
0.08–0.17	2,230	2,140	2,050	1,960	1,790	1,520	1,080	910	730
0.18–0.29	2,570	2,460	2,360	2,250	2,040	1,750	1,240	1,030	820
0.30–0.37	3,320	3,200	3,050	2,920	2,650	2,400	1,600	1,080	950
0.38–0.49	3,970	3,830	3,660	3,510	3,200	2,880	1,920	1,290	1,120
0.50–0.69	5,910	5,670	5,430	5,210	4,730	4,250	2,840	1,900	1,420
0.70–0.89	7,080	6,800	6,530	6,240	5,670	5,120	3,410	2,280	1,710
0.90–0.99	7,800	7,490	7,180	6,870	6,240	5,620	3,750	2,500	1,880
1.00–1.24	9,360	8,980	8,600	8,240	7,490	6,750	4,490	3,000	2,260
1.25–1.49	10,060	9,660	9,260	8,860	8,070	7,270	4,850	3,220	2,430
1.50–1.99	11,590	11,120	10,650	10,200	9,260	8,350	5,570	3,720	2,800
2.00–2.99	13,310	12,790	12,250	11,730	10,650	9,590	6,400	4,280	3,200
3.00–3.99	15,980	15,330	14,690	14,060	12,790	11,500	7,670	5,130	3,840

* Retail prices are based on information provided by Lucent Diamonds.

*Auction Prices of Fancy-Color Diamonds (A Sampling)**

Prices are per carat in U.S. dollars.

Color	Shape	Weight	Clarity	Approx. Price per Carat
Red	round	.95	not graded	926,000
Red	oval	.25	not graded	326,000
Vivid Purplish Pink	oval	3.10	not graded	592,000
Intense Pink	emerald-cut	24.78	VVS_2	1,860,000
Intense Pink	heart	2.05	VS_2	125,000
Intense Orangey Pink	emerald-cut	6.82	SI_1	68,000
Pink	radiant	1.12	not graded	56,000
Light Pink	cushion	4.27	VS_1	22,500
Light Purplish Pink	radiant	1.74	VS_1	29,000
Light Orangey Pink	pear	15.66	not graded	10,500
Very Light Pink	emerald-cut	2.52	VS_2	7,500
Vivid Blue (*Bulgari* Blue)	triangular brilliant	10.95	VS_2	1,590,000†
Vivid Blue	cushion	7.03	not graded	1,350,000
Vivid Blue	trilliant	3.32	IF	294,000
Deep Blue (Wittelsbach-Graff)	cushion	35.56 (recut 31.06)	IF	684,000
Vivid Greenish Blue	cushion	1.62	VVS_2	1,051,636
Intense Blue	round	3.17	not graded	796,000
Intense Blue	heart	.58	not graded	59,000
Blue	marquise	6.21	SI_2	224,000
Blue	round	.90	VS_1	80,000
Vivid Green	cushion	2.52	not graded	1,222,000
Grayish Yellowish Green	radiant	2.71	not graded	24,200
Vivid Yellow (pair)	round	4.57, 4.74	IF, VS_1	64,250
Vivid Yellow	radiant	30.39	SI_1	27,500
Vivid Yellow	radiant	1.02	SI_1	11,500
Intense Yellow	heart	17.29	IF	24,000
Intense Yellow (pair)	pear	2.13, 2.31	IF, IF	18,000
Intense Yellow	pear	2.16	SI_2	12,000
Yellow	emerald-cut	18.00	VS_2	43,000
Yellow	radiant	2.18	VS_2	16,000
Yellow	radiant	1.24	VVS_1	12,500
Yellow	radiant	6.21	SI_1	7,500
Yellow	oval	1.84	not graded	6,000
Brownish Yellow	emerald-cut	13.12	VVS_2	6,000

* Based on prices at Christie's and Sotheby's from 2005–2010.

† Price reflects cost of ring containing the vivid "*Bulgari* Blue" and a 9.87-carat near-colorless (G) VS_1.

CHAPTER FOURTEEN

A Word about Synthetic Diamonds

Synthetic diamonds are diamonds that are made in the laboratory; they are also called lab- or laboratory-*created*, lab- or laboratory-*grown*, or *cultured* diamonds. These terms, including the term *cultured diamond*, have been approved in some countries but not in all; in the United States any of these terms may be used (but "cultured" may be used only when it is clear that the diamond is made in a laboratory and not mined from the earth).

Unlike imitations such as cubic zirconia (CZ), gadolinium gallium garnet (GGG), yttrium aluminum garnet (YAG), synthetic moissanite, and all other diamond imposters (which differ from diamond physically and chemically), synthetic diamond *duplicates* the natural. That is, it is scientifically produced in a laboratory using nature's "recipe," so a synthetic diamond has essentially the same physical and chemical properties as natural diamond. In essence, synthetic diamond *is* diamond.

Synthetic jewelry-quality diamonds are now available in a range of sizes, shapes, and colors. Yellow stones ranging from lemon yellow to orange yellow are readily available in sizes up to 3 carats, and larger stones in the 4-carat range have also been produced, although these are not readily available. Pink stones are being produced up to approximately 1 carat, although most are smaller, and blue stones are now readily available from melee sizes up to under ½ carat, and some have even exceeded 1 carat. DeBeers recently obtained a patent for producing laboratory-grown blue diamonds, so we may find larger synthetic blue diamonds available in the not-too-distant future. Fancy-color synthetic diamonds are finding a niche in the marketplace because they provide very beautiful alternatives to their much rarer—and much costlier—natural counterparts.

Where colorless and near-colorless synthetic diamonds are concerned, major strides are now being made. Color is improving and stones are now being produced with much less tint to the body color. Sizes are also increasing. In 2010, Apollo Diamond produced the first near-colorless faceted diamond over one carat, using chemical vapor deposition (CVD) "single-crystal" growth techniques (as opposed to CVD *thin film*, from which gem diamonds cannot be cut). It was submitted to GIA for documentation and was identified as a laboratory-grown pear-shape diamond weighing 1.05 carats, G color, with a clarity grade of I_1. Another CVD near-colorless diamond was subsequently produced by Gemesis Diamond Company, weighing 1.11 carats, described by International Gemological Institute (IGI) as I color, VVS_2 clarity. Smaller stones are being produced with even higher colors—many in the G–H color range—and some have even been graded F color on the GIA scale. Clarity grades are also improving, with more stones being graded in the VVS, VS, and SI ranges.

Since synthetic diamonds are grown in laboratories, gemological testing reveals distinctive growth features not seen in natural diamonds. These features make it possible to distinguish all synthetic diamonds now being produced from natural diamonds. Some may be identified with relatively simple testing that can be done in any gemological laboratory, but many require sophisticated scientific instrumentation found only in major gem-testing laboratories. For this reason, I once again stress the importance of having laboratory documentation for any fine diamond represented as natural. *Note:* Electronic diamond testers have become very popular and are very effective in distinguishing diamonds from all diamond *imitations* (such as those mentioned above and in chapter 10). They cannot, however, distinguish between synthetic and natural diamonds, and testers *will* indicate "diamond" when testing synthetic diamond because synthetic diamond *is* diamond, physically and chemically.

Synthetic diamonds are still difficult to find in jewelry stores; most are being sold on the Internet by the companies producing them, usually already set in a lovely piece of jewelry and often using multiple stones to create distinctive designs.

The cost to produce synthetic diamonds remains high—the larger the costlier—so while less costly than their natural counterparts, synthetic diamonds are not inexpensive. Even so, producers are having trouble keeping up with demand, especially from those concerned about human rights violations in some diamond-producing countries or about the effects of mining on the environment.

Retail Prices of Colorless Synthetic Diamonds (A Representative Sampling)

Prices are per carat in U.S. dollars.

COLORLESS ROUNDS				
Weight	Shape	Color	Clarity	Price
.34	round	F	VVS_2	2,800*
.45	round	G	VS_1	2,380*
.54	round	I	SI_1	1,900*
.58	princess	I	IF	2,825*
.59	round	G	VS_1	3,800*
.64	round	G	VVS_1	4,600*
.65	round	H	SI_1	2,150*
.69	emerald	G	VS_1	3,040*
.70	round	G	VS_2	3,420†
.72	round	H	VVS_1	3,340†
.77	round	G	VS_1	3,450†
.79	round	I	VS_1	3,400*

* Retail prices are based on actual stones sold by Apollo Diamond. Apollo Diamond produces laboratory-grown diamonds sold as *Apollo Cultured Diamonds* with a notation that they are "man-made" to comply with FTC guidelines. They are producing colorless/near colorless, pink, chocolate brown, and yellow at this time, in both round and fancy shapes. Most of Apollo's colorless production is under 1.25 carats, although size is increasing and a 2-carat stone has been produced. Production is currently sold directly to consumers in finished jewelry, including earrings, multistone rings, tennis bracelets (up to 10-carat total weight), and assorted necklaces in which the stones have been carefully matched. All stones over .25 carats are laser marked with an Apollo Cultured Diamond serial number. All stones are graded by GIA-trained diamond graders and are based on criteria established for grading natural diamonds. Some have been issued GIA reports.

† Retail prices are based on actual stones sold by Gemesis Diamond Company, which produces lab-created (or *cultured*) diamonds in a range of shapes and sizes. They are focusing on producing stones with high clarity grades in the VVS–VS range. Their fancy-color yellow stones occur in a range of shades from lemon yellow to orange yellow; pink and blue colors are often "vivid" or "intense" in tone. Gemesis is also producing near-colorless stones ranging from G–I color. Yellow stones are readily available up to 3 carats, although larger stones have been cut; pink and blue stones are typically under 1 carat, although stones weighing 1 carat or more have also been produced. Near-colorless stones are also typically under 1 carat, although larger stones have been produced. Production is currently sold directly to consumers, often in finished jewelry but also loose (unmounted), with the inscription "Gemesis" on the girdle. Most stones are accompanied by laboratory reports issued by International Gemological Institute (IGI).

*Retail Price Guide for Fancy-Color Synthetic Diamonds**

Prices are per carat in U.S. dollars.

PINK ROUNDS			
0.01–0.99 carat	**VS**	**SI**	**I**
Pink to Raspberry	2,500–12,320	2,075–8,300	1,200–5,040
Peachy Pink	1,825–6,860	1,500–6,435	1,100–4,680
Champagne Pink	1,500–6,750	1,250–5,625	1,000–4,500
Vintage Pink	1,350–5,400	1,125–4,500	900–3,600
1.00–1.99 carats	**VS**	**SI**	**I**
Pink to Raspberry	14,140–17,900	11,740–14,880	5,400–6,400
Peachy Pink	7,380–10,040	6,160–8,360	5,040–6,080
Champagne Pink	6,480–8,880	6,075–7,400	4,860–5,920
Vintage Pink	5,940–7,200	4,950–6,750	3,960–5,400

BLUE ROUNDS			
0.01–0.99 carat	**VS**	**SI**	**I**
True Blue	2,500–12,320	2,075–8,300	1,200–5,040
Sky Blue	2,200–10,980	1,800–9,160	1,100–4,680
Navy Blue	1,500–7,500	1,250–5,625	1,000–4,500
Midnight Blue	1,350–5,400	1,125–4,500	900–3,600
1.00–1.99 carats	**VS**	**SI**	**I**
True Blue	14,140–17,900	11,740–14,880	5,400–6,400
Sky Blue	11,800–16,060	9,860–13,380	5,040–6,080
Navy Blue	6,480–8,880	6,075–7,400	4,860–5,920
Midnight Blue	5,940–7,200	4,950–6,750	3,960–5,400

YELLOW ROUNDS			
0.01–0.99 carat	**VS**	**SI**	**I**
Canary Yellow	2,375–6,580	1,975–6,165	1,100–3,800
Marigold Yellow	1,350–4,860	1,125–4,050	900–3,600
Amber Yellow	1,200–4,320	1,000–3,600	800–3,200
1.00–2.99 carats	**VS**	**SI**	**I**
Canary Yellow	7,260–10,360	6,060–8,640	3,780–5,400
Marigold Yellow	5,400–6,960	4,500–6,525	3,600–5,220
Amber Yellow	4,590–5,940	3,825–4,950	3,400–3,960

* Retail prices are based on information provided for Chatham Created Pink, Blue, and Yellow Diamonds; pink, blue, and yellow synthetic diamonds are also available from Apollo Diamond and Gemesis Diamond Company.

PART THREE

Design & Style

Getting the Look You Want ... and Keeping It That Way

CHAPTER FIFTEEN

Choosing the Right Metal

The color of the metal in a setting can affect the appearance of the color of the stone—sometimes adversely and sometimes beneficially. A very white diamond will look whiter in a white metal such as white gold, platinum, or palladium. If you prefer yellow gold, it's possible to have just the portion of the setting that holds the diamond itself fashioned in white metal. For example, a diamond can be set in a yellow gold design that uses a white metal "head" (the part that actually holds the diamond itself in the setting).

An all-yellow setting may make a very white diamond appear less white because the yellow color of the setting itself is reflected into the diamond. On the other hand, if the diamond you choose tends to be more yellow than you'd like, mounting it in yellow, with yellow surrounding the stone, may make the stone appear whiter in contrast to the strong yellow of the metal. Where fancy-color diamonds are concerned, a yellow environment may intensify the yellow appearance in a fancy yellow diamond, while it might adversely affect other fancy colors.

So the answer to "What is the right metal?" depends both on personal preference and the color of the diamond. Whenever buying an unmounted diamond—which we recommend when buying larger, rarer stones—try to view the diamond in both white metals and in the various shades of gold (yellow, rose, green) now available. Notice the impact of the color of the metal on the color of your diamond.

Once you decide on a color, the following information can help you decide which metal best meets your needs.

Gold—The Timeless Choice

Gold jewelry is very popular today and is available in more styles, colors, and finishes than ever before. It is also a very popular choice for setting gemstones. But it is very important to understand gold and the differences that affect price in order to avoid confusion about the wide range of prices that seems to pervade the market for what may *appear* to be the "same thing." As with gems, wherever there are significant price differences there are usually quality differences. The key to getting good value in gold is understanding what accounts for differences in quality and price.

Gold is one of the world's most precious metals. It is so soft and workable that one ounce can be stretched into a wire five miles long or hammered into a sheet so thin that it could cover a hundred square feet. It is one of our rarest metals, and since pure gold doesn't rust or corrode, it can last forever. Interestingly, gold is present almost everywhere around us—in the earth's crust, in seas and rivers, and in plants—but it is very difficult and expensive to extract. Approximately two-and-a-half to three tons of ore are needed to extract one ounce of gold.

Most Gold Used in Jewelry Is an Alloy

Gold is the most popular metal used for jewelry today. The simple gold wedding band probably accounts for more of the world's gold than any other single type of jewelry. But pure gold is very soft, so it is usually mixed with other metals to make it stronger and prevent it from bending too easily. When two or more metals are mixed together, we call the resulting product an *alloy*. Most gold used in jewelry is an alloy—and the metals added to the gold are also called alloys.

What Is a Karat? Or Is It Carat?

In jewelry, the term *carat* (or karat) has a double meaning: *carat* is used as a measurement of weight for gemstones, with one carat weighing ⅕ gram; *carat* is also used in countries around the world to indicate the amount of pure gold in a piece of gold jewelry. In the United States, however, when the word is used to indicate gold content rather than gemstone weight, it is spelled with a K—hence *karat*—to avoid confusion. Jewelry should always be marked to indicate how much pure gold it contains.

In the United States, a karat mark, abbreviated to K or KT, indicates the amount of pure gold present in the metal. The word *karat* (carat) is derived from the word for the fruit of the carob tree: in Italian, *carato*; in Arabic, *qirat*; in Greek, *keration*. The seeds of the fruit were used in ancient times for weighing gems. Also, the pure gold Byzantine coin called the solidus weighed 24 karats. Therefore, a 24-karat mark (24K or 24KT) became the mark used to indicate that something was pure gold.

To understand the concept as applied to gold, imagine that "pure gold" is a pie divided into 24 equal "slices," or parts. Each karat equals one part of the pie. So, 24K would mean that 24 parts (out of a total of 24) are gold. In other words, 24K would be 100 percent gold, or pure gold. In 18K gold jewelry, 18 parts are pure gold and 6 are another metal (or, 18/24 = ¾ = 75 percent pure gold); in 12K, 12 parts are pure gold, 12 parts another metal (12/24 = ½ = 50 percent pure gold). And so on.

In some cultures, 24K gold jewelry is required for certain jewelry pieces, but it's generally agreed that 24K (pure) gold is too soft for jewelry use. In some parts of the world, 18K or 20K is preferred because of its brighter yellow color and because it is considered "purer" and more precious. In the United States, 14K or 18K gold is preferred because it is more durable than higher-karat gold. We usually caution clients about the risk of high-karat gold (20K, 22K, or 24K) for a gem-studded setting because the prongs can be too easily bent open accidentally, resulting in loss of stones.

In some countries, such as Italy, the percentage of pure gold is indicated by a number representing how many parts—out of a total of 1,000 parts—are pure gold. One thousand parts would be the equivalent of 24K. Seven hundred fifty means that 750 parts out of 1,000 are pure gold: 750/1,000 = 75/100 = ¾ = 75 percent pure gold. This corresponds to 18K.

Comparison of Gold Content Markings

American Marking (Karatage)	Pure Gold Content (Fineness in Percent)	European Marking
24K	100	1,000
22K	91.6	916
20K	83	833
19K (used in Portugal)	79.2	792
18K	75.0	750
15K (seen in antiques)	62.5	625
14K	58.3	585
12K	50.0	500
10K	41.7	417
9K	37.5	375

New Titanium Alloy Increases Strength and Versatility

A new alloy—gold 990—combines gold with a very small amount of titanium. The result is almost pure gold (990/1,000 gold), with greatly increased durability. The titanium produces a color that is much less yellow than what one expects from such a high-karat gold, closely resembling straw and similar to the color of 14K gold. This has reduced its universal appeal. Nonetheless, it offers the preciousness of high-karat gold with added durability.

A Word about Russian Marks

Old timepieces made in Russia were marked to indicate the content based on its equivalent to a zolotnik. A piece marked 96 contained as much gold as 96 zolotniks, which equals pure gold; 72 equals 18K (750); 56 equals 14K (585).

To Be Called Gold, What Is the Minimum Gold Content?

Many countries have established minimum standards that must be met for items to be legally called gold. The laws governing the actual content of gold required in a piece of jewelry, however, vary. In the United States, to be called gold, the item must be at least 10K; in England and Canada, 9K; in Italy and France, 18K.

The Many Colors of Gold

Pure gold is always yellow. But because pure gold is too soft for most jewelry use and must be mixed with other metals (alloys) to increase its hardness, the color can also be modified by adding varying amounts of these other metals. Those usually added to gold for jewelry use include copper, zinc, silver, nickel, platinum, and palladium (a metal in the platinum family). Depending on which alloys are used, a variety of colors can be produced. Another practice is to plate 14K gold jewelry with 18K for an 18K look—that is, a stronger yellow color. White gold is also frequently plated with rhodium, a rare and more expensive metal from the platinum family, to create a whiter, brighter finish.

Using some combination of one or more metal alloys will result in various colors. Several avant-garde designers are now producing jewelry in exciting new colors—including *black* gold, *brown* gold, and *blue* gold—to create dramatic new looks.

What causes skin discoloration with some gold jewelry? Pure gold doesn't tarnish and won't discolor the skin, but *alloys* in the gold can corrode and produce discoloration to the skin in contact with the gold, especially under moist or damp conditions. The fats and fatty acids present in perspiration can set up a corrosive reaction, and the problem can be worse in warm, humid areas, especially where chloride (salt) is in the air.

Smog can also be a problem. Smog fumes can introduce chemicals that cause the alloys in gold to tarnish. The tarnish then rubs off, discoloring skin or clothing.

Cosmetics may be the culprit. Another common cause of discoloration is metallic abrasion caused by some makeup. Some makeup contains compounds that are actually harder than the jewelry with which it comes into contact. As the harder compounds rub against the jewelry they cause tiny particles of metal to flake off, forming a darkish-looking dust. When this dust makes contact with a soft, absorbent surface such as skin or clothing, it forms a black smudge.

There are several possible solutions to the problem of skin discoloration. First, get into the habit of removing jewelry often and cleansing the skin that has touched it with soap and water. Keep your jewelry clean as well, and wipe it periodically with a soft cloth to remove tarnish. Next, try using an absorbent body powder, one free of abrasives, on all areas of your skin that are in contact with jewelry.

How Alloys Affect Gold Color

Color	Composition
Yellow gold	Gold, copper, silver
White gold	Gold, nickel,* zinc, silver, platinum, palladium
Green gold	Gold, silver (much more than in yellow gold), copper, zinc
Pink (red) gold	Gold, copper (sometimes a small amount of silver is used)

* *Note:* Some people are allergic to nickel and should not wear white gold containing nickel. For this reason, a white gold alloyed with palladium is being used by some manufacturers. White gold that contains palladium will be more expensive than yellow gold or white gold containing another alloy, but it is still less expensive than all platinum.

Pay attention to the design of jewelry you select if skin discoloration seems to be a problem. Wide shanks can cause perspiration, and rings with an inner concave surface can cause moisture and contaminants to collect, causing both discoloration and dermatitis.

Finally, try switching to a higher gold content or to a different manufacturer. The higher the gold content, the less likely it is that discoloration will occur, because in the higher-karat gold there is less of the alloy—such as copper, silver, or nickel—that might corrode. People who have a problem wearing 14K gold jewelry may find that the problem disappears with 18K gold.

Sometimes simply changing to a similar product made by a different manufacturer may solve the problem. For example, a 14K yellow gold bracelet made by one manufacturer may cause discoloration, while a similar bracelet made by another manufacturer may not. This does not mean that one product is inferior to the other. Manufacturers often use different combinations of alloys, or different percentages or ratios of alloys. They may look the same, but you might find you can wear one manufacturer's line better than that of another.

Since different metals and different ratios are used to produce different colors, discoloration may result when you are wearing one particular color of gold but not with other colors. If there seems to be a problem with wearing white gold, try a white gold alloyed with platinum rather than nickel, since platinum won't corrode.

Determining Value Requires More Than a Scale!

Weight is one factor that goes into determining the value of a piece of gold jewelry. Gold is usually sold by weight, in grams or pennyweights. There are 20 pennyweights to one ounce; if you multiply grams by 0.643, you will have the number of pennyweights. Weight is important because it is an indication of the actual amount of pure gold in the piece. However, it is only one factor to consider. When you are buying gold from a gold manufacturer, for example, factored into the price per gram is the cost of gold *plus* the cost for labor and workmanship. The price always takes into consideration (1) the type of *construction,* (2) the means of *production,* and (3) how the piece is *finished.*

Design and construction are important not only because of the piece's finished look but also because specific details in the overall design and construction affect comfort, wearability, and ease in putting the piece on or taking it off. Good design requires excellent designers as well as extra care and attention to small mechanical details. This adds to the cost of any piece of jewelry.

In addition, jewelry design is also becoming recognized as an art, and jewelry designers as artists. Some award-winning designers command top dollar, as do top painters, sculptors, and other artists. A piece of gold jewelry made by a fine designer, especially if it is a one-of-a-kind or limited-edition piece, will sometimes sell for much more than another piece of mass-produced gold jewelry of the same weight and gold content.

In looking at a piece of gold jewelry, you must also consider the type of construction necessary to create a particular design or look. Is the construction simple or complex? Did the piece require extensive labor or minimal labor? Did it require special skill, talent, or equipment?

To ignore the design and construction factors and assign a value to a piece of gold jewelry based on gold content (i.e., 14K, 18K) and weight alone would be equivalent to placing a value on a painting based on the cost of paint and canvas alone.

Production can affect price significantly. Is the piece produced by machine or by hand? The type of construction required to create a particular design may require that it be made entirely, or in part, by hand, while others can be completely made by machine. Some designs may be produced either way, but those done by hand will have a different look, feel, and cost.

Finish is where we take into account the care and labor costs associated with the actual finishing of the piece. For example, are any special skills or techniques required to put on the final touches that make the piece distinctive, such as engraving, milgraining, hammering, or granulation? Here we also need to note whether or not the piece has been carefully polished to remove any scratches that might diminish its beauty, or rough edges that might be abrasive or catch or snag on fabric. Consider whether the item was hand polished or machine polished; some pieces are machine made but finished by hand. We must also take into consideration any special finishes to the metal itself, such as a florentine, matte, or sand-blasted finish. Each step in the process, and each special step or skill required, adds—sometimes dramatically—to the cost.

Adding It All Up

Many pieces of gold jewelry look alike at first glance. When they are examined carefully, however, it often becomes clear where the differences lie, both in quality and in cost. Ask your jeweler to help you understand these differences by comparing different qualities for you. Only after carefully evaluating all of these factors can you appreciate gold jewelry and recognize cost differences and real value.

Is That "Bargain" Really a Bargain?

Beware of *underkarating,* which is a serious problem around the world. If a piece of gold jewelry is underkarated, it means that the jewelry is marked to indicate a certain gold content but actually contains less than is indicated. Needless to say, retailers who knowingly sell underkarated gold jewelry create the impression that they are giving you a bargain because their prices are so low, but if there is actually less gold (and more alloy, so the piece would have a comparable weight to that of others you might be considering), you aren't getting any bargain. Unfortunately, most people never learn that they have bought underkarated gold. We know of people who bought gold jewelry marked 14K or 18K and found out later that it was only 8K or 10K—or less! Thus, it is very important to buy gold jewelry from a reputable source, one that makes the effort to check its gold shipments carefully.

Look for a manufacturer's registered trademark. Being sure gold is properly represented in terms of its value is what really matters; you should get what you pay for. Buying from a reliable source is the first step. In addition, be sure to look for a manufacturer's registered trademark: a mark stamped near the karat mark. To avoid being held liable themselves, more and more jewelers are buying only from manufacturers willing to stamp what they make with their own mark registered with the U.S. Patent and Trademark Office. Buying gold with a manufacturer's trademark is one way to help assure you get what you pay for, since the product can be traced to a specific manufacturer whose name and reputation are on the line.

Fine, expensive gold jewelry should always be tested. While testing for *exact gold content* requires assaying, it is usually relatively easy to detect any underkarating that is serious enough to affect the value of a specific piece of jewelry and the price paid. Any jeweler or gemologist-appraiser can make such a determination, in most cases, quickly and easily, with only a gold tester or by using the streak test. You should be aware that with an electronic gold tester, some very heavily plated pieces might give a false reading indicating gold when the piece is only base metal. For this reason the streak test is better, but the person doing the test must be sure to take a file or carbide scriber and make a very deep scratch in order to penetrate the plating for an accurate test.

There are strict laws pertaining to gold content and marks used to indicate it. Take the time to understand what you are buying, buy only from a reputable source, and be sure to have it tested. If you do, your gold jewelry will give you a lifetime of pleasure.

Platinum: Cool, Classic, and Contemporary

Platinum is even rarer and more valuable than gold. The platinum family is composed of six elements—platinum, palladium, iridium, osmium, rhodium, and ruthenium. These six silvery-white metals are generally found together in nature, with platinum and palladium the most abundant, and iridium and ruthenium the rarest (and most expensive). Platinum is rarer and heavier than other precious metals and is the purest metal—often referred to as the "noblest." Because platinum is so pure, it does not cause allergic reactions. This is very important to people who are sensitive to the base metals used in many other metal alloys, which can cause a wide range of reactions from skin irritation or discoloration to hay fever and asthma. In addition, platinum is much stronger than other precious metals, and more malleable, which makes it easier for a jeweler to maneuver around a fragile stone with less risk of damaging it. Because of these qualities, fine jewelers often prefer working in platinum, especially for intricate pieces.

Platinum Marks

Unlike gold, platinum is not identified by karat marks. The amount of pure platinum is indicated in *parts per thousand* (ppt) of pure platinum. In the United States, jewelry that contains at least 950 parts per thousand pure platinum can be referred to as "platinum," with no qualifiers. Such pieces will be marked with the word *platinum*, the abbreviation PLAT, or the numeric indicators pt950 or 950Plat. Platinum pieces that contain less than 950 ppt must be described accordingly and the pure platinum content indicated in the mark. For example, platinum jewelry that contains 900 parts per thousand pure platinum would be marked "900Plat" or "900Pt." Jewelry containing 850 ppt would be marked "850Plat" or "850Pt" (this usually applies only to platinum chain, which has been alloyed with a higher percentage of other metals for added strength and flexibility). In the United States, a two-letter or four-letter abbreviation for the word platinum is permitted. *Platinum consisting of 500 parts per thousand pure platinum or less cannot be called platinum or marked with the word platinum or any abbreviation for platinum.*

Platinum articles that combine pure platinum with other platinum group members will also be marked accordingly. For example, 900Pt/100Ir would indicate 900 parts per thousand pure platinum and 100 parts per thousand of iridium. This was once the most commonly used platinum *alloy* in the United States. Older pieces may be stamped "900Pt" or "900Plat" without any indication that there is also iridium because it was understood that "900 platinum" would always be alloyed with 100 parts of iridium. Some older pieces will still have the stamp IRIDPLAT or the stamp "90% platinum 10% iridium" inside.

Palladium. Palladium is a member of the platinum family and offers an affordable alternative to platinum or white gold. It is an attractive alternative to platinum because it is less rare and, therefore, more affordable. It is an attractive alternative to white gold because it is a pure metal and no known allergies exist to this metal. Its white color, hardness, and overall wearability are comparable to platinum, but the metal is lighter in weight—closer to the weight of white gold—making it attractive for earrings and pendants. It is also an attractive alternative for rings, especially those replicating some of the ornate rings of the early twentieth century.

Palladium is a metal to watch, and makes an excellent overall choice for anyone who prefers a white metal, and especially for those who need a pure, hypoallergenic white metal but can't afford its rarer cousin, platinum.

Platinum Alloys Old and New

Typically, platinum is alloyed for added strength, usually combining pure platinum with another rare platinum-group metal to maintain its purity. Today there are a growing number of new platinum alloys on the market that have been created for different functions that make platinum easier to manufacture for different types of jewelry. For example, there are *hard cast* alloys that are desirable for "tension" mountings, and *heat treatable* alloys can be hardened for extra durability, after the piece has been made. Platinum/iridium is used for fabrication of jewelry, platinum/ruthenium is used for machine-made wedding rings, and platinum/cobalt is designed to provide the finest detailing in castings. The specific alloy combinations are proprietary, but platinum is most often alloyed with other platinum family members (although copper, tungsten, cobalt, and gold can also be used in platinum alloys). Unlike gold alloys, there are very minor color differences regardless of the alloy used. More importantly, the pure platinum content in the various combinations found in today's platinum alloys has remained very high—at least 90 percent (except in platinum chain)—and primarily alloyed only with platinum-group metals to protect its reputation as the purest and most "noble" metal.

Low "Karat" Platinum? In recent years, several platinum alloys have entered the marketplace not for the purpose of adding strength or to make it easier to manufacture specific types of jewelry in platinum, but in an effort to provide more affordable white-metal alternatives to 950-platinum.

In our discussion of white gold we have already mentioned the platinum/gold alloy that provides a nickel-free "white" gold alternative. This product eliminates the risk of possible allergic reaction to the nickel used to create "white" gold, and it is also attractive because, while more expensive than nickel-alloyed white gold, it is still more affordable than platinum. This product, however, is not described as a "platinum" product but as a "white gold alternative."

Today, new "platinum" products such as "karat platinum" have been created and are expected to be available soon. These new alloys contain much less platinum (most have only 585 parts per thousand of pure platinum, or less), making them much more affordable than other platinum alloys and more affordable than the platinum-alloyed white gold. The proposed mark for the new "karat platinum" alloy is "585Plat.0PGM." This indicates that there are 585 parts per thousand of pure platinum and *no platinum group metals*; "karat platinum" is alloyed with a combination of copper and cobalt. This affordable new alloy is already finding retailers eager to offer it to customers. It could become a very attractive alternative to people looking for a nickel-free white-metal alternative that is even more affordable than the platinum/gold alloy currently available.

There is some concern that such platinum alloys will confuse consumers about what they are really buying. More importantly, because they don't meet the purity standards that have long set platinum apart from other precious metals, many jewelry industry groups are recommending that jewelry must contain at least 850 parts per thousand of platinum in order to be marked or sold as "platinum." The FTC is currently examining the issues surrounding "karat platinum" and similar alloys and reviewing its current platinum guide in regard to how such alloys should be described and marked in order to avoid confusion or misrepresentation. This may delay entry into the marketplace, but we expect to see exciting new jewelry creations fashioned from these new alloys in the not-too-distant future.

Rhodium Plating Adds Whiteness and Brightness

The brightest and most reflective of all the platinum family members is *rhodium*. Because of these qualities it is frequently used to coat silver, gold, and palladium jewelry, and as an electroplate finish. Rhodium is harder and whiter even than platinum and highly resistant to corrosion. Because rhodium is so hard, it does not wear off as quickly as yellow gold plating.

Rhodium plating can eliminate allergic reactions to base metals. White gold that has been alloyed with nickel or other base metals *should* be rhodium plated, especially 10-karat or 14-karat white gold. The rhodium plating eliminates skin contact with the base metal in the alloy and thus eliminates any possible allergic reaction that the wearer might have to one of the alloys used to transform the color of yellow gold to white.

Rhodium alchemy. Another use for rhodium plating is to change the color of yellow gold jewelry to "platinum" white. People who have inherited jewelry, for example, that is yellow gold rather than white, or whose own metal color preference has changed over time, can simply take it to a jeweler to have it rhodium-plated. This will change the color to platinum-white, and because of rhodium's hardness, the color transformation can last for a very long time. When the yellow begins to show through, you can simply have it replated with rhodium at a nominal charge.

A Yellow or White Metal—Which One?

The first choice you must make is one of color. This selection usually depends on personal preference, skin tone, and the color of other jewelry you may own. Remember when considering yellow gold that it is available in several different hues, which include a greenish yellow and a pinkish yellow.

If your choice is yellow, the only decision you must make is whether you prefer 14-karat, 18-karat, or a higher-karat gold. On a limited budget, 14-karat is more affordable. It is also harder than 18-karat. One noticeable difference is that 18-karat yellow gold is a brighter gold (and 20-karat to 24-karat has an even brighter, more vivid yellow color). If you prefer the brighter yellow but can't afford higher-karat gold, ask for 14-karat gold with an 18-karat finish. After several years the finish may wear off, but you can have a jeweler restore it at a reasonable price.

If you prefer a white metal, your choice may be more difficult. While white gold and platinum or palladium may look quite similar, they are distinctly different metals. As we have mentioned, platinum is the most expensive, so if you have a limited budget, palladium, low-karat platinum, or white gold may make a better choice. In addition to being more affordable, palladium offers the whiteness of platinum and the other attributes of platinum except for its lighter weight. However, you may have a more limited choice in terms of styles available in palladium. 18-karat white gold is harder and more resistant to scratches than most platinum alloys (see below). On the other hand, white gold often exhibits a brownish or yellowish cast which must be covered with rhodium plating; the plating will wear off over an extended period of time, but as with gold plating, a jeweler can have it replated at a modest cost.

One significant disadvantage of white gold is that it is more brittle than platinum, palladium, or yellow gold. Because of this, be sure to have your jeweler check the prongs of a white gold setting at least once a year. White gold is also subject to stress corrosion, which does not occur in platinum or palladium. And there is the allergy consideration; nickel-alloyed white gold can result in a range of allergic reactions, some serious, which has led many European countries to ban its use in jewelry. For this reason, platinum-alloyed white gold—or perhaps the new "585Plat" alloy—may make a better choice for those who cannot afford platinum.

Platinum is somewhat softer but it is more malleable than white gold, making it an ideal choice for very intricate settings that require intensive labor. It is much easier to use platinum for pavé work—that is, designs in which the stones are set as closely together as possible, as though the surface were "paved" with stones. With platinum, the jeweler can also make a safer setting because a larger prong can be used, since platinum conforms so easily to the shape of the stone, reducing the risk of damage. The most important benefit of platinum is that, while it is softer than white gold and can scratch, it is more durable and does not wear down or abrade like gold. Therefore, over time, platinum settings hold up and last longer than gold settings. Palladium has comparable benefits to all of the benefits of platinum discussed here.

Today there are more styles in platinum, and platinum and gold combinations, than ever before, and the introduction of the new platinum alloys we discussed earlier is also having a positive effect on the increasing availability of platinum designs. We are also seeing many more styles becoming available in palladium.

In the final analysis, it is up to you to weigh the advantages and disadvantages of each in terms of your own needs. Whichever precious metal you choose, you can find many beautiful styles and designs. With proper care, whatever choice you make should last a lifetime.

Nontraditional Metals Find a Jewelry Niche: Titanium, Stainless Steel, and Tungsten

Some of today's newest jewelry designers, seeking bold, comfortable, and often more affordable alternatives to gold, silver, and platinum, have focused the spotlight on nontraditional metals: titanium, stainless steel, and tungsten. These metals have a lot to offer. All three are very comfortable, wearable, and low maintenance. Designers are producing pieces made entirely of one of these metals, which have particular appeal to men as well as women, and also in combination with 14- or 18-karat yellow gold, platinum, and silver. Some incorporate diamonds and gemstones into their creations, while others are having fun with other nontraditional jewelry materials such as rubber, leather, and wood. These new metals are also becoming popular choices for wedding rings.

Ed Mirell's winning *titanium* and *blue anodized titanium* and diamond men's accessory collection.

Titanium

Best known for its uses in space exploration and bicycle frames, titanium is an affordable newcomer to the jewelry scene that has become very popular. It offers an attractive white-metal look when used alone, or a straw-yellow look when alloyed with gold. It can also be alloyed with other metals to create other colors, such as black, or to display incredible rainbow iridescence. It is lightweight, resistant to saltwater and sun damage, and hypoallergenic. In addition, it won't dent or tarnish.

William Richey's stainless-steel cuff links include all stainless steel or stainless steel and 18K yellow gold, with or without diamonds.

Stainless Steel

Stainless steel is becoming one of the hottest metals on the jewelry scene. Many designers like to combine it with gold because its gray color blends so well with pink gold and yellow gold to create interesting design contrast, but stainless steel is being used increasingly on its own. Forged stainless steel is maintenance-free—it will not rust or oxidize—and this durable metal makes a strong, clean statement at a very affordable price.

Tungsten

Tungsten is an unusually hard, dense metal. Its weight is comparable to 18-karat gold, which makes it especially attractive to men seeking a ring with heft. When processed with carbon and other elements to form tungsten carbide, it becomes a very durable, scratch-resistant metal. It is the world's hardest metallic substance—*approximately ten times harder than 18-karat gold, and four times harder than titanium*—and produces an intense polish that will last longer than other metals. For this reason, it requires special equipment and the use of diamond abrasives to work the metal. This adds significantly to its cost, and also limits the type of jewelry currently available. At this time, only rings are being produced from tungsten, and their price is significantly higher than titanium or stainless steel; the cost of tungsten is roughly comparable to the cost of 18-karat or platinum rings.

Rings from Trent West's TrewTungsten® by Trent West Permanently Polished™ line: tungsten carbide with yellow gold inlay and tungsten carbide with platinum inlay and diamond.

The tungsten customer is not drawn to tungsten for its cost, but rather for its character and durability. Its dark gray color is distinctive on its own, and it also provides a striking contrast when used with gold or platinum inlay. Used alone or in combination with other precious metals and diamonds, tungsten rings make a singular statement, one that seems destined to shine brightly into future generations.

CHAPTER SIXTEEN

Choosing the Design of the Setting

The setting you choose will be determined primarily by your personal taste. Nevertheless, it is a good idea to be familiar with a few of the most common settings so that you have a working vocabulary and some idea of what is available. Whatever type of jewelry you seek—a ring, earrings, pendant, bracelet—these terms are used to describe the setting style.

Types of Settings

Bezel-set center stones with "grosgrain textured" platinum and 18K gold

Bezel setting. With a bezel setting, a rim holds the stone and completely surrounds the gem. Bezels can have straight edges, scalloped edges, or any molded shape that accommodates the stone. The backs can be open or closed. The bezel setting can protect the girdle of the stone from chips and nicks, as well as conceal them; this can be a good or bad thing, depending on whether you know the chips are there and have paid an appropriate price.

Keep in mind that if you use yellow gold in a bezel setting, the yellow of the bezel surrounding the stone will be reflected into the stone, causing a white stone to appear less white. On the other hand, a yellow-gold bezel can enhance the color of some fancy-color diamonds.

A variation on the bezel setting is the collet setting, which has a similar appearance to the bezel setting but involves the use of gold tubing.

Partial bezel-set solitaire

Gracefully intertwined prongs hold these diamonds in five-stone bands.

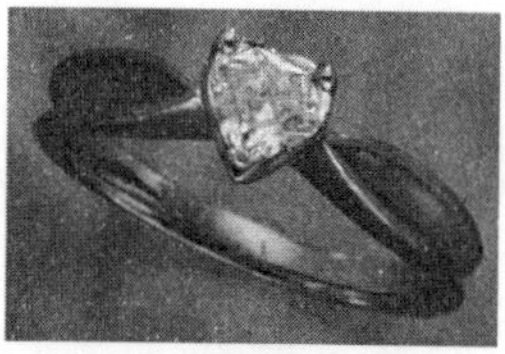

V-shaped prongs protect point of heart.

In this grouping, lower ring shows gypsy setting; upper ring shows collet setting.

Channel-set baguettes in a wedding band

Prong setting. Prong settings are perhaps the most common type of setting. They come in an almost infinite variety. There are four-prong, six-prong, and special styles such as Belcher, Fishtail, shared-prong, and six-prong Tiffany. In addition, prongs can be pointed, rounded, flat, or V-shaped. Extra prongs provide added security for the stone and can make a stone look slightly larger. However, too many prongs holding too small a stone can overpower the stone, making the stone look smaller and the mounting look heavy. When setting any shape with points, we recommend that the point or points be held by a V-shaped prong, which will best protect the point(s). For emerald-cut stones that have "canted" corners (a corner with a small diagonal edge rather than forming a 90° angle), flat prongs are the preferred choice.

Gypsy setting. In this type of setting, the metal at the top of the ring (around the stone) is much heavier than the shank. The stone is set flush into a hole at the top.

Illusion setting. The illusion setting is used to make the mounted stone appear larger. There are numerous styles from which to choose.

Flat-top and bead settings. In a flat-top setting, a faceted stone is placed into a hole in the flat top of the metal and then held in place by small chips of metal attached by solder at the stone's girdle. Sometimes these metal chips are worked into small beads, so this setting is sometimes called a bead setting.

Channel setting. This setting is used extensively today, especially for wedding bands. The stones are set into a channel with no metal separating them. In some cases, the channel can continue completely around the ring so that the piece has a continuous row of stones.

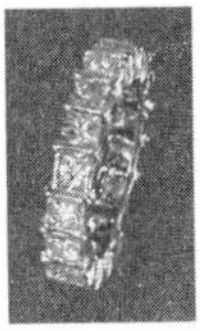

Bar-set bands

Bar setting. This setting, which resembles a channel setting, combines the contemporary and classic looks. It is used in a circular band, and instead of prongs, each stone is held in the ring by a long, thin bar, shared between two stones.

Fine pavé work in diamond and pearl engagement rings and in a wedding band

Pavé setting. This setting is used for numerous small stones set together in a cluster with no metal showing through. The impression is that the piece is entirely paved with stones. The setting can be flat or dome-shaped, and can be worked so that the piece almost appears to be one large single stone. Fine pavé work can be very expensive.

Cluster setting. A cluster setting usually consists of one large stone and several smaller stones as accents. A cluster setting is designed to create a lovely larger piece from several small stones.

Very tiny diamonds cover all visible metal—even the prongs—in this *micro-pavé* ring.

Micro-pavé. This describes intricate pavé work using extremely small diamonds set into delicate frames, the baskets holding the stones, the front and side sections, and even into the prongs themselves. Micro-pavé settings are beautiful, but the diamonds are not as secure in this type of setting and regular wear may result in loss of stones, especially in rings.

Distinctive Contemporary Settings

Today there are many interesting and distinctive designs offering something for everyone. Fine casting houses produce top-quality settings that simply await the stones to finish them off. Some firms produce semi-mounts: settings complete with side stones, awaiting only your center stone. These can provide affordable and easy solutions to creating a new ring or remounting stones from another piece.

An increasing number of custom jewelry designers also cater to today's market (see color section). International jewelry design competitions such as the Spectrum Awards designer competition sponsored by the American Gem Trade Association (AGTA), or the Diamonds-International Awards sponsored by the Diamond Information Center, provide a showcase for their work. The result is an almost limitless choice, ranging from bold sculpted gold and platinum combinations to intricate antique reproductions.

Settings to Suit Your Lifestyle

It is important to consider your lifestyle when selecting any piece of jewelry. Be realistic about the wear and tear a ring or bracelet might take, and remember that no piece of jewelry is indestructible. Remember that even diamond, the hardest natural substance known, can chip or break if exposed to a sharp accidental blow.

Active outdoor types, for example, might be better off avoiding jewelry like a ring containing a marquise or pear-shaped stone, since both these shapes have points. Points are more vulnerable to chipping or breaking, which could result from the kind of sudden or sharp blow an active person might subject a stone to.

In addition, the shank as well as the prongs of a ring will show the effects of wear; any detailing on a ring will blur over time as the result of gardening, playing on the beach, mountain climbing, handling ski equipment or bicycles, or any other kind of repeated contact or use.

Classic four- or six-prong settings served a less active generation well but may not be as suitable for today's woman. If your daily schedule features a great deal of activity, you would be wise to consider a sturdier jewelry style, keeping in mind that *sturdy* and *graceful* are not mutually exclusive. For example, a bezel setting might be better suited to your activity level. This choice won't detract from a gemstone's brilliance, yet it will afford you and your fine gems greater security.

Since everyday activities can loosen a setting as easily as more strenuous ones can, it is important to have a reputable jeweler check mountings and settings once every six months. Chlorine attacks soldering links and stress points, so if you swim regularly in a chlorinated pool, take your jewelry off first.

In terms of ring design, while rings are usually round, fingers aren't. Top-heavy rings will turn on the finger unless the diameter, or outline, is square or stirrup-shaped to conform to the shape of the finger. Also, remember that rings worn together side by side quickly begin to wear on each other.

Tips for Selecting the Right Style

1. Set a realistic budget range to eliminate confusion and temptation that can result in disappointment.
2. Shop around and familiarize yourself with current styles to educate your eye and learn what really appeals to you.
3. Try on different styles. Jewelry looks different when you see it *on*. This holds true of rings especially. We've seen many men and women insist they don't like a particular ring in a showcase, and then love it when they try it on.
4. If you're trying to achieve an impressive look with smaller stones, consider interesting jackets for earrings, or inserts or wraps for rings. These enable you to slip your ring or studs into another piece (usually gold, platinum, or silver, sometimes with stones) and instantly create a larger look.
5. If selecting an engagement ring, remember that you will also be wearing a wedding band. Be sure to select a style that will complement the type of wedding band you are considering.

International Ring Size Equivalents

American	English	French/Japanese	Metric
½	A	–	37.8252
¾	A½	–	38.4237
1	B	–	39.0222
1¼	B½	–	39.6207
1½	C	–	40.2192
1¾	C½	–	40.8177
2	D	1	41.4162
2¼	D½	2	42.0147
2½	E	–	42.6132
2¾	E½	3	43.2117
3	F	4	43.8102
3¼	F½	–	44.4087
3¼	G	5	45.0072
3½	G½	–	45.6057
3¾	H	6	46.2042
4	H½	–	46.8027
4¼	I	7	47.4012
4½	I½	8	47.9997
4¾	J	–	48.5982
5	J½	9	49.1967
5¼	K	10	49.7952
5½	K½	–	50.3937
5¾	L	11	50.9922
6	L½	–	51.5907
6¼	M	12	52.1892
6½	M½	13	52.7877
6¾	N	–	53.4660
7	N½	14	54.1044
7	O	15	54.7428
7¼	O½	–	55.3812
7½	P	16	56.0196
7¾	P½	–	56.6580
8	Q	17	57.2964
8¼	Q½	18	57.9348
8½	R	–	58.5732
8¾	R½	19	59.2116
9	S	20	59.8500
9¼	S½	–	60.4884
9½	T	21	61.1268
9¾	T½	22	61.7652
10	U	–	62.4026
10¼	U½	23	63.0420
10½	V	24	63.6804
10¾	V½	–	64.3188
11	W	25	64.8774
11¼	W½	–	65.4759
11½	X	26	66.0744
11¾	X½	–	66.6729
12	Y	–	67.2714
12¼	Y½	–	67.8699
12½	Z	–	68.4684

CHAPTER SEVENTEEN

Caring for Your Diamond Jewelry

A key to enjoying your jewelry over the years is knowing how to care for it and protect it. I've come to realize, however, that most people don't know what proper care entails. So, here are some tips to help you derive even greater pleasure from your diamonds and jewelry—after you buy!

Store Jewelry Carefully

Keep jewelry pieces separated from each other to prevent scratching. Keep fine jewelry in soft pouches or wrapped in soft cloth to help protect it.

Don't overcrowd your jewelry box. This can result in misplacing or losing pieces that might fall unnoticed from the case. Forcing jewelry into the box may cause damage, such as bending a fragile piece.

Handle and Wear Diamond Jewelry with Care

Every twelve to eighteen months have a reliable jeweler check each fine jewelry piece to make sure the setting is secure, especially the prongs. If you ever feel (or hear) the stone moving in the setting, it's a warning that a prong or bezel needs tightening. Failure to fix this may result in loss of or damage to the stone.

Get into the habit of removing jewelry before showering or bathing. Soap can deposit a film that can diminish the liveliness and beauty of diamonds, and necessitate more frequent cleaning. Also, remove jewelry before putting on makeup or powder, and wash your hands after applying makeup (to remove dulling residues) before handling your jewelry.

Never wear diamonds mounted in 14K gold (or lower) in chlorinated swimming pools or soak your diamond and gold jewelry in chlorine bleach. Chlorine attacks the gold and weakens it, possibly resulting in lost stones.

Avoid wearing fine jewelry while doing any type of rough work, especially where abrasives or chemicals are used. Abrasives can scratch your jewelry—both softer stones used to offset a diamond and the metal in settings. Chemicals such as chlorine and ammonia can cause discoloration of metals used in settings and dull the polish on many stones (necessitating having the stone repolished to restore its full beauty). Chlorine can cause some settings to pit and discolor.

Avoid exposing fine jewelry to intense heat (for example, while *cooking*). Exposure to extreme heat—from contact with a hot pot handle or from getting too near a flame or hot steam—can cause damage to many gems. *Note:* Enamel may be ruined by contact with heat. I know someone who ruined an antique diamond ring that had lovely enameling on the shank by picking up a pot with a handle that was too hot—the enamel came into contact with the handle and melted.

Avoid storing diamond jewelry that contains other gemstones in safe deposit boxes for extended periods of time. While diamonds, rubies, and sapphires won't be adversely affected, other gems—such as opal and emerald—may suffer from the extreme dryness. With these gems, if long-term storage in a safe deposit box or bank vault is unavoidable, place a damp cloth in the box with the jewelry (check from time to time to be sure the cloth is still damp).

A Few Special Words about Rings

Try not to touch the stones in your rings when putting them on or taking them off. Instead, take rings on and off by grasping the metal portion that encircles the finger (called the shank). Slipping rings on and off by grasping the metal shank rather than the stones will prevent a greasy buildup on the stones' surface, which greatly reduces the brilliance and sparkle of a stone.

To keep rings sparkling, get into the habit of "buffing" them. This is a little trick we use to remove the dirt and oily film on the stone's surface (which occurs from putting rings on and off incorrectly, or from occasionally fingering them—which most of us do without even realizing). Each time the stones are touched, a layer of oily film is applied to the top, and the stone's beauty is reduced. To restore its sparkle, simply hold the ring close to your mouth and "huff" on it with your breath—you'll see the stone fog up—and wipe it off with a soft, lint-free cloth, such as a handkerchief, scarf, or coat/blouse sleeve. You'll be amazed to see how much better jewelry can look simply by removing even the lightest film of oil from the surface!

Don't take rings off and lay them on the side of the sink unless you are sure the drain is closed. Also, never remove your rings to wash your hands when away from home (all too many have been forgotten and lost).

Take Extra Precautions When Traveling

If you take jewelry with you when traveling, don't pack it in luggage that you plan to check or in luggage to be given to the bell captain at a hotel or a ship's porters. Keep it with you.

Never leave jewelry in your hotel room. Whenever possible, obtain a safety deposit box in which to store your jewelry, even for part of a day. Be wary of in-room safes that are operated by programming your own private code; professionals can quickly and easily override your code and remove the contents of the safe.

Purchase a "body pouch" that can be concealed under clothing for when you *must* carry a valuable piece. Never go sightseeing with valuables in a purse or pocket.

For customs purposes, it can be useful to take a photo (a simple Polaroid) of the jewelry pieces you take with you. Have the photo dated and notarized before departure, so you can prove that you did not purchase it abroad. Otherwise you may be asked to pay duty on it.

Keep a photo inventory of your jewelry. You don't need professional photos; simply lay your jewelry out on a flat surface and take several snapshots. They will be invaluable should there be a robbery, providing detectives with a visual record that will make it easier to recognize the stolen pieces and claim what is yours should the jewelry ever be recovered. Photos are also important for insurance purposes and can aid in replacement. Where a piece is one of a kind and you want to have someone make a replica, a photo can provide a custom jeweler with the necessary details in order to duplicate it.

How to Clean Your Jewelry

Keeping your diamond jewelry clean is essential if you want it to sparkle to its fullest. Film from lotions, powders, and your own skin oils will dull stones and reduce their brilliance. You will be amazed at how much a slight film can affect the brilliance of your gems. So, learn how to keep them clean, and clean them on a regular basis.

The simplest and easiest way to clean any kind of jewelry is simply to wash it with warm, sudsy water. Prepare a small bowl of warm, sudsy water, using any kind of *mild* liquid detergent. Soak the piece a few minutes and then brush gently with an eyebrow brush or soft toothbrush, keeping the piece submerged in the sudsy water. Rinse thoroughly under running water (make sure the drain is closed—some prefer to place jewelry in a wire strainer before placing under the running water) and pat dry with a soft lint-free cloth or paper towel.

Diamond jewelry pieces that do not contain any other gemstones can be immersed in a solution of equal parts of hot water (not boiling—you should be able to put your fingers in it without pain!) and ammonia. This can be especially effective at removing built-up dirt and grime. Let the jewelry soak for a few minutes, brush gently, rinse well, and pat dry with a lint-free cloth. Remember, however, that ammonia should *not* be used on most other gems, and washing with warm, sudsy water is usually sufficient for *all* gemstones.

Use Jewelry Cleaners and Ultrasonic Cleaners with Caution

Commercial jewelry cleaners usually are no more effective than the methods suggested above. They seem to be popular because they are convenient. In any case, *never soak diamond jewelry that contains other gemstones in commercial cleaners for more than a few minutes.* Leaving stones such as emerald or amethyst in some commercial cleaners for any length of time can cause etching of the surface, which reduces the stone's luster (shine). *Never use commercial cleaners containing ammonia or harsh chemicals on diamond jewelry that contains pearls.* For difficult pieces, try the new *ionic* cleaners. These are safe for all gems and are fast, convenient, and affordable.

Diamonds can also be cleaned using an ultrasonic cleaner. However, *I do not recommend ultrasonic cleaning for most gems*—the new ionic cleaners are safer and equally effective. Washing in sudsy water or using an ionic cleaner is simple, effective, and safe for all jewelry.

Protecting Your Diamond with Gemprint

Gemprint is a unique service. Once offered by appraisers nationwide, it is now offered exclusively through Gem Certification and Assurance Lab (GCAL). While not totally foolproof (recutting the diamond may affect Gemprint's reliability), it is playing an increasingly important role in the recovery and return of lost and stolen diamonds.

Gemprint offers a fast and practical way to identify a diamond, even one already mounted, by capturing the image of the pattern of reflections created when the diamond is hit by a low-level laser beam. Each diamond produces a unique pattern, which is documented by this technology. As with human fingerprints, no two Gemprints are ever alike. The unique Gemprint information of your diamond is kept in GCAL's international database, whereby interested law enforcement agencies can verify ownership of a diamond when recovered.

If your stone is ever lost or stolen, you or your insurer sends a notice-of-loss form to Gemprint, which will then notify appropriate law enforcement agencies. Police can then verify with the registry the identification of recovered diamonds, many of which are thereby returned to the rightful owners. As another safeguard, Gemprint also checks each new registration against its lost-and-stolen file before confirming and storing the registration. Gemprint can also be useful in checking a diamond that has been left for repair, cleaning, or resetting, to assure you that your stone has been returned.

Increasingly, jewelers today are providing not only GIA reports but also GCAL certificates with the diamonds they sell, and every GCAL certificate includes a Gemprint. If you are purchasing a diamond that does not have one, or if you have previously bought a diamond that does not have one, I recommend getting it. A fine jeweler or appraiser can submit your diamond to the GCAL lab for a nominal fee. For this fee you will receive not only a Gemprint for your stone, but a certificate providing supplemental documentation on its quality and cutting (see page 101), adding another layer of quality assurance.

Whether purchasing a diamond or repairing, resizing, or remounting an heirloom, getting a Gemprint is another way to secure your investment.

A similar fingerprinting service called ImaGem Secure has recently become more widely available. For more information or to find a provider of this service, visit www.imageminc.com.

Laser Inscriptions—Security and Romance

Laser inscription services are available at many gem-testing laboratories for a nominal charge. In the United States, laboratories offering inscription services include Gem Certification and Assurance Lab (GCAL), Professional Gem Sciences (PGS), and the Gemological Institute of America (GIA); in Europe, Hoge Raad voor Diamant (HRD) and the Swiss Gemmological Institute (SSEF) (see appendix). Laser inscriptions can be useful in providing an identifying mark or a brand name, or to record the number of a corresponding laboratory report. Many companies selling branded diamonds now inscribe their own company logo and registration number for the particular stone on the girdle.

A romantic laser inscription

For the romantic, laser inscriptions also provide a way to add a secret, intimate message or to mark a special moment, occasion, or personal image of some type. The service can usually be completed within forty-eight hours, and the cost is usually under fifty dollars unless you have an unusually high number of characters or a complex image.

PART FOUR

Important Advice Before & After You Buy

CHAPTER EIGHTEEN

What to Ask When Buying the Stone

Asking the right questions is the key to knowing what you're getting when it comes to buying diamonds. It is also the only way you can be sure what you are comparing when considering diamonds from different jewelers. Be sure the jeweler can answer your questions or can get the answers for you. Then, be sure the jeweler is willing to put the answers *in writing* on your bill of sale. Finally, verify the facts—double-check that the stone is as represented—by having it examined by a qualified gemologist-appraiser. In this way you'll be able to make an informed choice about quality and value, you'll have no doubt about what you are getting, and you'll begin to develop a solid relationship with the jeweler from whom you make the purchase, based on confidence and trust. And, in the event the stone is not as represented, you'll know in time—and have the information you need—to get your money back.

Questions to Ask When Buying a Diamond

You should always have very specific information before purchasing a fine diamond weighing one carat or more. For smaller stones, the information may not be so readily available, since most jewelers don't take the time to grade them precisely. An experienced jeweler, however, should be able to provide information regarding quality for stones from a half carat and up, or offer to find it for you. Indeed, some laboratories are now providing grading reports for diamonds as small as half a carat or smaller.

Also keep in mind that since it is not possible to grade mounted diamonds accurately, I recommend that fine diamonds weighing one carat or more be purchased unmounted, or removed from the setting and then remounted. In jewelry containing numerous small diamonds, the stones are graded before they are set, and the information may be on the sales tag. If not, it is extremely difficult to know for sure what the true quality is, and much can be concealed by a setting. I recommend buying such pieces only from a knowledgeable jeweler with a good reputation.

Here are the basic questions to ask and the information that needs to be included on the bill of sale of your diamond:

1. *What is the exact carat weight?* Be sure the stone's *weight* is given, not its *spread* (see chapter 8).
2. *What is its color grade?* And what grading system was used? (See chapter 6.) Is the color natural?
3. *What is its clarity (flaw) grade?* Again, ask what system was used (see chapter 7).
4. *What shape is it?* Round, pear, marquise? (See chapter 5.)
5. *Is it well cut for its shape?* How would the make be graded: ideal, excellent, good? (See chapter 5.)
6. *What are the exact millimeter dimensions of the stone?*
7. *Is this stone accompanied by a diamond grading report or certificate?* Ask for the full report (see chapter 9).

Be sure to find out what system was used to grade the stone. If Gemological Institute of America (GIA) terms are used, ask if GIA standards and methods have been applied to grading the stone.

Be sure to get the *exact* millimeter dimensions of the stone; the dimensions can be approximated if the stone is mounted. For a round stone, be sure you are given *two* dimensions for the stone's diameter; since most are not round, you need the highest and lowest dimensions. For fancy shapes, get the dimensions of the length and width. Always get the dimension from the table to the culet as well, that is, the depth of the stone.

Be especially careful if the diamond is being taken out on consignment, on a jeweler's memorandum or sales slip, or on a contingency sale. Having the measurements in writing helps protect you from being accused of switching, should you have to return the stone for any reason.

Always ask if the stone has a certificate or diamond grading report. If so, make sure it accompanies the stone; if you are taking the stone on approval, ask for a copy of the report. If there is no report or certificate, find out who determined the color and flaw grades, make sure the seller puts that information on the bill of sale, and insist that the sale be contingent on the stone's actually having the grades represented.

Additional Questions to Help You Make Your Selection

Is it large enough? This is a valid question and one you should be honest with yourself about. If you think the diamond is too small, you won't feel good about wearing it. Remember that such other factors as clarity and color can be juggled several grades with little visible difference, and this might enable you to get a larger diamond. And remember that the color and type of setting can also help you achieve a larger look.

Does this stone have a good make? Does this stone have good proportions? How do its proportions compare to the "ideal?" Remember, much variance can exist and a stone can still be a beautiful, desirable gem even if it does not conform to the ideal. Nonetheless, you won't want a stone with poor proportions, so if you have any question about the stone's brilliance and liveliness—if it looks lifeless or dull in spots—you should ask specifically about the proportioning of the cut. In addition, you should ask if there are any cutting faults that might make the stone more vulnerable to chipping or breaking, as, for example, an extremely thin girdle would.

Has this stone been clarity enhanced? Be sure to ask whether or not the diamond has been laser treated or fracture filled (see chapter 7). If it is accompanied by a GIA report, the report will indicate lasering, if present. However, the GIA won't issue a report on a fracture-filled stone, and some jewelers don't know how to detect them. If there is no GIA report, be sure to ask explicitly, and get a statement in writing that the diamond is or is not clarity enhanced, whichever the case may be. Getting this fact in writing may save you a big headache should you learn later that the stone is enhanced.

Does this stone show any fluorescence? If a diamond fluoresces blue when viewed in daylight or under daylight-type fluorescent light, it will appear whiter than it really is. This can be a desirable quality—it may even cost a little less, though it may look a little better—so long as the stone has not been graded or classified incorrectly. A diamond may also fluoresce yellow, which means that in certain lights its color could appear worse than it actually is. If the stone has a diamond grading report, any fluorescence will be indicated there. If there is no report, and if the jeweler can't tell you whether or not the stone exhibits any fluorescence, the stone's color grade may be incorrect.

Special Tips When Buying a Diamond

Ask the Jeweler to Clean the Stone

Don't hesitate to ask to have the stone cleaned before you examine it. Cleaning will remove dirt, grease, or indelible purple ink. Cleaning is best done by steaming or in an ultrasonic cleaner. Cleaning also helps to ensure that you'll see the full beauty of the stone; diamonds can become very dirty just from customers handling them and, as a result, look less brilliant and sparkling than they really are.

View the Stone against a Dead-White Background

When looking at unmounted stones, look at them only against a *dead-white background* such as white blotter paper or a white business card, or on a grading trough. Examine the stone against the white background so that you are looking at it through the side, not down through the table (see chapter 6). Tilt the stone toward a good light source; a daylight fluorescent lamp is best. Examining the stone in this manner makes it easier to see the subtle tint of color that can dramatically affect price. If the stone shows a readily apparent yellow body tint when viewed through the girdle, it is not "colorless" or "near colorless" but "slightly tinted" or "tinted." A truly "colorless" diamond ("D") will be as colorless as an ice cube; with E–F colors, it will be very difficult to pick up the slight tint.

Get the Facts on the Bill of Sale

Ask that all the facts concerning the stone be put on the bill of sale. These include the carat weight, the color and flaw grades, the cut, and the dimensions. Also, be sure you obtain the report on any certificated stone, as diamonds accompanied by laboratory reports are sometimes called.

Other information that should be included for jewelry. If the piece is being represented as being made by a famous designer or house (Van Cleef and Arpels, Tiffany, Caldwell, Cartier, etc.) and the price reflects this, the name of the designer or jewelry firm should be stated on the bill of sale. If the piece is represented as antique (technically, an antique must be at least a hundred years old) or as a period piece from a popular, collectible period like art deco, art nouveau, or Edwardian (especially if made by a premier artisan of the period), this information should be stated on the bill of sale, with the approximate age or date of manufacture and a statement describing the condition. If the piece is made by hand or custom designed, this should be indicated on the bill of sale. If the piece is to be taken on approval, make sure millimeter dimensions—top to bottom, as well as length, width, or diameter—are provided, as well as a full description of the piece. Also, check that a time period within which the piece can be returned is indicated, such as "two days." Before you sign anything, be sure that you are signing an approval form and not a binding contract for purchase.

Verify Facts with a Gemologist

If a stone is one carat or larger and is not accompanied by a respected laboratory report, make the sale contingent on verification of the facts by a qualified gemologist, gem-testing lab, or the GIA. While the GIA will not estimate dollar value, it will verify color, flaw grade, make, fluorescence, weight, and other physical characteristics. If it already has a report, the gemologist can confirm that the quality of the diamond matches the information on the report and assure you of the "genuineness" of the report itself. It is essential to verify the facts with an independent gemologist, whether or not the stone is accompanied by a laboratory report (see chapter 21).

Weigh the Facts

Decide what is important to you, and then weigh the facts. Most people think color and make are the most important considerations when buying a diamond, but if you want a larger stone, you may have to come down several grades in color, choose a slightly spread stone, or select one of the new shapes that look much larger than traditional cuts. The most important thing is to know what you're getting and to get what you pay for.

CHAPTER NINETEEN

How to Select a Reputable Jeweler & Gemologist Consultant

It's very difficult to give advice on this matter, since there are so many exceptions to any rules I can suggest. Size and years in business are not always absolute indicators of the reliability of a firm. Some one-person jewelry firms are highly respected; others are not. Some well-established firms that have been in business for many years have built their trade on the highest standards of integrity and knowledge; others should have been put out of business years ago.

One point worth stressing is that for the average consumer, price alone is not a reliable indicator of the integrity or knowledge of the seller. Aside from variations in quality, which often are not readily discernible by the consumer, significant price differences can also result from differences in jewelry manufacturing processes. Many jewelry manufacturers sell mass-produced lines of good-quality jewelry to jewelers all across the country. Mass-produced items, many of which are beautiful, classic designs, are usually much less expensive than handmade, one-of-a-kind pieces, or those on which there is a limited production. The work of some designers may be available in only a few select establishments and may carry a premium because of skill, labor, reputation, and limited distribution. Handmade or one-of-a-kind pieces are always more expensive, since the initial cost of production is paid by one individual rather than shared by many, as in mass-produced pieces.

Furthermore, depending on the store, retail markups also vary based on numerous factors unique to each retailer, including differences in insurance coverage, security costs, credit risks, education and training costs, special services such as in-house design and custom jewelry production and repair, customer service policies, and more.

The best way to select wisely is by shopping around. Go to several fine jewelry firms in your area and compare the services they offer, how knowledgeable the salespeople seem, the quality of their products, and pricing for specific items. This will give you a sense of what is fair in your market area. As you do so, however, remember to ask the right questions to be sure the items are truly comparable, and pay attention to design and manufacturing differences as well. As part of this process, it may be helpful to consider these questions:

- *How long has the firm been in business?* A quick check with the Better Business Bureau may reveal whether or not there are significant consumer complaints.
- *What are the gemological credentials of the jeweler, manager, or owner?* Is there a gemologist on staff? Does the store have its own laboratory?
- *What special services are provided?* Are custom design services, rare or unusual gemstones, educational programs, or photographic services for your jewelry available?
- *How would you describe the store window?* Is the jewelry nicely displayed? Or is the window a mélange of incredible bargains and come-on advertising to lure you in?
- *How would you describe the overall atmosphere?* Is the sales staff's manner professional, helpful, tasteful? Or hustling, pushy, intimidating?
- *What is the store's policy regarding returns?* Full refund or only store credit? How many days? What basis for return?
- *What is the repair or replacement policy?*
- *Will the firm allow a piece to be taken "on approval"?* It won't hurt to ask. Some jewelers will. However, unless you know the jeweler personally this is not often permitted today, since too many jewelers have suffered from stolen, damaged, or switched merchandise.
- *To what extent will the firm guarantee its merchandise to be as represented?* Be careful here. Make sure you've asked the right questions, and get complete and accurate information on the bill of sale, or you may find yourself stuck because of a technicality.

If the jeweler can't or won't provide the necessary information, I recommend that you go to another store, no matter how much you've fallen in love with the piece. If you're making the purchase on a contingency basis, put the terms of the contingency on the bill of sale.

Never allow yourself to be intimidated into accepting anyone's claims. Beware of the person who says "Just trust me" or who tries to intimidate you with statements such as "Don't you trust me?" A trustworthy jeweler will not have to ask for your trust; he or she will earn it through knowledge, reliability, and a willingness to give you any information you request—in writing.

Again, in general, you will be in a stronger position to differentiate between a knowledgeable, reputable jeweler and one who isn't if you've shopped around first. Unless you are an expert, visit several firms, ask questions, examine merchandise carefully, and then you be the judge.

Using a Gemologist Consultant

Somewhat new to the gem and jewelry field is the arrival of the gemologist consultant. People interested in acquiring a very fine diamond, a fancy-color diamond, or a fine piece of period or antique jewelry that may be difficult to find in traditional jewelry stores are now seeking the professional services of experienced gemologist consultants. A gemologist consultant can provide a variety of services, including general consulting to help you determine what you really want, what it will cost, and how to best acquire it; how to dispose of jewelry you already own, or from an estate; how to design or redesign a piece of jewelry and have it made. A gemologist consultant can also provide the expertise needed to help you safely purchase diamonds or jewelry at auction or from private estate sales. An experienced gemologist consultant can expand your view of the possibilities in terms of diamonds and also suggest ways to make jewelry more personal and distinctive.

As with all else in the sparkling world of diamonds and jewelry, be sure to check the credentials of anyone offering services as a gemologist consultant. Do they have a gemological diploma? How long have they been working in the field of gems? Do they have a laboratory? Can they provide references within the field? Can they provide client references? If you have jewelry you wish to sell, arrange meetings at a safe place, such as a bank vault.

Fees vary depending on the gemologist consultant's level of expertise and experience and the nature of the assignment. For example, for general consulting about how to buy or sell diamonds or jewelry, you should expect to pay about $150 to $300 per hour for someone with good credentials.

For assistance in the acquisition or sale of specific gems or pieces of jewelry, some gemologist consultants work on a fixed fee for the project, some on a percentage of the purchase or sale amount, and some at an hourly rate. When I am retained by clients, my work is done on one of the bases noted above, or even a combination of them, depending on the nature of the work to be done and what best meets the client's needs.

If You Want to File a Complaint

If you have a complaint about a firm's practices or policies, please contact the Better Business Bureau in your city. In addition, if any jeweler has misrepresented what was sold to you, please contact the Jewelers Vigilance Committee (JVC), 25 West 45th Street, Suite 1406, New York, NY 10036, (212) 997-2002, www.jvclegal.org. This group can provide invaluable assistance to you, investigate your complaint, and take action against firms believed to be guilty of fraudulent activity in the jewelry industry.

CHAPTER TWENTY

Buying on the Internet

E-Commerce & Online Auctions

E-commerce is the current buzzword, and diamond and jewelry websites are springing up almost daily, along with online auction sites. The Internet offers an endless array of merchandise from around the world—a virtual international flea market—and opens doors to more choices than ever imagined, at prices often represented to be much lower than what can be found in traditional jewelry stores. Buying on the Internet can be fun, and there are some good opportunities for knowledgeable buyers, possibly even a real "treasure" at a bargain price. But e-commerce and online auctions are not for everyone, and the risk of buying something that is not properly represented is very high. Before flying off into cyberspace, take a few moments to consider some of the pros and cons.

For many, the major attraction of shopping online is convenience. It is fast and easy, enabling you to make decisions in private, but without the assistance of salespeople. For those who live in remote areas far from fine jewelry stores, it provides an opportunity to see what is available, see what's new and exciting, and keep current about everything from gemstones to the latest award-winning designers. Many online vendors also provide educational sites to help you understand more about what you are buying. And for people who leave important gifts to the last minute, the Internet can bring the world of jewelry directly to the screen, in time to be a real lifesaver!

It is easy to see the allure of Internet shopping, but in all too many cases it is not all that it appears to be. Where diamonds and jewelry are concerned, the disadvantages may quickly outweigh the advantages, especially on auction sites.

The first disadvantage is the inability to see and compare diamonds and jewelry firsthand. As I hope you've learned from previous chapters, this is a serious shortcoming, since it is impossible to accurately judge beauty and desirability from a static photo. Furthermore, you can't determine how well made a piece of jewelry might be or how it might compare with the alternatives. Be sure to ask about the vendor's return policy, and read the fine print. Find out how quickly merchandise must be returned and whether you will receive a refund. Be leery of vendors who will only give a credit toward future purchases.

Another serious problem is the absence of any screening mechanism to help you determine the reliability of information provided. Sales information pertaining to diamonds or jewelry being sold is often incomplete and inaccurate, and many "educational" sites are also filled with inaccurate, incomplete, or misleading information. It is also difficult to find reliable information about the competence or trustworthiness of many online vendors, and written representations may be meaningless unless you can work out a way to verify the facts before making payment to the vendor.

In general, everything I have warned about in previous chapters applies to purchases from an online vendor or auction. As I have stressed repeatedly, many of the factors affecting quality and value cannot be accurately judged without gemological training, experience, and proper equipment, and many online vendors are so deficient in requisite knowledge and skill that their representations may be unreliable.

I cannot emphasize too strongly the importance of taking every precaution to protect yourself and ensure you are getting what you think you are getting, at an appropriate price. Remember that many Internet companies and individual vendors are unknown entities, without reliable track records or well-established reputations. This means that problems might be more difficult or impossible to resolve satisfactorily, regardless of "guarantees" made before purchase. You must also remember that it may be difficult or impossible to find the seller off-line, and you cannot rely on vendor ratings because they can be easily rigged by the unscrupulous.

Appraisals and Laboratory Reports Provide a False Sense of Security

Appraisals and gem-testing laboratory reports are being used increasingly by online sellers to increase confidence among prospective buyers.

Unfortunately, they are also being used increasingly by the unscrupulous. I am seeing an increase in bogus appraisals and fraudulent lab reports that have duped unsuspecting buyers into purchasing something that has been misrepresented. I have also seen diamonds accompanied by reports from highly respected labs where the quality of the stone does not match the description on the report. Be sure to get independent verification of any documentation provided by the seller (see chapter 10), before payment if possible.

Remember also that you cannot properly judge a gem on the basis of a lab report or appraisal alone. I've seen many diamonds with "great reports" that were not beautiful (and should sell for less than one might surmise based on the report alone), and others with "questionable" reports that were exceptionally beautiful (and should cost more than the report would indicate). In other words, you really must see the stone along with the report.

Other problems that are surfacing on the web include the following:

- *Failure to comply with Federal Trade Commission (FTC) guidelines.* The FTC has found extensive failure to comply with its guidelines. Most notably, descriptions provided by sellers often omit critical information pertaining to quality factors, exact weight, and treatments used on diamonds.
- *Prices are often higher than fair retail.* Don't assume you will pay a lower price, and beware of fictitious "comparative retail" prices that lead you to believe you are getting a bargain. Prices are often no lower than those at a local jewelry store, and many e-retailers sell jewelry at prices significantly higher than what you would pay for comparable quality from knowledgeable independent jewelers. Before buying online, check prices from a variety of sources, including your local jeweler.
- *"Wholesale" claims may be misleading.* "Wholesale" online offerings present even greater risks to consumers than buying in any wholesale jewelry district (see chapter 10), because you do not see the actual diamond or jewelry firsthand and have no guarantee you are buying from a bona fide wholesaler. Many people buying "wholesale" through online sources are not getting the bargains they believe they are getting, and many mistakes would have been avoided had the buyer seen the jewelry first or had an opportunity to compare it with alternatives.

In some cases, arrangements can be made to allow you to view the stone before the vendor receives payment, using a local bank or gemological laboratory, for example, as an intermediary. I recommend this be done whenever possible.

- *Here today, gone tomorrow*. In numerous reported cases, buyers have never received the merchandise for which they paid, or received merchandise that was not as represented. Often there is no recourse because vendors cannot be located once the transaction is complete.

Online Auctions—Rewards and Rip-Offs

Fine auction houses are an important source of exquisite jewelry from bygone eras, often exhibiting elaborate workmanship that cannot be duplicated today. They are also an important source of some of the finest, rarest, and most magnificent natural gemstones—gems that surpass even the best material being mined today—which are no longer available in the jewelry trade. Such gems may fetch handsome prices—possibly even a new record—or some knowledgeable buyer may recognize a treasure that others have missed and pay very little. This, for many, is what makes the auction arena so fascinating.

Items offered at auction may also come to the auction block to settle estates, or as a means to dispose of unclaimed property, and usually must be sold at whatever the highest bid might be, regardless of value. While this is no guarantee that you'll get a bargain, because knowledgeable buyers know the value of pieces on which they are bidding, sometimes these pieces are sold at very low prices because no one obtained proper certification and they get overlooked, even by the pros!

Buying at auction can be a rewarding experience, but keep in mind that even at the best firms there is an element of risk. One must be very knowledgeable, or work with an expert consultant, to recognize opportunities and spot pitfalls. Over the years I've seen many pieces acquired from reputable auction firms that contained synthetic stones, fracture-filled diamonds, and diffusion-treated sapphires.

As I have stressed throughout this book, no one can properly judge any fine gem without seeing it firsthand and examining it with proper gem-testing equipment. Where auctions are concerned, proper examination is even more critical because the auction house has limited liability.

I never bid on any item at auction without having personally viewed the piece and examined it with proper gem-testing equipment. Firms such as Antiquorum, Christie's, and Sotheby's provide opportunities to view the items at exhibitions held at various locations around the country before the auction, and bidding takes place both on-site and online, as a convenience to people who cannot be present. However, this is not the case with all online auction sites, and in many cases there is no opportunity to view the item before bidding on it. In such cases, more than anything else, success is dependent on having incredible luck!

Protection May Be Illusion

Where some auction sites are concerned, you may be under the impression that you are protected against misrepresentation and have recourse should there be a problem, but this may be just an illusion. In reality, you may have no recourse at all. Never forget that in situations where proper examination is not possible, the risk is dramatically increased: you are bidding on a blind item from a blind source. Even among legitimate sources, not seeing the diamond or jewelry before purchase can result in disappointment when you receive your purchase. Be sure to read the "terms and conditions" very carefully, especially the fine print pertaining to "representations, warranties, and limits of liability."

I was recently contacted by a woman regarding a diamond purchased from an individual through an online auction site. She had previously purchased a diamond through an Internet auction and arranged for us to confirm that the diamond was properly represented before she paid for it. She did very well and obtained a very nice diamond at a price comparable to legitimate wholesale. In the second case, she thought she had arranged a similar transaction. She was very excited about the diamond, which she thought she had purchased at a "bargain" price. She expected to be able to confirm the quality, as she had in the earlier transaction, before paying for it. Here is where the problem began.

The diamond was described as having a certain color, clarity, and weight, but it was not accompanied by any lab report or appraisal. The buyer was aware of this when she bid, but she had been told by the seller that she could have it verified by a third party. She became alarmed and suspicious when the seller would not accept a credit card or agree to an escrow arrangement, especially since she, the buyer, was willing to pay all costs related to the escrow arrangement or credit card fee. The seller had agreed that the buyer could send the stone to a third party for verification, but what was never made clear before the bidding was that the seller would send the stone to a third party only *after* receiving full payment!

I tried to be helpful, but when I spoke with the owner, I also became very suspicious. I asked the owner how she was able to provide such a precise description of the diamond without any appraisal or lab report, and she responded that she knew "by looking." So I asked her if she was a gemologist or in the jewelry trade and I was told no, but that she had looked at "hundreds of diamonds" and "knew what she was looking at." She then told me she was a lawyer and began her litany about the buyer having entered into a legally binding contract, and that the buyer knew before bidding that the description was only her "opinion," and so on. I quickly realized that this woman was an experienced "pro" who knew how to legally exploit the auction arena ... and the unsuspecting.

To sum it all up, the seller used the "terms and conditions, warranty, and limits of liability" clauses established by the auction site to construct a situation in which she was able to rip off the inexperienced. She knew that representations made in the auction arena without documentation are not guarantees and fall outside the legal constraints placed on other online vendors, and once payment had been received, she had no intention of ever refunding one penny, regardless of what any independent evaluation revealed.

Buying at auction can be an exciting and exhilarating experience with compelling financial incentives, but there are always risks for the unknowledgeable, and buying through online auction sites poses even greater risk. The FTC has warned that Internet auction fraud has become a significant problem. According to the FTC, most consumer complaints center on these situations:

- Sellers who don't deliver goods
- Sellers who deliver something far less valuable than they described
- Sellers who don't deliver in a timely way
- Sellers who fail to disclose all the relevant information about the product or terms of sale

Form of Payment May Provide Protection

There are several payment options that might provide some protection. Credit cards offer the most consumer protection, usually including the right to seek a credit through the credit card issuer if the product isn't as delivered. If the seller won't agree, other options include setting up an escrow arrangement (for which there is usually a nominal fee) or using a reliable third party for verification, such as a well-known gem-testing laboratory, before an exchange of products or money.

To sum up, whether you are buying or selling diamonds or jewelry online—from e-retailers, auction sites, or individuals—the rewards may be great, but the risks are much higher than buying from traditional sources. To file a complaint (see page 198) or for additional information on how to reduce the risk in buying or selling online, write to the Federal Trade Commission, Consumer Response Center, 600 Pennsylvania Avenue, NW, Washington, DC 20580, or see their website: www.ftc.gov.

Online Sources of Information

There are many sources of online information but no screening mechanism to separate reliable from unreliable information. Consider the source and be wary of information provided by sellers of gems or jewelry. The following sites may provide helpful information:

1. www.accreditedgemologists.org (Accredited Gemologists Association)
2. www.americangemsociety.org (American Gem Society)
3. www.antoinettematlins.com (Antoinette Matlins, P.G.)
4. www.ftc.gov (Federal Trade Commission)
5. www.gia.edu (Gemological Institute of America)
6. www.jic.org (Jewelry Information Center)
7. www.roskingemnews.com (The Roskin Gem News Report)

CHAPTER TWENTY-ONE

Choosing the Appraiser & Insurer

Why Is It Important to Get an Appraisal?

If you have bought a diamond or diamond jewelry, getting a professional appraisal and keeping it updated is critical. An appraisal is necessary for four reasons: (1) to verify the facts about the jewelry you have purchased (especially important with the abundance of new synthetic materials and treatments); (2) to obtain adequate insurance to protect against theft, loss, or damage; (3) to establish adequate information to legally claim jewelry recovered by the police; and (4) if items are lost or stolen, to provide sufficient information to make sure they are replaced with jewelry that actually is of comparable quality, if that is what your insurance policy provides.

The need for appraisal services has increased greatly because of the high incidence of theft and sharp increases in the prices of diamonds. It has become necessary to have any fine gem properly appraised, particularly before a purchase decision, given today's costs and the potential for financial loss if the gem is not accurately represented.

It is also important, given recent rising prices, to update value estimations from old appraisals. This will ensure adequate coverage should gems that have been in your possession for several years or more be lost or stolen. In addition, current and accurate appraisals may be needed in connection with inheritance taxes, gifts, or the determination of your net worth.

How to Find a Reliable Appraiser

The appraisal business has been booming over the past few years, and many jewelry firms have begun to provide the service themselves. I must point out, however, that there are essentially no officially established guidelines for going into the gem appraising business. Anyone can represent himself or herself as an appraiser. While many highly qualified professionals are in the business, some others lack the expertise to offer these services, so it is essential to select an appraiser with care and diligence. Further, if the purpose of the appraisal is to verify the identity or genuineness of a gem as well as its value, I recommend that you deal with someone who is in the business of gem identification and appraising and not primarily in the business of selling gems.

To find a reliable gem-testing laboratory, see the appendix for a selected list of laboratories that issue internationally recognized reports. To find a reliable gemologist-appraiser in your community, contact:

Accredited Gemologists Association
c/o G-Force Services, 3315 Juanita St., San Diego, CA 92105
(619) 501-5444 • Ask for a list of *Certified Gem Laboratories* or *Certified Master Gemologists.*

American Gem Society (AGS)
8881 W. Sahara Ave., Las Vegas, NV 89117
(866) 805-6500 • Ask for a list of *Certified Gemologist Appraisers* or *Independent Certified Gemologist Appraisers.*

American Society of Appraisers
555 Herndon Pkwy., Ste. 125, Herndon, VA 20170
(800) 272-8258 • Ask for a list of *Master Gemologist Appraisers.*

Association of Independent Jewellery Valuers
Algo Business Centre, Glenearn Road
Perth, Scotland, PH2 0NJ United Kingdom
+44 (0) 1738 450477 • See www.independent-jewellery-valuers.org for a list of valuers and appraisers.

International Society of Appraisers
737 N. Michigan Ave., Ste. 2100, Chicago, IL 60611
(312) 981-6778 • Ask for a list of *Certified Appraisers of Personal Property.*

National Association of Jewelry Appraisers
P.O. Box 18, Rego Park, NY 11374
(718) 896-1536 • Ask for a list of *Certified Master Appraisers* or *Certified Senior Members.*

In addition, when selecting a gemologist-appraiser, keep the following suggestions in mind:

- *Obtain the names of several appraisers and then compare their credentials.* To be a qualified gemologist-appraiser requires extensive formal training and experience. You can conduct a preliminary check by telephoning the appraisers and inquiring about their gemological credentials.
- *Look for specific credentials.* The Gemological Institute of America (GIA) and the Gemmological Association of Great Britain provide internationally recognized diplomas. GIA's highest award is G.G. (Graduate Gemologist) and the Gemmological Association of Great Britain awards the F.G.A.—Fellow of the Gemmological Association (F.G.A.A. in Australia; F.C.G.A., Canada). Some hold this honor "With Distinction." In Germany, the D.G.G. is awarded; in Asia, the A.G. Make sure the appraiser you select has one of these gemological diplomas. In addition, when seeking an *appraiser,* look for the title C.G.A. (Certified Gemologist Appraiser), which is awarded by the American Gem Society (AGS), or M.G.A. (Master Gemologist Appraiser), which is awarded by the American Society of Appraisers. Some fine gemologists and appraisers lack these titles because they do not belong to the organizations awarding them, but these titles currently represent the highest awards presented in the gemological appraisal field. Anyone holding these titles should have fine gemological credentials and adhere to high standards of professional conduct. Where possible, seek someone who is a *Registered Master-Valuer*™, an additional certification that helps identify reputable, knowledgeable gem and jewelry appraisers. (See www.mastervaluer.com for more information.)
- *Check the appraiser's length of experience.* In addition to formal training, to be reliable a gemologist-appraiser needs extensive experience in the handling of gems, use of the equipment necessary for accurate identification and evaluation, and activity in the marketplace. The appraiser should have at least several years' experience in a well-equipped laboratory.
- *Ask where the appraisal will be conducted.* An appraisal should normally be done in the presence of the customer, if possible. This is important in order to ensure that the same stone is returned to you and to protect the appraiser against charges of "switching."

> Recently I appraised an old platinum engagement ring that had over twenty years' filth compacted under the high filigree-type box mounting typical of the early 1920s. After cleaning, which was difficult, the diamond showed a definite brown tint, easily seen by the client, which she had never noticed when the ring was dirty. She had just inherited the ring from her deceased mother-in-law, who had told her it had a blue-white color. If she had not been present when this ring was being cleaned and appraised, it might have resulted in a lawsuit, for she would certainly have suspected a switch. This particular situation does not present itself often, but appraisers and customers alike need to be diligent and watchful.

If there are several pieces, the process can be very time-consuming. It normally takes about a half hour per item to get all of the specifications, and it can take much longer in some cases. Several appointments may be required for a proper job.

Appraisal Fees

This is a touchy and complex subject. As with any professional service, there should be a suitable charge. Fees should be conspicuously posted or offered readily on request so that the customer knows beforehand what to expect to pay for this service. Fees are essentially based on the expertise of appraisers and the time required of them, as well as the secretarial work required to put the appraisal in written form, since all appraisals should be done in writing. While it used to be standard practice to base appraisal fees on a percentage of the appraised value, this practice is no longer acceptable. Today, all recognized appraisal associations in the United States recommend that fees be based on a flat hourly rate, or on a per-carat charge for diamonds.

There is usually a minimum appraisal fee, regardless of value. The hourly rate charged by a professional, experienced gemologist-appraiser can range from $50 to $150, depending on the complexity of the work to be performed and the degree of expertise required. Find out beforehand what the hourly rate is and what the minimum fee will be.

For certification or special gemological consulting that requires special expertise, rates can easily be $125 to $150 per hour. Extra services such as photography, radiography, Gemprint, or spectroscopic examination of fancy-color diamonds will require additional fees.

Be wary of appraisal services offering appraisals at very low rates and of appraisers who continue to base their fee on a percentage of the "appraised valuation." The Internal Revenue Service, for example, will not accept appraisals performed by appraisers who charge a percentage-based fee.

Some appraisers can photograph jewelry, which I suggest. On the photo, the appraiser should note the approximate magnification and the date, along with your name as the owner. This provides a means of identifying merchandise that may have been stolen or lost and subsequently recovered by police. The photo can also be useful with the U.S. Customs Service should you take your jewelry with you on a trip outside the United States and find yourself having to prove that the jewelry was not purchased abroad.

Choosing an Insurer

Once you have a complete appraisal, the next step is to obtain adequate insurance. Most people do not realize that insurers differ widely in their coverage and reimbursement or replacement procedures. Many companies will not reimburse the "full value" provided in the policy, but instead exercise a "replacement" option by which they offer a *cash sum less than the amount for which the jewelry is insured,* or offer to replace it for you. Therefore, it is important to ask very specific questions to determine the precise coverage offered. I recommend asking at least the following:

- How do you satisfy claims? Do you reimburse the insured amount in cash? If not, how is the amount of the cash settlement determined? Or do you replace the jewelry?
- What involvement do I have in the replacement of an item? What assurance do I have that the replacement will be of comparable quality and value to the original?
- What is your coverage on articles that cannot be replaced?
- Exactly what risks does my policy cover? All risks? Mysterious disappearance? At all times?
- Does the policy have any geographic restrictions?

- Are there any exemptions or exclusions? What if the loss involves negligence?
- What are the deductibles, if any?
- What documentation do you expect me to provide?

To help with insurance claims, keep a photo inventory of your jewelry. Take a photo and store it in a safe place (a bank safe deposit box). In case of theft or fire, a photo will be useful in helping you describe your jewelry, and also in remembering other pieces that are missing, and in identifying them if recovered. A photo is also useful for insurance documentation. In addition, when planning a trip, whatever jewelry you will be taking should be photographed. Just put it on a table and take a snapshot.

APPENDIX

A Selected List of Recognized Laboratories

American Gemological Laboratories (AGL)
580 Fifth Ave., Ste. 706
New York, NY 10036

American Gem Society Laboratories
8881 W. Sahara Ave.
Las Vegas, NV 89117

CISGEM-External Service for Precious Stones
Viale Achille Papa, 30
20149 Milano, Italy

Gem Certification and Assurance Lab (GCAL)
580 Fifth Ave., Ste. LL
New York, NY 10036

GEMLAB Laboratory for Gemstone Analysis and Gemological Reports
Gewerbestrasse 3
FL-9496 Balzers, Principality of Liechtenstein

Gemological Institute of America (GIA)
580 Fifth Ave., Ste. 200
New York, NY 10036
and
5345 Armada Dr.
Carlsbad, CA 92008

German Gem Lab (DSEF)
Prof.-Schlossmacher-Str. 1
D-55743 Idar-Oberstein, Germany

Gübelin Gem Lab
Maihofstrasse 102
6006 Lucerne, Switzerland

Hoge Raad voor Diamant (HRD)
Hoveniersstraat 22
BE-2018 Antwerp, Belgium

Professional Gem Sciences (PGS)
5 S. Wabash Ave., Ste. 1905
Chicago, IL 60603

Swiss Gemmological Institute (SSEF)
Falknerstrasse 9
CH-4001 Basel, Switzerland

Selected Readings

Bronstein, Alan, and Stephen C. Hofer. *Forever Brilliant: The Aurora Collection of Colored Diamonds*. New York: Ashland Press, 2000. An excellent guide to the world of colored diamonds.

Bruton, Eric. *Diamonds*. 2nd ed. Radnor, Pa.: Chilton, 1978. An excellent, well-illustrated work for amateur and professional alike.

Hofer, Stephen C. *Collecting and Classifying Coloured Diamonds*. New York: Ashland Press, 1998. A lavish, comprehensive work essential for anyone with a serious interest in the subject.

Koivula, John I. *The MicroWorld of Diamonds: A Visual Reference*. Northbrook, Ill.: Gemworld International, 2000. Presents an intriguing look at diamonds through the microscope in four hundred color photographs.

Matlins, Antoinette. *Colored Gemstones: The Antoinette Matlins Buying Guide—How to Select, Buy, Care for & Enjoy Sapphires, Emeralds, Rubies and Other Colored Gems with Confidence and Knowledge*. 3rd ed. Woodstock, Vt.: GemStone Press, 2010. Covers every aspect of colored gemstones in detail, from their symbolic attributes to current frauds.

———. *Jewelry & Gems at Auction: The Definitive Guide to Buying & Selling at the Auction House & on Internet Auction Sites*. With Jill Newman. Woodstock, Vt.: GemStone Press, 2002. Everything anyone needs to know to buy gems and jewelry at auction.

———. *The Pearl Book: The Definitive Buying Guide—How to Select, Buy, Care for & Enjoy Pearls*. 4th ed. Woodstock, Vt.: GemStone Press, 2008. Covers every aspect of pearls, from lore and history to complete buying advice. An indispensable guide for the pearl lover.

Matlins, Antoinette, and A. C. Bonanno. *Engagement & Wedding Rings: The Definitive Buying Guide for People in Love*. 3rd ed. Woodstock, Vt.: GemStone Press, 2003. Everything you need to know to select, design, buy, care for, and cherish your wedding or anniversary rings—his and hers. Beautiful photos of rings.

———. *Gem Identification Made Easy: A Hands-On Guide to More Confident Buying & Selling*. 4th ed. Woodstock, Vt.: GemStone Press, 2008. A nontechnical book that makes gem identification possible for anyone. A must for beginners, and the experienced may pick up a few tips, too. Practical, easy to understand.

———. *Jewelry & Gems: The Buying Guide—How to Buy Diamonds, Pearls, Colored Gemstones, Gold & Jewelry with Confidence and Knowledge*. 7th ed. Woodstock, Vt.: GemStone Press, 2009. The only book of its kind ever offered by *Consumer Reports*; in use in over one hundred countries.

Pagel-Theisen, Verena. *Diamond Grading ABC*. 10th ed. New York: Rubin & Son, 1990. Highly recommended for anyone in diamond sales.

Roskin, Gary A. *Photo Masters for Diamond Grading*. Northbrook, Ill.: Gemworld International, 1994. A good reference with extraordinary photos for anyone interested in diamonds.

Color Plates and Exhibits

Charts

All the charts and the tables that appear here were especially designed and executed for use in this book; however, some from other publications were used as inspiration and reference. Grateful acknowledgment is given to the following for use of their charts as references:

The chart on page 77, "Sizes and Weights of Various Diamond Cuts," with permission of the Gemological Institute of America, from its book *The Jewelers' Manual.*

The chart on page 78, "Diameters and Corresponding Weights of Round Brilliant-Cut Diamonds," with permission of the Gemological Institute of America, from its book *The Jewelers' Manual.*

The chart on page 123, "Comparison of Diamonds and Diamond Look-Alikes," with permission of the Gemological Institute of America, from its publication *Diamond Assignment* No. 36, page 27.

Black-and-White Photographs and Illustrations

Illustrations by Kathleen Robinson.

Page 27: EightStar® from EightStar Diamond Company (photo/Richard von Sternberg).

Page 29: Diamonds seen through viewer from EightStar Diamond Company (photo/Richard von Sternberg).

Page 36–37: Radiant, princess, and Biro88™ from Eugene Biro Corp.; Crisscut® from Christopher Designs (photo/Christony Inc.); Quadrillion™ from Ambar Diamonds; trilliant from MEFCO Inc. (photo/Sky Hall); Noble Cut™ from Doron Isaak; Gabrielle® from Suberi Brothers (photo/Peter Hurst); Spirit Sun® and Context® from Freiesleben; Lucida™ from Tiffany and Company (photo/Monica Stevenson); Tiana™ from Brite Star Diamond Co., Ltd.

Page 39: Old Asscher from J. Birnbach; old cushion from Antiquorum Auctioneers.

Page 40: Trapezoids and half-moons from Doron Isaak; briolette from Rough and Ready Gems (photo/Azad).

Page 67: Flawless and SI_2 diamonds from Suberi Brothers.

Pages 172–173: Titanium men's collection by Ed Mirell. Stainless steel cufflinks by William Richey. Tungsten rings by Trent West.

Pages 175–177: Bezel-set rings by Robin Garin from Kwiat Couture; partial bezel-set ring from George Sawyer Design; five-stone bands from Lazare Kaplan, Inc.; heart-shaped diamond ring from Suberi Brothers; rings in gypsy and collet settings from Circle Round the Moon; channel-set baguette wedding band from JFA Designs; bar-set band (left) from Kwiat Couture; bar-set band (right) from J. Birnbach (photo/Peter Hurst); pavé rings from Barnett Robinson; micro-pavé ring from J. Birnbach.

Page 186: "I Love You Sara" ring from European Gemological Laboratory.

Cover Photographs

Royal Asscher® from Royal Asscher Diamond Company Ltd. (photo/Donald Barry Woodrow); classic gem shapes (round, pear, heart, emerald-cut, oval and marquise) from Bellataire Diamonds, Inc.; Tiffany-style solitaire from Diamond Information Center; yellow diamond and platinum ring from Oscar Heyman; "bouquet" ring from Janet Alix (photo/Hap Sakwa); colorless and yellow diamond necklace from Joshua J. Fine Jewelry.

Color Photographs

I wish to thank the following persons and companies for the color photographs appearing in this edition:

Page 1: Classic shapes from Bellataire Diamonds, Inc.

Page 2: Radiant from Eugene Biro Corp.; Gabrielle® rectangle and square from Suberi Brothers (photo/Peter Hurst); Crisscut® from Christopher Designs (photo/Christony Inc.); Royal Asscher® from Royal Asscher Diamond Company Ltd. (photo/Donald Barry Woodrow); Quadrillion™ from Ambar Diamonds; Lucida™ from Tiffany and Company (photo/Monica Stevenson); Tiana™ from Brite Star Diamond Co., Ltd.; Reiss cushion cut from Jack Reiss, LLC.

Page 3: Biro 88® and trilliant from Eugene Biro Corp.; Spirit Sun® from Freiesleben; EightStar® from EightStar Diamond Company (photo/Richard von Sternberg); Lily Cut® from Lili Diamonds (design/Siman-Tov Brothers); Gabrielle® heart from Suberi Brothers (photo/Peter Hurst); briolette and rondelles from Manak Jewels, Inc.; earrings, half-moons, and trapezoids from Doron Isaak; Crisscut® baguettes from Christopher Designs (photo/Christony Inc.).

Page 4: Bulgari blue and colorless diamonds from Christie's (photo/Christie's Images Ltd. 2010); six colored diamonds from NCDIA (photo/National Color Diamond Association); natural-color green, blue, and pink diamonds from Aurora Gems Inc. (photo/Tino Hammid); fancy-color diamond floral brooch from Sotheby's, NY.

Page 5: Black and white diamond rings from Manak Jewels, Inc.; platinum wirework and diamond rings by Janet Alix (photo/Hap Sakwa); necklace from NOVA by Gruber; ring and bracelet with inset colored diamonds from Etienne Perret (photo/Ralph Gabriner). All other jewelry from designers listed.

Page 6: Ring and necklace (middle right) from Bellataire Diamonds, Inc.; suite at bottom from John Buechner (photo/*The Jewelry Book*). All other jewelry from designers listed.

Page 7: Gabrielle jewelry from Suberi Brothers. All other jewelry from designers listed.

Page 8: Earrings (bottom right) by Joshua J. Fine Jewelry. All other jewelry from designers listed.

Page 9: Three rings (top right) from Barnett Robinson; bracelet (middle right) from Yossi Harari (photo/Doug Rosa); Scott Keating ring (upper left) from Scott Keating Design. All other jewelry from designers listed.

Page 10: Three-stone rings: top, from private collection of David and Agnes Sarns (design/Carvin French and Antoinette Matlins; photo/Tibor Ardai); middle and bottom from J. Birnbach. Classic solitaires: top (Tiffany-style), from the Diamond Information Service; middle right, from Lazare Kaplan International. Side stones: Ring with tiny channel-set stones from a private collector (design/Carvin French and Antoinette Matlins; photo/Tibor Ardai); classic round with tapered baguettes and yellow radiant rings from J. Birnbach; Diana® collection ring courtesy of Frederick Goldman. Heirloom reproductions: left, from Mark Silverstein for Varna. All other jewelry from designers listed.

Page 11: Top left, from Designs by Jean-François Albert; top right, from Kwiat; right, second from top, from Alex Primak; middle left, Nina Collection by H. Stern Jewellers Inc.; middle from Artcarved by Frederick Goldman; middle right from Kwiat; bottom left from Scott Keating Design. All other jewelry from designers listed.

Page 12: Luminari™ and Ultimate Created Diamonds™ from Lucent Diamonds (photos/Tino Hammid).

Index